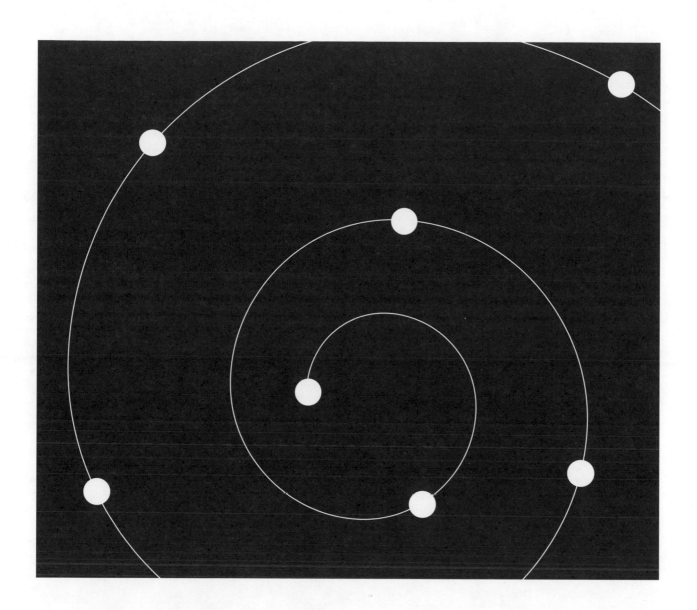

AIMprint

NEW RELATIONSHIPS ▮ **IN THE ARTS AND LEARNING**

AIMprint

NEW RELATIONSHIPS IN THE ARTS AND LEARNING

AIMprint

**NEW RELATIONSHIPS
IN THE ARTS AND LEARNING**

CO-EDITORS   Cynthia Weiss and Amanda Leigh Lichtenstein
COLUMBIA COLLEGE CHICAGO'S CENTER FOR
COMMUNITY ARTS PARTNERSHIPS (CCAP)

ASSISTANT EDITOR   Shawn Renee Lent

COPY EDITOR   David Peak

DESIGNER   Jehan Abon
CREATIVE & PRINT SERVICES,
COLUMBIA COLLEGE CHICAGO

AIMPRINT ADVISORY TEAM   David A. Flatley
Cynthium Johnson Woodfolk
Shawn Renee Lent
Amanda Leigh Lichtenstein
Leah Mayers
Jenn Morea
Sadira Muhammad
Joanne Vena
Cynthia Weiss

PANEL OF READERS   Luke Albrecht
Arnold Aprill
Deborah Brzoska
Gail Burnaford
Jo Cates
David A. Flatley
Kenda Hallman
Nick Jaffe
Shawn Renee Lent
Rachel McIntire
Mary Clare McCarthy
Jenn Morea
Nick Rabkin
Joanne Vena

Funding for the publication of AIMprint was provided by the
US Department of Education's Fund for the Improvement
of Postsecondary Education (FIPSE), the Oppenheimer
Family Foundation, and Columbia College Chicago.

Table of Contents

INTRODUCTION

CHAPTER ONE
THE LEARNING SPIRAL:
A MODEL FOR ARTS INTEGRATION

CHAPTER TWO
DIVERSE PORTRAITS
OF CLASSROOM LIFE

CHAPTER THREE
PROFESSIONAL DEVELOPMENT
AS REFLECTIVE PRACTICE

CHAPTER FOUR
THE ART OF PARTNERSHIPS

CHAPTER FIVE
FEATURED CURRICULUM

APPENDIX

arts in·te·gra·tion

1. an educational field that specializes essentially in relationships – between people, ideas, curricula, places, themes, and areas of study, with an emphasis on arts learning at the center of these relationships.

2. working with curricular intention to merge learning in the arts with learning in other academic subject areas.

Taking AIM, Reaching the Mark

Eric Booth

ARTS EDUCATION CONSULTANT
FOUNDING EDITOR, *TEACHING ARTIST JOURNAL*

It is the experiment of our lifetimes, so we had better get it right. Thank you, Project AIM, for giving us this book to sharpen the AIM of our work—work which we believe can recreate the future.

In the hundred-plus years that the arts have held a formal place in American schools, arts educators have worked toward the same two basic goals: teaching young people to be able to create works of art, and building their capacity to enter into, decode, and learn from works of art made by others. These are worthy goals. Our team of players, arts teachers, teaching artists and other contributors, have worked diligently, heroically—usually in constrained and ungenerous circumstances—to bring generations of young hearts and minds into the rich learning which the arts provide. The arts-learning community believes in this work as a mission to ensure that every young person has his/her chance—an almost-sacred birthright—to inculcate the ancient wisdom and perennial vitality and relevance of the arts.

And now, as the arts continue the endless argument for a better place at the school curriculum table—more hours, more resources, more opportunity to transform lives, classroom communities, and school culture—the great experiment has begun. That great experiment is *Arts Integration*. There is something new under the arts learning sun. The gamble is that by bringing learning in the arts (*through* the arts) together with other subject matters, students can go further in *both* areas, and students' lives and classroom culture can be transformed in the process.

Much of the early experimentation I see misses the mark—the arts get used as a handmaiden to pep up a boring curriculum (but a curriculum that gets tested and so holds priority), without really engaging and teaching arts-essentials like personal voice, brainstorming, making creative choices and reflecting on their impact. Or, conversely, a dynamic arts project, full of good arts learning, is connected to subject matter in a literal way, but doesn't really spark students' curiosity to delve into that subject matter as raw material for their personal expression or self-motivated exploration. Project AIM consistently hits the mark, and diligently studies the following: what the mark is, how the various players can talk about it and work together to expand the target, and what constitutes successful teaching and learning practice.

Project AIM has been rigorously dedicated to exploring the right balance. I have followed and been inspired by their work because they have been so careful, so wise, and so brave in applying themselves to the foundation work our whole field needs in order to grow.

The work presented in these pages is so important partly because it strengthens the case that the arts have earned more time in the chrono-economy that is the hardest currency in American schools. But even more, these essays, together, make the bigger case that the arts belong at the very center of schools. There are two things every revolution requires: a lot of dialogue, and examples of what liberated life looks like. My deepest thanks to the dedicated and innovative people who undertook the Project AIM experiments (and to their enlightened funders), and to our colleagues whose high-quality writing in these pages makes it possible for us all to learn from their work. This volume guides our next steps toward bringing arts learning to the center of schooling—where it belongs.

Project AIM's Art Integration Learning Spiral brings together, researches, articulates and shares the best of what our field knows in order to take the next step: the goals and practices we must use, the ways to build classroom communities that become arts environments, the ways to grow strong partnerships, and the essential processes like embedding big ideas, revising, reflecting, presenting and assessing.

The guidance from these essays builds on what we know from other experimentation around the country, such as in A+ Schools, Chicago Arts Partnerships in Education (CAPE), the Empire State Partnerships, and 150 other bold and thoughtful experiments across the country from Maine to Hawaii. This is how our field can finally grow toward its transformative potential. What I particularly love about the learning shared in this volume is the way that a fierce dedication to artistic processes and language informs the whole endeavor. Thank you, Project AIM, for your vision and guidance—thank you readers for learning from their good work.

The word *culture* has long been used in arts education, largely as a justification for bringing kids into art. In the 21st century the word has connotations of elitism and privilege that belie the equity and access issues that lie at the heart of Project AIM. The original etymological meaning of the word *culture* is closer to agriculture, more like the agar-agar in the Petri dish you dealt with in ninth-grade science class than the highbrow trappings of $200 night at the opera. The ancient meaning of *culture is the medium in which we grow,* and *AIMprint* provides us a guidebook for creating that healthy medium in 21st century schools. *AIMprint* helps us redefine the culture of schools through the culture of the arts, to grow a new generation of students with art at the heart of its learning, and thus the rest of their lives.

Eric Booth

"There are two things every revolution requires: a lot of dialogue, and examples of what liberated life looks like."

–ERIC BOOTH–

Notes
from the Field

THE EDITORS' WELCOME

Cynthia Weiss and
Amanda Leigh Lichtenstein

Our passion for arts integration is tied closely to our own practice as artists and writers—we bring our experiences to the frameworks for the editing of this book.

From Amanda

Alongside editing and writing this book, I am completing a book of poems entitled "Anthro(a)pology: Poems Written from an Apologetic Distance." These poems express over seven years of travel and speak to a perpetual longing for home. Poet Elizabeth Bishop once asked of travel, "Should we have stayed at home and thought of here?" And yet her poems affirm the absolute necessity of travel—to challenge one's perceptions, press one's whole body up against the extraordinary, think and think again of one's assumptions and notions of reality. My work strives to turn the world inside-out as a way of locating the self in a complex world. Travel is about entering new "fields of experience," and I believe that in heightening our senses of awareness within these fields, we grow and connect in ways we could not have imagined had we not left one field for another. Arts-integrated teaching is a lot like traveling, in that all of us travel the great terrain of ideas in search of ourselves, encountering and creating new realities that help us cope with, and embrace, the world in which we live.

From Cynthia

Alongside editing and writing this book, I have been working in my studio on a series of landscape paintings for an exhibition called, "Field Study." Working on the book and paintings concurrently has allowed me to borrow images and metaphors from one project to the other.

The ideas for my painting show are inspired by British art historian, John Berger's essay, "Field," from his essay collection, *About Looking.* In this essay, Berger proposes that when we enter the four boundaries of a natural field (and become conscious of ourselves within this enclosed space), we have the opportunity to see everything that happens within this frame as an *event*. A crow flying overhead, for example, or an insect landing on a leaf leads to a heightened consciousness and a renewed aesthetic appreciation of our lives.

My paintings are an investigation of fields very dear to my heart. I have spent a decade of summers painting in the Michigan dunes at Oxbow, the School of the Art Institute of Chicago's summer artist program, as well as working in a restored Illinois prairie, at the Ragdale Foundation, a residency for writers and artists. Both of these fields are in protected spaces; their fragile ecosystems are being preserved from future development. The artist communities, as well, offer a protected space and time for artists to bring a new work of art to life.

We believe that arts integration is a field that offers teachers, artists, and students a protected space within school buildings and school systems for nascent ideas, emergent curriculum, personal and collaborative inquiry, engaged learning, abstract thinking and relevant practice to take root, be nourished and grow.

A Field Guide
^{to} AIMprint

**HOW TO READ
THIS BOOK**

Cynthia Weiss and
Amanda Leigh Lichtenstein

AIMprint *tells the story of Project*
AIM, an arts integration mentorship
project of the Center for Community
Arts Partnerships at Columbia
College Chicago.

From chapter to chapter you will hear the varied voices of teaching artists, teachers, principals, students and program staff who create a theory of practice even as they write their essays.

The process of assembling this book has compelled us to take a very careful look at the core beliefs and common threads that run through Project AIM. We originally began this project as a tool-kit to disseminate the Project AIM model, but the book took shape more as a reflective narrative and less as a directive system. We hope that the working models and stories found in *AIMprint* will provide a useful guide to both long-time and new colleagues eager to engage in the complex work of arts integration.

The field of arts integration is vast and deep. Many books have already explored the big picture of arts education policy and theory, but few have told the more personal stories. In *AIMprint* we investigate the field of arts integration very close to the ground. We hope you will recognize yourself within these stories and seek out the chapters most relevant to your work.

Chapter One

The Learning Spiral: A Model for Arts Integration introduces the AIM Arts Integration Learning Spiral, which describes the why and how of doing the work. We address eight points for successful arts-integrated teaching and learning, including:

- Discovering intentions for teaching and learning
- Creating a safe community of learners
- Learning in the language of the arts
- Immersing in big ideas through art-making
- Revising and sharing
- Performing and exhibiting
- Reflecting and assessing
- Discovering new intentions for students in learning

This chapter also highlights interdisciplinary arts literacy pedagogy, moving between text and image, and parallel processes in arts and literacy.

Chapter Two

Diverse Portraits of Classroom Life invites you to step inside Project AIM classrooms. Each first person story is a testament to the arts as a catalyst for change. These stories speak from diverse cultural and artistic perspectives, and their unique voices and writing styles make a case for Project AIM's stance on the value of individual voices within education. Embedded in these stories are deeply eloquent examples of student work.

Chapter Three

Professional Development as Reflective Practice introduces Project AIM's multiple structures and opportunities for Professional Development, including:

- Monthly Teaching Artist Cadre Meetings
- Project AIM Annual Orientation
- Teacher Arts Integration Workshops at Individual Schools
- Cross-school Workshops at Museums and Cultural Institutions
- Curriculum Sharing at the End of the Year
- Classroom Residencies with Artist/Teacher Partners
- Teacher/Artist Summer Institute

The chapter includes an essay on the AIM Teaching Artist Cadre, the Anatomy of a Summer Institute, and an essay by consultant Deborah Brzoska on Assessment in Project AIM. Chapter Three ends with a collection of Arts Integration Strategies, written by AIM artists, that have been presented with great success in various professional development venues. The through-lines for all professional development are hands-on learning in the arts, supporting a professional community of peers, and engaging in reflective practice.

Chapter Four

The Art of Partnerships takes a look at relationships as an organizing principle for arts-integrated teaching and learning. The essays and interviews speak from the point-of-view of the many partners that support this work, including:

- College faculty
- Program directors
- School principals
- Program evaluators
- School teachers
- Students

We examine a range of partnerships from one-on-one relationships to complex infrastructures needed to support and sustain this work.

Chapter Five

The Art of Curriculum features samples of arts-integrated unit plans as well as discipline specific strategies for igniting arts-integrated learning. Disciplines represented include:

- Poetry & mathematics
- Poetry, math & architecture
- Documentary filmmaking & social studies
- Book making & language arts
- Visual arts & history
- Theater & literature
- Photography, writing & botany
- Animation & the writing process

Epilogue

The Epilogue raises essential questions about arts integration pedagogy and practice.

Appendix

The Appendix offers hand-outs, guidelines, blank forms, templates, and other useful tools that can be adapted and replicated by other practitioners.

Acknowledgements

Caminante no hay camino,

se hace el camino al andar.

Traveler, there is no road,

you make the road by walking.

– **Antonio Machado,** poet

We are fortunate to walk down a road that has been paved by exemplary national and international art educators, scholars, artists and students. We would like to acknowledge the following people and organizations that have greatly supported the work of Project AIM and have deepened our understanding of the power of learning in and through the arts.

Project AIM is a school partnerships program of the Center for Community Arts Partnerships at Columbia College Chicago. Our programs are greatly enriched by the vast resources of this vital arts and media college. We thank the President of Columbia College Chicago, Dr. Warrick L. Carter; Provost Steve Kapelke; Vice President of Academic Affairs, Louise Love; and Associate Vice President of Academic Research and Dean of the Library, Jo Cates, for their vision and continual support. A special thanks to Associate Vice President and Chief of Staff, Paul Chiaravalle, and to Associate Vice President and Chief Marketing Officer, Mark Lloyd, for providing support towards the publishing of this book.

At the Center for Community Arts Partnerships (CCAP), we thank Executive Director, David A. Flatley and the dedicated staff, whose collective good work supports every program: Joanna Barrios, Monica Boyd, Mecca Brooks, Rachel Culich, Kimeco Dodd, Nora Dunlop, Julio Flores, Nicole Garneau, Jose Gomez, Kenda Hallman, Sharon Harrell, Abijan Johnson, Joe Hulbert, Jason Lambert, April Langworthy, Dana LoGiudice, Edna Radnik-Madonia, Sarah Ogeto, Liz Parrott, Lea Pinsky, Melissa Soberanes, Paul Teruel, Joanne Vena, and Leslie Woods.

To the Project AIM team, a special thank you to Director of School Partnerships, Joanne Vena, and to Project AIM Program Coordinator, Sadira Muhammad, as well as Arts Integration Program Specialist, Shawn Renee Lent, who create an atmosphere of fun and dedication, and roll up their sleeves to make the work happen. Thank you to Lisa Hutler, former Project AIM staff, for her early, valuable contributions to Project AIM and to this book. Thank you to April Langworthy for her administrative support in the first years of Project AIM.

Thank you to Barbara A. Holland, Ph.D., our external evaluator for our grant from the United States Department of Education's Fund for the Improvement of Postsecondary Education (FIPSE), who gave us her wit and wisdom while encouraging us to stay on track to write a book for the field. Thanks also to Emmy Bright, Project AIM/FIPSE Observation Specialist, for her classroom observations that first illuminated the Project AIM approach.

A special thanks to Julie Simpson, Founder and former Executive Director of the Office of Community Arts Partnerships (now the Center for Community Arts Partnerships). Without her support and enthusiasm for Project AIM, and for arts education partnerships, the funding from FIPSE and the development of this program, would not have been possible.

Thank you to our internal evaluator, Lara K. Pruitt, and to our evaluation team: Vanessa McKendall-Stephens, Mary Ellen Murphy, and Beverly J. Dretzke of FaceValu Evaluation Consulting, Inc., for bringing us insightful perspectives on Project AIM's work funded by the Department of Education's Arts-in-Education Model Demonstration and Dissemination grant.

Deepest gratitude to our *AIMprint* contributors: Marisol Alcala, Meg Arbeiter, George Bailey, Barlow, Somya Bergman, Eric Booth, Emmy Bright, Deborah Brzoska, Julie Buzza, Michelle Cericola, Ai Lene Chor, Luis Crespo, Guillermo Delgado, Judith Diaz, Julie A. Downey, Luz Elena Escobar, David A. Flatley, Khanisha Foster, Margarita Garcia, Dan Godston, Alfea Denise Gordon, Dr. Betty J. Allen-Green, Candace Guevara, Deborah Guzmán-Meyer, Tricia Hersey, Barbara A. Holland, Margaret Jones, Leonor Karl, Rebecca Katsulis, Theresa Kern, Valerie King, Shawn Renee Lent, Jean Linsner, Bryan Litt, Michelle Lugo, Leah Mayers, Cecil Mcdonald Jr., Maria Mertz, Jenn Morea, Sadira Muhammad, Melissa Padilla, Lisa Redmond, Sophia Rempas, Tony Sancho, Mathias "Spider" Schergen, Jamie Lou Thome, Martha Torres, Suree Towfighnia, Joanne Vena, Joel Wanek, Cynthium Johnson-Woodfolk, and avery r. young. Thank you to Jenn Morea, who's essay, *Surprising Relationships: The Ooh's and Ahh's Between Poetry, Art, Music and Mathematics,* helped inspire our definition of arts integration for this book.

Thank you to all our principals, coordinators and school partners that make for well-run and joyful residencies: Academy of Communications and Technology (A.C.T.) Charter School – Principal, Terri Millsap, Founder Sara Howard, Meg Arbeiter, and Doug Van Dyke; Robert Crown Community Academy – Principal, Dr. Lee M. Jackson, Shontae Allen-Higginbottom, Virginia Jurcys, Andrea Mays, Walter Ornelas, and Lessia Wilson; Robert Healy Fine Arts Academy – Principal, Mary-Ellen Ratkovitch, Barbara Sisto, and Kellie Sorrell; Theodore Herzl Elementary School – Principal, Dr. Betty J. Allen-Green and Patricia Surgeon; Edward Jenner Academy of the Arts – Principal, Zelma Woodson, Berliner Fry, and Mathias "Spider" Schergen; Thurgood Marshall Middle School – Principal, Jose C. Barillas and Mary Ann Brandt; Casimir Pulaski Fine Arts Academy – Principal, Leonor Karl, Wilma Velazquez, Luz Jorges, Debbie Sanchez, Anne O'Malley, and Arturo Magaña; Albert R. Sabin Magnet School – Principal, Barton A. Dassinger and Former Principal, Christine Arroyo; Dr. Bessie Rhodes Magnet School – Principal, Patricia Mitchell and Mary Beth Koszut; and Martin Luther King Jr. Laboratory School – Principal, Keir A. Rogers, Ilyse Brainin, and Anne Lefkovitz.

And to our entire extraordinary Project AIM Artist Cadre, past and present, whose vision, imagination and dedication make this work sing: Maria Abraham, Barlow, Ai Lene Chor, Luis Crespo, Guillermo Delgado, Lydia Diamond, Julie A. Downey, Khanisha Foster, Dan Godston, Crystal Griffith, Deborah Guzmán-Meyer, Tricia Hersey, Amanda Leigh Lichtenstein, Bryan Litt, Dana LoGiudice, Daniel Lopez, John Lyons, Leah Mayers, Cecil McDonald Jr., Jenn Morea, Ron Pajak, Dia Penning, Lisa Redmond, Archie Roper, Tony Sancho, Agnes Starcewski, Megan Stielstra, Tone Stockenstrom, Jamie Lou Thome, Suree Towfighnia, Joel Wanek, Ian Weaver, Qween Roy-Wicks, Cynthium Johnson-Woodfolk, and avery r. young.

Project AIM, as part of CCAP, depends on collaborative partnerships and programs across Columbia College Chicago. Thanks to Randall Albers, Chairperson of the Fiction Writing Department; George Bailey, Faculty in the English Department; Anita Garza, Director of Community Programs at the Center for Book and Paper Arts; Lott Hill, Acting Director of the Center for Teaching Excellence; Deborah Holdstein, Dean of Liberal Arts and Sciences; Mark Kelly, Vice President of Student Affairs; Dimitri Moore, Facilities Coordinator for C-Spaces; Eliza Nichols, Dean of the School of Fine and Performing Arts; Neil Pagano, Associate Dean of Liberal Arts and Sciences; Dominic Pacyga, Faculty in the Liberal Education Department; Leonard Lehrer, former Dean of the School of Fine and Performing Arts; Brian Shaw, Faculty in the Theater Department; Bruce Sheridan, Chairperson of the Film and Video Department; Rod Slemmons, Director, along with Corinne Rose, Manager of Education, and the entire staff of the Museum of Contemporary Photography (MoCP); Kari Sommers, Vice President of Student Life; Jeff Spitz, Faculty for the Michael Rabiger Center for Documentary Film; Carol Ann Stowe, Director of the Harris Center for Early Childhood Education; and Ann Wiens, Director of Institutional Communications.

Thank you to Nick Rabkin, Robin Redmond, Irma Friedman and Victoria Malone of Columbia College Chicago's Center for Arts Policy, and to Nick Jaffe, Chief Editor of *Teaching Artist Journal* (housed at the Center for Arts Policy), for helping us to see the exciting synergies between research, policy and practice.

We gratefully thank our long-time, dear colleagues at Chicago Arts Partnerships in Education (CAPE) who have set the bar high in creating inspired arts integration partnerships, and have led the way with seminal work around the country and the world. A warm thank you to Arnold Aprill, Amy Rasmussen, Scott Sikkema, Erica Tryon, Kelly Nespor, Yanira Cirino, Lara Tan, Jessica Hudson, Stephanie Pereira, and Dr. Gail Burnaford, Florida Atlantic University.

We thank our brilliant colleagues and professors connected to the Arts in Education (AIE) Program at Harvard Graduate School of Education (HGSE): Steven Seidel, Rubén Gaztambide-Fernández, Eleanor Duckworth, Maura Clarke, Rachel McIntire, Beth Sondel and Tony Day, who shaped many of our ideas on curriculum theory and design and who fueled far-reaching conversations on the arts and learning.

We greatly appreciate the support from Chicago Public Schools arts administrators, David Roche, Director of Fine and Performing Arts; as well as Mario R. Rossero and Evan E. Plummer of the Fine and Performing Arts Magnet Cluster Program, Office of Academic Enhancement.

So many colleagues in the field are doing parallel work that inspires our practice and renews our spirit. A warm thanks to Eric Booth, whose tireless work has elevated the status and recognition of teaching artistry around the country. To our deeply admired colleagues: Debra Ingram of the University of Minnesota; Richard Deasy and Karen Gallagher of Art Education Partnerships AEP; John Abodeely of Americans for the Arts; Larry Scripp of Music-in-Education National Consortium; Lynette Emmons, Harvey "Smokey" Daniels, Marilyn Bizar and Steve Zemmelman of National-Louis University; Kathryn A. Humphries and Sinéad Kimbrell of Hubbard Street Dance Chicago; Antonia Contro of the Marwen Foundation; and Jackie Murphy, Jackie Terrassa, Deidre Searcy, Jackie Samuels, Lauren Lauter, Jamie Topper, Michael Warr and Anna West, extraordinary artists and educators. And thanks to David Schein, Ron Bieganski, Anita Evans, Bryn Magnus of Free Street Programs; Paul Sznewajs of Snow City Arts Foundation; Dr. Robert Boone and Shinae Yoon of Young Chicago Authors; and Tim Sauers and Marissa Reyes.

A huge embracing thank you to our panel of readers whose generous insights gave elegant shape and purpose to this book: Luke Albrecht, Arnold Aprill, Deborah Brzoska, Dr. Gail Burnaford, David A. Flatley, Kenda Hallman, Nick Jaffe, Shawn Renee Lent, Rachel McIntire, Jenn Morea, Lara K. Pruitt, Nick Rabkin, Joanne Vena, Mary Clare McCarthy and Jo Cates.

Love always to our families, Nick, Emily and Claire Rabkin; Howard, Harriet, Amy, Dan and Rick Weiss and their families; as well as Pam, Rich, Hillary and Nina Joy Lichtenstein, and David and Manuel Nacham Washington, whose humor patience, great cooking, and loving support has kept us moving toward the finish line.

Thank You
to Project AIM Supporters

It is with deep appreciation and gratitude that the Center for Community Arts Partnerships thanks the following organizations:

Without the support of several key fund contributors, Project AIM would have never advanced to the model presented in this book. With much appreciation for their early support, in 2000, of the Center for Community Arts Partnerships (CCAP), I want to thank the Chicago Public Schools' Office of Language and Culture, Polk Bros. Foundation and Kraft Foods for giving us initial funding to pilot work in several Chicago Public School classrooms; this greatly helped us to utilize the talents of our teaching artists, drawn from Columbia College Chicago faculty and community-based arts organizations. We also want to thank the Field Foundation, the Chicago Community Trust, the Oppenheimer Family Foundation, and the Prince Charitable Trusts for their support, of our professional development work with all ten Project AIM schools. More recently, the Lloyd A. Fry Foundation has helped CCAP evaluate and document the Project AIM work with their generous support.

With deep gratitude for their ongoing generosity, I would like to acknowledge the JPMorgan Chase Foundation for helping to build program stability and continuity at three schools: Robert Crown Community Academy Fine Arts Center, Theodore Herzl Elementary School, and Albert R. Sabin Magnet School. These schools are the first of six Community School Initiatives that involve Project AIM and we thank the leadership of Dr. Lee Jackson, Dr. Betty J. Allen-Green, Christine Arroyo, Barton Dassinger, and all the teachers for their energy and support. We warmly thank Diane Austin and the US Department of Education's Arts in Education Model Development and Dissemination Program for current support of Project AIM.

Finally, we acknowledge the enormous endorsement we received from the United States Department of Education's Fund for the Improvement of Postsecondary Education (FIPSE). Being a FIPSE grantee allowed us to grow and develop with input from our FIPSE program officer Bette Dow. It also encouraged innovation, new kinds of engagement with college faculty and students, and the creation of a vital cadre of teaching artists central to the Project AIM Model. Without their support, we would not be presenting *AIMprint* today.

With deep regards for all our contributors,

Joanne Vena
Director of School Partnerships

Expanding the Realm of Learning

David A. Flatley

EXECUTIVE DIRECTOR
CENTER FOR COMMUNITY ARTS PARTNERSHIPS

Arts Integration. The buzz is out there. We've got various definitions floating about, and everyone in the arts education field has an opinion about it. In an attempt to clarify the issue of certification, for example, some states are debating whether arts integration is even a "field" worthy of study.

For those of us working in the midst of it, it's important to consider the paths that led us to the world of arts education and to ask ourselves, how do we contribute to the question of how the arts impact learning while the jury is still out? For me, this issue goes deeper than the very important task of collecting evidence as to whether or not the arts play a role in impacting *achievement*.

I stumbled somewhat serendipitously into the world of education. I landed at a Chicago theatre company in the early nineties that had a successful, cutting edge young playwrights program and found myself moving seamlessly, if not unknowingly, into the world of education. I joined forces with a core group of idealistic arts folks that began what ultimately grew into a real arts integration movement. It took root nationwide, and Chicago remains to this day a fulcrum point of best practice in the field of arts education.

As Executive Director of the Center for Community Arts Partnerships (CCAP) at Columbia College Chicago, I have the good fortune of being charged with extolling the value that the arts play in the lives of youth. CCAP is an outreach arm of the nation's largest arts, media and communications college and we facilitate, implement, design and support arts education programming for the city's youth. We work with K-12 students, collaborating with community based arts organizations throughout the city, providing both in-school and out-of-school programming.

The debate that pits arts integration against teaching arts for its own sake is an unfortunate false dichotomy. We provide both arts-integrated instruction as well as discipline specific arts programming. And in any case, much of the arts education programming I have witnessed over the years is "integrated"—in the sense that good teachers understand that value of connecting to students' personal and social worlds. Good inquiry, the root of genuine learning, requires that the learner make some connection to the concept of relevance.

My point is that there's high quality and mediocre quality teaching. Across the board. The crux of the matter is the teaching and learning that unfolds in the classroom. A principal at a recent Arts Education Partnerships national forum held at Columbia College Chicago made the delightful remark that we should always refer to this as "learning and teaching," in that order, to help clarify the focus with which we should explore and understand what's important in education.

Are the students engaged? Do they care about the material? Do they find it relevant to them on some level? Is the teacher "delivering" the curriculum or is the curriculum being engaged in a fashion that requires students to delve into their own questioning? Do students have an opportunity to make their learning visible? This is, after all, a trademark quality that the arts bring to any classroom regardless of the subject matter being taught.

Arts integration helps bring this pedagogy alive, and it had a surge of public recognition in the late 90's with the publication of *Champions of Change* and subsequently *Critical Links*. The U.S. Department of Education started funding model dissemination projects that focused on using the arts as a vehicle for learning across content areas. Funders began to take notice of programs that not only increased student engagement in the classroom through creativity and the arts, but also those that placed arts integration strategies and similar pedagogies at the center of professional development for teachers. The emergence of the teaching artist and their work as a viable and respected field points to the need for educators to take seriously the opportunities the arts provide for urban school reform.

CCAP and Columbia College Chicago are deeply involved in this conversation and in this work. The Center for Arts Policy at Columbia, our sister Center down the street, is spending energy and resources to explore the evolving *profession* of the teaching artist. It is looking closely at the implications of an evolving field that is becoming more recognized throughout all corners of the country. How do artists who stumble into this work, and discover that they are brilliant at it, move into conversations about benefits, quality control and training, and equity of pay?

The Center for Arts Policy now houses and edits the *Teaching Artist Journal,* which is an important development for Columbia as it increasingly takes on the commitment of supporting the very concept of the teaching artist, and the integration of arts into learning.

We're delighted at CCAP that this debate is under way. Our practitioners, some of whom were colleagues of mine long before I came to Columbia when this work started in great earnest in 1993, are dedicating their involvement in CCAP partner schools to the notion that:

- YES. Arts integration does impact how learning happens in the classroom (in a powerful and more sustaining manner).
- YES. Arts integration has profound value in providing professional development and inspiration to teachers who have long held the belief that their creativity and passions for learning have been pushed down by the system.
- AND YES. Arts integration taps into imagery that helps build literacy for students starving for higher order thinking skills.

CCAP believes that there is a need to cultivate the teaching artist. Because it is a growing field, we should take care to build and support this evolving force for change. It holds the promise of shifting education into a new way of thinking. While some wait for a critical mass to

address the inadequacies of standardized testing, these artists are boldly embarking on their own mission. To demonstrate to the world that, not only are there different ways of knowing and learning, but that the arts are a prime vehicle for providing a viable path to assessing those myriad ways of thinking.

What have perhaps struck me most are the epistemological issues associated with how the arts impact education as a whole.

Elliot Eisner, one of our more articulate advocates of arts education, impressed me early on in this regard. In his latest book, *Arts and the Creation of Mind,* he speaks of the multiple ways in which education can learn from the arts. One of these lessons is that the way something is formed matters. As he sees it, because we tend to differentiate in our culture between content and form, we consider that what is said constitutes content and how it is said constitutes form. He continues:

> "What is said cannot be neatly separated from how something is said. Form and content interpenetrate. The way in which something is spoken shapes its meaning; form becomes content… Actors have learned this lesson well. So too have poets, painters and musicians… What would the attention to the relationship of form and content mean in the teaching of mathematics?… Attention to such matters would help students understand the sources of our experience, how the ways in which a form is crafted affects our experience and, therefore, how we relate to what we pay attention to…" *(The Arts and the Creation of Mind, pages 197–198).*

One of our first objectives when we teach must be that students pay attention to what is being taught. It's simple and something that good teachers have always understood; but if *how* we teach is actually more closely connected to *what* we teach, then using the arts and creativity to spark interest, passion, self expression, and relevance for students—no matter what the content—that's going to have an impact on real learning.

Eisner also reminds us that judgment depends on feeling: "The body is engaged, the source of information is visceral, the sensibilities are employed to secure experience that makes it possible to render a judgment and to act upon it," (Eisner, pg. 201). We can't separate emotion from intellect. And yet the educational system in the U.S. leaves little room for acknowledging the role of emotion in the classroom.

The arts provide safety and space to express emotion. All the arts enable students to let their emotions merge with their exploration and inquiry. Storytelling is arguably the oldest art form. Who among us believes that good story telling is devoid of emotion? Who can argue that form and content do not "interpenetrate" when someone tells a really good story?

Educational philosopher Maxine Greene writes in *Releasing the Imagination* about the profound nature of imagination and the arts and its impact on our evolution as a society. For Greene, her attention continually turns back to the importance of "wide-awaked ness," the awareness of what it is to be fully present in the world.

> "Meanings spring up all around as soon as we are conscious, and it is the obligation of teachers to heighten the consciousness of whoever they teach by urging them to read and look and make their own interpretations of what they see. We must use our imagination to apply concepts to things. This is the way we render the world familiar and therefore manageable." *(Releasing the Imagination: Essays on Education, the Arts, and Social Change, page 35).*

For Greene, it ultimately connects back to the idea of Dewey's notion that if we are going to produce a democratic society, our educational system must reflect the ways that democracy is formed. *Releasing the Imagination* is critical to the endeavor of designing curriculum, the classroom, and ways in which we interact in schools:

> "Democracy, we realize, means a community that is always in the making. Marked by an emerging solidarity, a sharing of certain beliefs, and a dialogue about others, it must remain open to newcomers, those too long thrust aside. This can happen even in the local spaces of classroom, particularly when students are encouraged to find their voices and their images." *(Releasing the Imagination: Essays on Education, the Arts, and Social Change, page 39).*

Text and image, voice and expression. Within the framework of our work in education, our journey has brought us here, creating a community that honors and develops the students' artistic inclinations. One can argue whether or not we are all artists deep inside, but clearly a student's creativity should play a central role in his or her path toward inquiry, and ultimately, meaningful learning.

I have great passion for the unearthing of new evidence that will highlight the power and efficacy of integrating the arts into learning. But we have a much bolder agenda than just proving that arts integration increases student achievement—one that helps policy makers understand how broadly achievement can be imagined, and therefore assessed. We need to rise to the challenge of understanding that the process of measuring a young person's ability to learn and to think critically deserves much more attention than the entirely too narrow view afforded by a number 2 pencil.

This portfolio, developed by the teaching artist brain trust that makes up Project AIM at CCAP, will be an invaluable resource for those interested in walking down this path. It is a strategic resource that should be embraced as such. Our supposition is that each community, each classroom, and each teacher/teaching artist team will supply its unique dynamics. This is no package off the shelf. It is a brainstorming chemistry set for educators to explore how to take their teaching to the next level.

Eisner, Elliot. The Arts and the Creation of Mind. Yale University Press, New Haven & London, 2002.

Greene, Maxine. Releasing the Imagination: Essays Education, the Arts and Social Change. Jossey-Bass, a Wiley Company, San Francisco, 1995.

About
Project AIM

THE ARTS INTEGRATION MENTORSHIP PROJECT

The Center for Community Arts Partnerships (CCAP) at Columbia College Chicago plays an important leadership role in the arts integration movement through its acclaimed Arts Integration Mentorship (AIM) project. Gaining increased national attention, arts integration is a unique teaching practice that weaves the visual, media, performing and literary arts into classrooms in order to engage students in their own learning. This approach has a proven impact on a school's curriculum and helps to build students' critical thinking, problem-solving and team building skills—often underdeveloped in traditional classrooms. It also provides invaluable professional development for teachers and artists, and builds school-based leadership infrastructure to sustain and support this practice.

ARTS

Project AIM introduces public school teachers and students to the authentic arts practice of artists by partnering teaching artists from Columbia College Chicago and community-based art organizations with public school teachers. The talented Project AIM Teaching Artist Cadre brings professional expertise in: creative writing, spoken-word performance, theatre, music, visual arts, book and paper arts, photography, dance and film to the classroom.

Artists and teachers work together to infuse the classroom with creativity and experiential learning that connect arts processes and personal experiences to the core curriculum. Using inquiry-based teaching methods, these teams guide their students through each step of the creative process from brainstorming, writing first drafts, revision and rehearsal, to exemplary performances, exhibitions, and documentation of their work.

INTEGRATION

Focusing on the integration of word and image, Project AIM explores the parallels between arts and literacy learning. Artists and teachers jointly create arts-integrated curriculum that promotes reading and writing through the arts. Classrooms are transformed into studios and performance spaces where students are engaged in a powerful learning cycle in and through the arts. As a result, students learn higher-order thinking skills by translating their ideas across mediums.

MENTORSHIP

Project AIM provides many opportunities for mentorship between teachers, artists, students and college faculty. It establishes reciprocal learning communities that provide professional development through hands-on workshops, cooperative classroom learning laboratories and summer institutes. Monthly artist meetings are a key feature and an invaluable opportunity for teaching artists to share, and learn from, their peers. Project AIM works with principals, school-based steering committees, and local school councils to develop arts programming that supports positive, whole school change. Project AIM also enriches the arts integration practice of participating faculty at Columbia College Chicago.

Project AIM/
FIPSE Goals

Project AIM was founded in the fall of 2002 with the support of a United States Department of Education Fund for the Improvement of Postsecondary Education (FIPSE) grant. The core goals for the FIPSE grant became the blueprint for the creation of a comprehensive assessment matrix and the development of the Project AIM program (see Appendix for the Project AIM/FIPSE assessment matrix).

The Project AIM/FIPSE Goals are to:

1. Establish sustainable infrastructures for arts integration at targeted Chicago Public Schools.
2. Train Chicago Public School teachers and administrators to deliver arts integration programming to elementary students.
3. Train Columbia College Chicago faculty and artists to partner effectively with Chicago Public School teachers and staff.
4. Enhance Chicago Public School student engagement and achievement in learning (in and through the arts).
5. Develop and disseminate an arts-integrated model for teaching and learning.

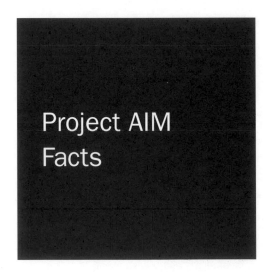

Project AIM
Facts

Project AIM currently works in 10 Chicago and Evanston Public Schools:

*   Academy of Communications and Technology (A.C.T.) Charter School*
*   Crown Community Academy*
*   Robert Healy Elementary School
*   Theodore Herzl Elementary School*
*   Edward Jenner Academy of the Arts*
*   Thurgood Marshall Middle School
*   Casimir Pulaski Fine Arts Academy*
*   Albert R. Sabin Magnet School*
*   Dr. Bessie Rhodes Magnet School, Evanston
*   Martin Luther King Lab Magnet School, Evanston

* Center for Community Arts Partnerships (CCAP) Community Schools' partners

Project AIM typically offers:

- Teacher/artist orientation at the beginning of the year
- The development of 14-week arts-integrated units, in 6-9 classrooms at each school
- Ongoing planning meetings between teachers and artists
- 3 school-based steering committee meetings per year
- 1 whole school arts integration professional development session
- 2-3 cross-site workshops at cultural institutions
- Culminating events, exhibitions, anthologies, performances of student work
- Monthly Teaching Artist cadre meetings
- Curriculum share event to feature arts integration projects
- Annual summer institute for teachers and artists
- Partnerships with the faculty and facilities of Columbia College Chicago
- Support for the documentation and dissemination of project work

Project AIM:

- Employs 30 teaching artists from five major arts disciplines, drawn from Columbia College Chicago departments and community-based arts organizations
- Works with over 80 public school teachers
- Serves over 2,000 students each year

Project AIM Focuses on the Middle School Student

Project AIM has primarily worked in middle school classrooms. These early adolescent years are a time when students are grappling with issues of authority, autonomy, identity and self-actualization. They are hungry to develop their own voice and perspectives. Project AIM artists and teachers have been very successful at creating learning environments that provide positive peer-support and offer safe structures for experimentation and risk-taking. Nancy Atwell, in her book *In the Middle: Writing, Reading, and Learning with Adolescents* writes, "By nature, adolescents are volatile and social, and our teaching can take advantage of this, helping kids find meaningful ways to channel their energies and social needs instead of trying to legislate against them," (Atwell, 25). Project AIM has found that the vehicles and structures of arts-integrated learning, and the ambitious themes, big ideas and opportunities for developing personal perspectives are particularly meaningful to our students at this age.

About
CCAP

**THE CENTER FOR COMMUNITY ARTS PARTNERSHIPS
AT COLUMBIA COLLEGE CHICAGO**

About the Center for Community Arts Partnerships (CCAP)

Since 1998, the Center for Community Arts Partnerships (CCAP) at Columbia College Chicago has been transforming the lives of thousands of Chicago's young people through its unique approach to building partnerships between college and community. Founded on a mission to link the academic departments of Columbia College Chicago with diverse communities throughout the city, CCAP brings the concepts of community-based learning, arts-integrated curricula and reciprocal partnerships into the spotlight. It unites artists, educators, students, corporations, schools and community-based organizations to form meaningful, sustainable partnerships in the arts.

CCAP develops and implements arts education programming that cultivates ongoing, reciprocal relationships—true partnerships—among Columbia College, Chicago schools and community-based organizations. These unique partnerships not only extend the resources of the college into the community, but also bring the knowledge of the community into the learning environment. Working together, college and community partners create mutually beneficial programs that promote service-learning, professional development, creativity and community enrichment through the arts. In turn, CCAP and its partners are building stronger schools and communities, and ultimately better educated students.

Community Partnerships

At Columbia College, students embrace the entire city of Chicago as their classroom, and CCAP helps bring that experience to realization through its Community Partnerships programs. CCAP's Urban Missions program, and Arts in Youth and Community Development (AYCD) graduate program work to connect the college and its urban communities—forging relationships that enhance the learning experience for students of all ages. These partnerships provide unique opportunities for civic engagement, service-learning, employment, artistic practice, and personal and professional growth for all those involved.

College Readiness

CCAP is committed to making the possibility of higher education a reality for Chicago youth, by providing them with life skills and leadership opportunities they might not have had in the past. Through effective college readiness programs, hundreds of Chicago students not only have gained awareness of Columbia College, but also have gained the skills and experience necessary to bring the dream of a college education to fruition.

The Saturday Scholars program is a critical component of CCAP's college readiness initiatives. Founded in 1989, Saturday Scholars is dedicated to empowering Chicago youth by developing strong mentoring relationships that focus on college and workforce readiness, educational and cultural programs, and personal motivation. Supported by JPMorgan Chase and Columbia College, Saturday Scholars helps level the playing field for students from Chicago neighborhoods, most of whom are the first in their families to attend college.

Community Schools

As part of the Chicago Coalition for Community Schools, the Center for Community Arts Partnerships (CCAP) plays a vital role in the development, success and sustainability of this initiative in the city's public schools. Through the Community Schools initiative, CCAP is shaping the schools of tomorrow through its commitment to improved student learning, stronger families and healthier communities. By uniting the most important influences in children's lives—school, family and community—this initiative fully supports their learning and development. The programs and projects offered in Community Schools provide a full-service approach to education by addressing the whole child, including physical, social and emotional, as well as academic needs. Schools become the center of their community, ensuring that students have the creative, supportive environments necessary to succeed.

Working with the Chicago Public School's Office of After Extended Learning Opportunities and the Illinois Federation of Community Schools, CCAP serves as the lead agency partner for six community schools throughout the city.

Illinois Parent Information Resource Center (PIRC)

Parents around the state of Illinois now have a new way to support their child's education. In partnership with Columbia College Chicago's Harris Center for Early Childhood Education, the Center for Community Arts Partnerships (CCAP) will operate the Illinois Parent Information Resource Center (PIRC). Funded by the United States Department of Education (USDE), Illinois PIRC will continue the USDE's efforts to meet the education needs of children in both rural and urban areas. Illinois PIRC will implement and support a variety of programs and policies, and will provide resources to increase parental involvement, improve student academic achievement, and strengthen partnerships among parents, teachers, school administration and communities. Through workshops, presentations and summer institutes, parents will have access to information designed to improve their skills and knowledge, and to help support their child's success at school.

AIMspeak

**WORKING DEFINITONS
OF ARTS INTEGRATION TERMS**

anchor organization

the lead arts or educational organization that manages and facilitates an arts partnership and often serves as the fiscal agent to the project.

artist cadre

an intentional learning community of artists who meet on a regular basis to dialogue and debate the theoretical and practical questions and concerns of their work in schools and communities.

arts integration

1. an educational field that specializes essentially in relationships—between people, ideas, curricula, places, themes, and areas of study, with an emphasis on arts learning at the center of these relationships. 2. working with curricular intention to merge learning in the arts with learning in other academic subject areas.

arts partnership

intentional relationships initiated and developed between institutions and individuals who share programmatic and philosophical visions related to the arts and learning.

assessment

opportunities to measure and understand the effectiveness and impact of arts integration teaching and learning.

big idea

a generative, over-arching concept that helps shape an entire arts-integrated unit of study. The big idea is explored through multiple lenses across the curriculum and through various art forms as a way to generate new questions and deepen learning on a particular subject or concept.

community-based arts organizations (C.B.O.'s)

community organizations that have as their mission the development and delivery of youth development and arts programming, and who partner with schools to co-create arts integration programs.

critical response

a method of positive critical feedback developed by choreographer Liz Lerman to inspire and encourage all artists to return to their art making with a sense of purpose and confidence.

culminating event

a final showing to signify the end of a residency and celebrate both the process and product of arts-integrated learning.

curriculum coach

an experienced third party that mediates discussions between arts partners, teachers and artists to support the development of integrated curriculum.

curriculum share

a final, culminating event showcasing the collective efforts of an arts program to document and highlight the processes and products of arts-integrated learning.

documentation

the collection of project artifacts including student artwork, journal entries, process photography, audio clips, interviews, videos, written reflections, pre- and post-samples of student work, that serves to narrate an arts integration unit of study.

exit slip

a form used for assessment and reflection at the end of a classroom session, workshop or residency, typically comprised of three short questions about the learning experience.

inquiry

specific questions that help shape curriculum planning around a big idea. Inquiry questions are curiosity-threads woven into the arc of an arts-integrated unit.

inquiry-based learning

a teaching methodology that embeds participants' questions and curiosity into the design and delivery of integrated curriculum.

lead teacher

the teacher/leader within a school that has been identified as the point person and site coordinator of an arts partnership.

model works of art

examples of professional, historical, and student works of art that serve as informative structures for inspiration and creation of new work.

parallel processes

a theory of arts and literacy learning that supports and investigates the ways in which learning in and through the arts parallels the reading and writing process.

school steering committee

a leadership committee at the school level that helps to guide, set policy and manage the arts integration program at a given school. This committee usually includes the school principal, assistant principal, classroom teachers, art and literacy specialists, teaching artists, and anchor organization partners.

teaching artist

1. a professional artist who values teaching in and through the arts as much as art-making and seeks out opportunities to teach and learn in schools and communities. 2. a professional artist who views art-making as pedagogically valuable to all members of society.

text & image

engaging text as image and image as text as a way to "read" and interpret a world of symbols and meanings through art-making.

The Learning Spiral

A MODEL FOR ARTS INTEGRATION

The
Learning
Spiral

A MODEL FOR ARTS INTEGRATION

Cynthia Weiss and
Amanda Leigh Lichtenstein

How broadly can achievement be imagined?

As broadly as… a sixth-grader who finds a surprising corollary in her writing between a mailman who moves from house to house and a bird that flies from tree to tree, considering the idea of narrative perspective for the first time…

As broadly as… a seventh-grader who creates a hand-made book in the form of an ascending staircase to represent his growing acceptance for his newborn baby brother…

As broadly as… fifth-graders who use details from their own daily lives, along with sophisticated camera angles, to create a documentary film about immigrant life in Chicago.

As broadly as… an eighth-grader learning to algebraically represent the death rates of HIV/AIDS in South Africa, and then using those graphing skills to chart her own emotions.

In this chapter, we consider the relationship between the imagination, achievement and pedagogy. In the previous essay, "Expanding the Realm of Learning," David A. Flatley asks: "How broadly can achievement be imagined?" We propose that arts-integrated teaching and learning helps us imagine student achievement as broadly and richly as possible. We have chosen the form of the spiral as a metaphor—and working model—for the infinite possibilities of arts integration. The spiral allows us to imagine children, teachers, and artists continually revisiting materials, ideas, and curriculum, each time with a deeper understanding.

This Arts Integration Learning Spiral model emerged as a theory of practice in the course of writing this book. We looked at the lessons learned in our own practice as well as those of national arts education partnerships.

We hope the Learning Spiral model speaks to the need for a working theory broad enough to encompass the many different approaches to arts education. Every point on the spiral leads to deep and meaningful learning in and through the arts, regardless of variations on particular program goals, because they offer structures that make the learning process visible. It names the qualities of teaching and learning that allow us to become more intentional and conscious when developing and implementing arts-integrated curriculum. With the Learning Spiral, achievement is imagined not just at the end of things, but from its inception and at every stage of the learning process.

We offer a model of arts-integrated learning that helps us find a radical middle ground in the debates between the intrinsic and instrumental purposes of arts teaching. We believe that high quality arts education is a complex, dynamic process that connects form and content, history and aesthetics, craft, tools, vocabulary, methodology and studio practice. High-quality arts education connects students' lives across the curriculum. It provides tools, languages and methods to make meaning of the complex issues of our times. The AIM Arts Integration Learning Spiral hopes to begin to name a process that can access the broadest definition of student achievement including academic, social, emotional, spiritual, historical, ethical and aesthetic learning that cultivates empathy, insight and humanity.

Why wouldn't we want to help children by giving them every possible tool for making meaning out of a complex world?

We invite you to apply the AIM Arts Integration Learning Spiral in your own programs and let us know how the Learning Spiral works for you in your own teaching and learning in the arts.

Beginning
with the End
in mind

THE ARTS INTEGRATION LEARNING SPRIAL

Cynthia Weiss

I begin this introduction to the AIM Arts Integration Learning Spiral moving backwards from a culminating event at Crown Community Academy. It is always exciting to imagine, at the start of our work, what the impact of an arts-integrated curriculum, and the possibilities of a given school year, might hold for our students.

On the very last day of school in June 2006, I had the distinct pleasure of being among school children at Crown Community Academy. The last day of school in Chicago is traditionally very hot. Students eat pizza and *red hots* at class parties, help teachers clean their rooms, and make plans for the summer. Middle school students spend considerable time flirting with each other. All of these events were in full swing at Crown.

In addition to this, I had come to Crown—along with writer and Teaching Artist, Lisa Redmond—to bring students culminating products of their work. Lisa's students swarmed around her as she entered the classroom, and gathered with enthusiasm to listen to a CD recording of their work being read aloud. I was also bringing Crown seventh-graders copies of their student anthology, *Keepin' It Real,* edited and directed by Project AIM artist Cynthium Johnson-Woodfolk. Teachers Lessia Wilson and Luke Albrecht invited me to join the party with their students.

Students were thrilled to see their stories, poems and essays in print. I asked if anyone would like to read their work out loud. Everyone wanted to read. In one piece, the author spoke from his heart to his girlfriend. A girl in the class beamed with the private knowledge that the piece might be directed to her. She asked permission to visit the room next door, hoping to confirm her intuition. She returned grinning from ear to ear.

Another student, Aleisha, had written a piece chastising certain adults for caring more about name brand clothes than caring for their kids. She wrote:

I see your daughter going to school with grocery store rubber bands in her hair, the kind that holds the greens together. Chile, I look in her ponytail and see collards! You can't even pay the rent, but you rockin' Gucci, forcing your kids to eat water with their cereal instead of milk. Girl, please! You need to face the fact and stop fooling yourself. You're BROKE and ain't no amount of name brand gonna change that.

Aleisha's poignant, honest and funny writing gave rise to a spirited conversation about keeping up appearances. The conversation was full of give and take. Mr. Albrecht interjected with a connection of his own. He told the class that his father worked in a grocery store when he was growing up, and always brought home the produce rubber bands. The rubber bands were everywhere, and used for everything. He laughed in recognition of the collards in the girl's hair. We all appreciated his story, and could not pull ourselves away from the readings and tellings that followed.

We knew that in one hour, the spell would be broken; seventh-grade would be over, kids would disperse for the summer, this group would never return in the same configuration or age or perspective again. The anthology held us captive, like the magic of stories, marking this last hour, in the last day of seventh-grade at Crown Community Academy with a ritual we would all remember.

Keepin' it Real is a beautifully written collection by African American teenagers whose searing and hilarious observations are often neglected contributions to the larger discourse on American life today. The joy in our impromptu sharing reminded me of the core reasons to do arts integration work. We hope that our work will inspire our students to find their own voices, respect the point-of-view of others, and learn to be attentive to the world around them.

The Arts Integration Learning Spiral begins, much like a new school year, with the hopes of what might be accomplished with a given set of students, teachers and artists working together with an intentional and artful purpose.

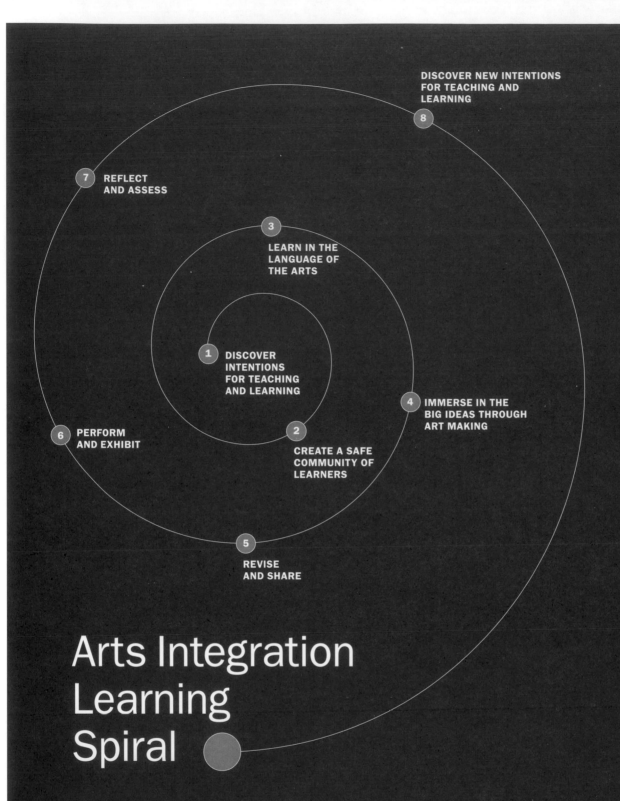

DISCOVER NEW INTENTIONS
FOR TEACHING AND
LEARNING

8

7 REFLECT
AND ASSESS

3

LEARN IN THE
LANGUAGE OF
THE ARTS

1 DISCOVER
INTENTIONS
FOR TEACHING
AND LEARNING

4 IMMERSE IN THE
BIG IDEAS THROUGH
ART MAKING

6 PERFORM
AND EXHIBIT

2

CREATE A SAFE
COMMUNITY OF
LEARNERS

5

REVISE
AND SHARE

Arts Integration Learning Spiral

Columbia
COLLEGE CHICAGO
CENTER FOR COMMUNITY ARTS PARTNERSHIPS

The Why and How

The

Why and How

of doing the work

Cynthia Weiss and
Amanda Leigh Lichtenstein

1 DISCOVER INTENTIONS FOR TEACHING AND LEARNING

... I believe that to address our

literacy issues we should adopt

a teaching model that supports

the process of writing. This means

that writing becomes a part of your

classroom, not just a book report

or essay on a topic you have chosen

to assign to students. Storytelling,

poetry, essays, newspapers, lyrics

to the latest hip hop song, love notes—

all become opportunities to teach writing.

Make your classroom breathe words.

— **Tricia Hersey**
   Poet, writer & AIM Teaching Artist

What do you believe? What do you want your students to know and be able to do? Why is this important to you? Sharing "I believe" conversations between teaching partners is a great place to begin collaborative work. Initial planning meetings are the opportunity for teachers and artists to share core values and visions. Dialogue about social, emotional, intellectual and aesthetic intentions for the project deepen the conversation and bring exciting ideas to the table. This is the time to be very candid and expansive. Most importantly, this is a time to get to know each other. Teachers and artists find that meeting away from school—in a café or someone's home—offers a more relaxed atmosphere to plan the work ahead. The importance of making this time cannot be underestimated; these conversations pay off greatly in both the ease and depth of collaboration between teaching partners.

What's the Big Idea?

Big conceptual ideas provide a framework for both art and academic content strands. The big idea provides a container—or frame—to unify the parts into a meaningful whole. Chicago Arts Partnerships for Education (CAPE) has developed good criteria for meaningful big ideas (www.capeweb.org). Teachers are coached to find overarching big ideas that are open-ended and generative. To ensure that these ideas will have both breadth and depth, teaching partners ask and answer the why questions: Why is this idea important to me? Why will this idea be important to my students?

Educator Steve Seidel, in his key note address for the ArtsConnection 2005 Symposium: Beyond Arts Integration, speaks to the challenges of contemporary educators in a time of war. He asks his audience to consider the fundamental question, what is worth learning? He proposes six subjects worth learning, including: Human Rights, Languages, Globalization, Monuments, Sadness, and Density. Seidel says, "If there's a simple equation to guide us here, it might be that the more complex the problem, the more important to study it from various perspectives." (www.artsconnection.org)

PROJECT AIM ARTSTS, CECIL MCDONALD, JR. AND GUILLERMO DELGADO, WITH CYNTHIA WEISS,
SHARE AND DISCUSS STUDENT WORK AT THE PROJECT AIM CURRICULUM SHARE.

Some of the big ideas that have framed AIM units include Democracy, Coming of Age, Identity, Community, Survival, Relationships, Transformation, and Time. Successful big ideas are typically conceptual, as well as content driven—as opposed to skills-driven. The focus on such big ideas requires deep interconnection among all curricular areas.

A good way to field test the power of a big idea is to facilitate a brainstorming session with teaching partners and see if it leads to a rich conversation among partners. The excitement generated mirrors what an artist feels at the inception of a creative project. Constructing curriculum is an art form; two or more people, and two or more content areas, are coming together to build something new. The great challenge—and beauty—of this work is how tailor-made each unit is to a specific place, time, classroom of learners; as well as to the relationships forged by the teachers and artists.

Ask Essential Questions

When teachers, artists and students articulate their own curiosities, a spirit of surprise and discovery infuses the curriculum. Essential questions might explore the content or process of a unit; they might connect to the big ideas or look at the impact of specific arts processes. Questions explored in Project AIM units include: *What are the social concerns that fifth-graders face? How can documentary film represent these concerns? What do ensemble members need from each other? How can story writing be enhanced by theater and book-making? What can we learn from looking closely at the world around us? Where are relationships found?*

Project AIM is intrigued by the many kinds of questions that come up within the arc of an arts-integrated unit of study. Overarching essential questions provide a focus for the project. There are also many other kinds of questions that arise. Artists ask teachers about their content area and teachers have questions about art-making. Students' questions may lead to emergent curriculum within the unit. We encourage partners to keep track of the questions that arise in the course of their collaboration. We are continually learning from leading arts organizations around the country about the ways in which essential questions develop and deepen arts-integrated learning.

Set Art/Social/ Content Goals

Well-designed arts-integrated units provide educators ways to teach to the standards, as well as go beyond the standards. When teachers and artists have developed the Essential Questions and Big Ideas to study, they can easily identify and establish specific art and content area goals that fit within the larger frame. The standards offer a guide on *what* to teach; arts integration can help us figure out *how* to teach and engage our students when trying to meet those standards. It is useful to write social and emotional goals for a unit, as the arts always reach those students that are often not reached in more conventional teaching practice.

Curricular Coaching

An experienced third person sitting at the table can facilitate, support and mediate the exchange of ideas between teachers and artists. This curricular coach, often a program staff member, listens for themes and connections, and encourages both parties to find commonalities in their ideas. A coach helps teachers make conceptual connections from academic to art content, and supports artists in translating the intuitive knowledge of their art form into a sequential program plan.

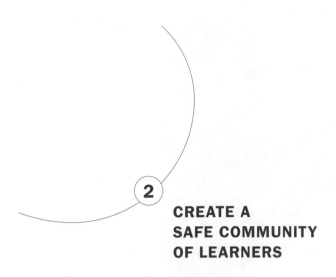

2

CREATE A
SAFE COMMUNITY
OF LEARNERS

I want the year my students and I spend

together to be one that we will forever

remember… It is in the building of this

community that we will lay the foundation

for a year of academic learning but also

for learning about people and the way we

live in the world together.

— **Joanne Hindley**
In the Company of Children

Develop an Atmosphere of Respect

Project AIM takes the expression: *a place for everyone at the table* both literally and metaphorically. The seating or desk arrangements in every gathering should offer everyone a seat and a clear line of vision. Every participant should feel that they have the time and opportunity to express their ideas. The attention invested in creating a community of learners will pay off in students' investment in the art-making process and all participants' investment in the partnership venture.

Arts-integrated instruction inspires and invites teachers, artists and students to take risks in their own learning process. Teachers and students have to participate in new and unfamiliar art lessons; teachers and artists experience the complex give and take of collaborative teaching, students will be asked to be presenters as well as audience in the public showings of their work. It is absolutely essential to create a safe community of learners to ensure engaged participation of everyone involved. An atmosphere of respect should be nurtured and cultivated at every teacher/artist meeting, faculty gathering, artist cadre meeting, classroom residency session, and culminating performance.

Establish a Set of Working Rules for Arts Learning

Every classroom has a culture and a stated, or unstated, set of rules that govern behavior and procedures. Visiting artists need to get to know the teacher's established set of rules and rituals, and also share their own rules and philosophy of practice. Teachers and artists often have different ideas about appropriate behavior, noise levels, and expectations for student participation. Different art forms also require new physical arrangements of the classroom space. Visiting artists might want to arrange chairs in semicircles for writing workshops or move desks for movement lessons. Teachers and artists should come to agreements about classroom management before a residency begins. New rules might need to be established between teachers, artists and students as the unit evolves.

Honor Every Voice
in Learning

The arts invite personal connections to learning that help
shape a shared sense of responsibility in the classroom.
There is a risk of exposure in doing real and meaningful
work. Arts integration challenges students to put their
curiosities, doubts and questions forward and to make
their learning visible to the group. Arts-integrated strategies
including theatre games, creative writing exercises, and
pair-shares all have the goal of honoring the voice of every
student. Artists and teachers can work with their students
to create respectful protocols for student sharing that set
the stage for a safe learning experience. In an increasingly
complex and intolerant world, arts-integrated teaching at its
best encourages acceptance of multiple perspectives, and
the celebration of diverse cultural experiences.

3

LEARN IN THE LANGUAGE OF THE ARTS

The forms we use to represent what we think—literal language, visual images, numbers, and poetry—impact how we think and what we can think about... Minds, then, in a curious but profound way are made. Their shape and capacities are influenced by what the young are given an opportunity to learn.

— **Elliot Eisner**
The Kinds of Schools We Need–Personal Essays.

Get Started

Once the unit plan has been developed, artists and teachers move back and forth between specific arts instruction, core curricular instruction, and the fusion of both within any given lesson. Depending on the needs of the unit and an art form, the language of the arts are either embedded in every lesson or taught as stand-alone sessions that precede immersion in a big idea. Each discipline requires its own rhythms of instruction. Many theatre artists need to teach the fundamentals of warm-up exercise, respect for personal space, and expression of the body and voice, before beginning to connect to theatre games and strategies to other content areas. The point we would like to make is that strong arts integration pays serious attention to the discipline, vocabulary and artistic habits of mind that lead to a high-quality arts experience.

Create a Studio in the Classroom

Teaching Artists offer their own art-making practices to the classroom to create studio/workshop environments. They bring high-quality art materials and equipment, well-organized supplies, bulletin boards with visual ideas, writing portfolios, which all lead to the message that this classroom is transformed into a space for exploration.

Establish a Working Arts Vocabulary

The working vocabulary of any art form is more than just vocabulary words. Within each word there is a complex history, an inventory of techniques, structures, and ideas that are the building blocks for curricular lessons. They are the tools of the trade of professional artists and provide students with a mastery of terms that will help their learning.

Utilize Professional Models of Artwork

Make use of strong model poems, films, songs, writing passages, and photographs that demonstrate examples of high quality art. These models scaffold the learning process in so many ways: they provide images and structures

STUDENT PHOTOGRAPHER
CONSIDERS SHOT ANGLE AND
LIGHTING DURING PHOTO
RESIDENCY AT ALBERT R. SABIN
MAGNET SCHOOL. PHOTO BY
JOEL WANEK.

that help teachers and artists demonstrate quality work to students. They stretch and inspire students to reach beyond their repertoire of ideas. They expand students' awareness of new writers, cultures, and voices—which can be used in order to develop their own.

Engage Student Models that Make Learning Visible

Student work, created in response to professional work, becomes in turn, a powerful model for inspiring new classrooms of students. There is a lovely cycle of modeling when artists and teachers use professional work to inspire their students, and their students offer back rich models of their own to inform future practice. Models of student work also serve as powerful documentation of the learning process. Arts integration partnerships around the country have had great success convening peer groups of educators to carefully study student work and inquire about the implications of this work on teaching and learning.

A Space for Connections

The space between points 3 and 4 on the learning spiral is the most exciting and difficult to capture. This is the space where integration is sought and connections are made. This is the space where the intersection of curriculum, content, and process come together.

Arts integration serves to connect the parts and the whole; there is an interdependence between acquiring skills in the art forms, and using those skills to respond expressively to the big ideas of our time. Some educators may begin with the vocabulary of the arts, some with big ideas and inquiry questions, the learning standards, or a model poem. The art of curriculum writing is to create a plan that brings all the pieces together in a dialogical whole.

Link Art Making to the Big Idea

The Big Idea is the bridge between learning in the arts and learning in the content area. AIM teaching artists often introduce the big idea at the beginning of a residency and then spiral that idea even as students learn basic skills in the arts. In order for students to be able to transfer knowledge from one domain to another, the conceptual ideas must be revisited continuously in the unit. This can happen by asking, "What did this lesson today have to do with our big idea?" Provide an opportunity for reflection at the end of every classroom session.

Transition Between Text and Image

Project AIM utilizes the power of image to illuminate text, and the power of text to illuminate image. When students are given opportunities to translate ideas across modes of expression, they are better able to think abstractly and metaphorically. Arts Integration offers students the chance to engage in a full range of images: theatrical, aural, photographic, kinesthetic and visual. For example, AIM artists commonly coach their students to create *tableau,* a theatrical image-making exercise where students take physical poses in response to the action or emotional content of a story. Through tableau, students can imagine the inner-feelings and thoughts of a character in their own bodies. Moving from text to tableau supports the learning of empathy, inference and perspective taking.

Book and Paper artist Jamie Lou Thome shows her students how to create visual images and book structures that will give shape to their written ideas. In the curricular unit, *Housing Our Stories,* Jamie's students used objects of personal significance (a father's tool box) or created new structures (game boards, stair forms, mazes) to house their autobiographical writing. Jamie explains,

> I want my students to focus on how the structures of their books can push their writing forward. Creating structures to house their stories allows students to shape their writing—literally and metaphorically. Working in both the literary and visual arts helps them to discover the essence of their work.

4) IMMERSE IN THE BIG IDEAS THROUGH ART MAKING

Literacy experts have long considered the importance of *transmediation* (moving back and forth between mediums of expression). Educator Jean Anne Clyde, in an essay on story and subtext strategies, refers to literacy experts Berghoff, Egawa, Harste, and Hoonan who write, "Transmediation pushes beyond metaphor by taking what is known in one sign system and recasting it in another… Moving from sign system to sign system is like turning an artifact so that we can suddenly see a new facet that was previously hidden from view, *(Beyond Reading and Writing: Inquiry, Curriculum, and Multiple Ways of Knowing, 2000).*

Work with Parallel Processes in Literacy and the Arts

In Project AIM we have focused on the integration of art and literacy **processes** as well as the integration of arts and core subject **content.** We have built on a theory of **parallel processes** that Cynthia first developed with colleague, Lynette Emmons, Center for City Schools at National Louis University, and Gail Burnaford and Arnold Aprill, Chicago Arts Partnership in Education (CAPE). *(Renaissance in the Classroom: Arts Integration and Meaningful Learning, Lawrence Erlbaum Associates, 2001).*

The parallel processes approach is rooted in the belief that the schools can teach students how to write like professional writers, create art like professional artists, study science like scientists, and history like historians. Many teachers have embraced the idea of Reading and Writing Workshop process; their students are familiar with working through brainstorming, making first drafts, revising, refining, and publishing their work. Teaching artists can find common language with classroom teachers when they name the steps they use to make work in their own artistic discipline. Lynette Emmons has helped Project AIM artists further articulate what proficient readers, writers and artists do **before**, **during** and **after** reading, writing and art-making, to construct meaning in their work. There are elegant connections to be found—structurally, synthetically and metaphorically, when processes across disciplines are delineated and taught. (See Appendix)

The arts process—sensory based and expressive—engages the whole student and helps them enter the curriculum. Teachers and artists can coach their students to pick a step in the reading/writing process and expand upon it through the arts. Collage compositions may serve as an exercise to precede composition in writing or in music; theatre exercises help students to visualize a difficult text. The learning is a two-way street, the reading and writing process helps students create more nuanced artwork as they engage material on a cognitive, expressive, and imaginative level in endless permutations of learning.

Activate Prior Knowledge and Research New Information

Making personal connections is absolutely essential for engaged learning. Starting with students' own lives and interests is a way to enter the world of text. Theatre artists and dancers begin with self, body, and voice as entry points for learning. Other artists and teachers tap the rich foundations of students' family life, neighborhoods, and traditions as entry points.

Students are also challenged to research new information in order to complete arts-integrated projects. In a curricular unit at Albert R. Sabin Magnet School, teaching artists Deborah Guzmán-Meyer and Julie Downey, along with their fifth-grade teaching team, looked closely at plants through botany, photography, and writing lessons. The strength and beauty of their project depended on students' careful library and internet research that informed and expanded their photographic and written interpretations.

CROWN COMMUNITY ACADEMY
STUDENTS CONSIDER THE BIG IDEAS
OF THEIR CLASSMATES. PHOTO BY
AMANDA LEIGH LICHTENSTEIN.

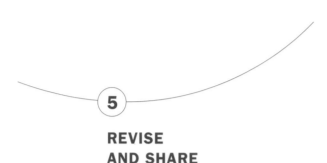

5

REVISE
AND SHARE

One's sense of rightness involves

absolutely the whole person...

if the artist doesn't make his

work right he has no idea what

he has left out.

— **Richard Diebenkorn**
American painter

Compare Drafts
with Intentions

How do we know when our work is finished? How does our work arrive at a rightness of fit? When does our work become the idea we hold in our mind's eye? The impulse to make work *right* is a driving force in an artist's creative process. This impulse is a gift that the arts bring to education; it offers an intrinsic reason and motivation for students to revise and refine their work. The goal of the revision in this context helps students to bring their work closer to what they want it to be. Revision helps them take a critical look and find the tools they need to make their work better. Comparing drafts with intentions compels students to strive for more nuanced expressions of their ideas.

Revise

Project AIM artists and teachers encourage their students to edit and revise their work as an ongoing investigation into their own learning. The products made by students narrate a learning journey, and through deep editing and revision, students hone in on the meaning of quality and communication. Revision is where new questions and visions arise—it is an essential part of the learning spiral. With an emphasis on process itself as a kind of product, revision is where students really learn to grapple with the artistic skills and the big ideas at the same time.

CASIMIR PULASKI FINE ARTS
ACADEMY STUDENT SHARES HIS
WRITING WITH POET, JENN MOREA.
PHOTO BY LISA HUTLER.

Share

The opportunity to share work in mid-process with an audience is one of the best ways to access the coherency of ideas. If we think of learning as a cycle, a natural part of the cycle is to present work in the world and gather responses from others. Project AIM has adapted critique strategies developed by choreographer, Liz Lerman, and her company, the Liz Lerman Dance Exchange. Her process is unique in the sense that it asks artists, and students, to improve upon their work—without shutting them down with negative criticism. In Critical Response, the most important step is asking students to notice what they find memorable in their fellow students' work. In doing so, students learn to assume that there will be something memorable and that their fellow students will notice it. Students realize that their voice matters—that it impacts other people. The basic idea with a partnership, like a relationship, is that an audience will be responsive to what an artist creates.

Improvise and Experiment

Play is an essential part of the creative process. The arts invite experimentation, trial and error, and improvisation at all stages of the learning process—beginning, middle, and right up to the end. This open-ended investigation is often a new experience for students and for teachers. At first they may be impatient with not knowing where their work or a given lesson will take them. Throughout the process, students learn to trust the impulse to experiment and take risks with new ideas. In doing so, they learn to generate new questions as they problem-pose and solve the puzzles of their art-making and thinking.

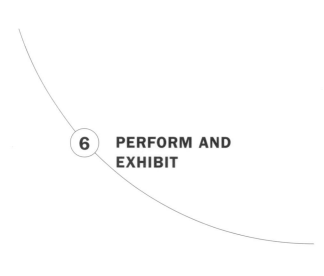

6 PERFORM AND EXHIBIT

When I made my book, I learned how to make an autobiography and how to be a better writer and artist. Now I want to become a professional artist.

— **Takira**
  Edward Jenner Academy of the Arts

Process and Product

Project AIM believes that the process and product are indispensable to each other, and that creating high-quality artwork is an essential part of the learning spiral. But that being said, it also important to avoid the *perfect assembly syndrome,* where performance preparation overtakes good teaching practice. In reflective arts integration, artwork is viewed as evidence of learning. Art products become the mediating focus that teachers, artists and students can learn from, appreciate and discuss.

Prepare Work for Culminating Events

In the classroom, as in the professional art world, performances and exhibitions raise the bar for aspiring artists. Rehearsals and preparation for culminating events let students know that adults believe their work deserves careful attention. When students get positive feedback they feel a strong sense of accomplishment that often surpasses their own expectations of what they thought possible.

Present Work to an Audience

Arts-integrated teaching offers students a greater audience for their ideas. In each step of the learning spiral, from creating a community of learners, to encouraging peer reviews and positive critical response, students learn to become more attentive audiences for each other. Students will want to share their work, and may want to expand their audience to include parents, other classrooms or the whole school community. Our belief is that when students gain a sense of agency through success in the arts, this will transfer to a greater sense of agency in other parts of their lives.

DURING A CULMINATING EVENT, A STUDENT
AT EDWARD JENNER ACADEMY OF THE ARTS
PRESENTS HER WORK WITH TEACHING ARTIST,
IAN WEAVER. PHOTO BY JULIO FLORES.

High-Quality Exhibitions and Performances

Exhibitions and presentations demand that students seek a well-formed articulation of their ideas. It is often in the very preparation towards exhibition that curricular projects come into focus. Arts partnerships can extend their audience and impact by joining forces with local galleries, museums, libraries or colleges to present student work outside of the school setting. The exhibition opening or performance is an opportunity for students across the city to celebrate their achievements with family, friends, and a wider public. High-quality of student work in a professional venue will always exceed everyone's expectations.

(See Chapter Four for a description of Talkin' Back: Chicago Youth Responds—an annual collaborative exhibition between Project AIM and the Museum of Contemporary Photography at Columbia College Chicago.)

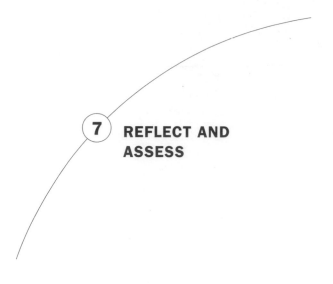

7 REFLECT AND ASSESS

"To exist humanly is to name

the world, to change it. Once named,

the world in its turn reappears to the

namers as a problem and requires

of them a new naming. [We] are not

built in silence, but in word, in work,

in action-reflection."

— **Paolo Freire**
Pedagogy of the Oppressed

Reflective Practice

Reflection at each step of the learning spiral allows students to name and re-frame their own understanding of their work. Project AIM makes a commitment to create a culture of reflective practice. Reflections and debrief discussions are a regular part of the work—in the classroom, at artist and teacher meetings, at professional development sessions, the summer institute, staff meetings, and end of the year evaluations. Inspired by the many creative writers that are in the artist cadre, there is also a culture of writing across Project AIM. Students are given residency journals, teaching artists write journal entries after classroom sessions, and teachers fill out exit slips after each professional development series. It is a challenge to find time for thoughtful reflection in the hectic lives of schools, but the insights gained in the process are well worth the constant effort to hold this time sacred.

Curricular Sharing among Peers

When teachers, students, and artists reflect on their work, they become researchers—as well as creators. Just as students need to step back and appreciate their own learning, teachers and artists come to understand the impact of their teaching through the audience of a supportive peer community.

Project AIM organizes curriculum fairs at the end of the year that provide opportunities for educators across school sites to share their arts-integrated units. Documentation of student learning in videos, photographs, and Power Point presentations, shared over food, drink, and conversation, have afforded a rich exchange of ideas.

Recently, Project AIM has revised the format of this culminating event to support deeper and more meaningful peer-to-peer interactions. Teachers and artists from different schools come together to share artifacts of student work in small peer groups. Educators briefly present the context for their students' work and then ask their peers to consider these questions:

- What captures your attention in the work?
- What does this make you wonder?
- What are the implications for teaching and learning?

Documentation as Occasions for Reflection and Assessment

Documentation of the arts integration process offers rich evidence of learning and invaluable opportunity for reflection. Documentation can be collected at each step of the learning spiral. Documentation of the teacher/artist collaboration might include:

- Planning meeting notes
- Initial unit plans
- Action research questions
- Journal entries and
- Teacher exit slips

Documentation of student learning might include:
- Student journal entries and reflective writing samples
- Pre- and post-samples of student work
- Video clips of lessons at the beginning, middle and end of a unit
- Audio recordings of students' reflections
- Photos of culminating artwork

Each of these artifacts can serve as eloquent evidence of student growth in the course of a unit of study. Plans for documentation should be made in the initial partnership meetings. Practitioners use documentation to revisit goals and assess student learning. Documentation is also an excellent way for practitioners to share the story of their practice with the school community, arts education researchers and policy makers.

AT CASIMIR PULASKI FINE ARTS ACADEMY, A STUDENT KEEPS A WEEKLY JOURNAL TO REFLECT ON HER LEARNING IN THE THEATRE ARTS. PHOTO BY JULIO FLORES.

DISCOVER NEW INTENTIONS FOR TEACHING AND LEARNING

(8)

At the end of an arts integration unit, it is ideal for artists and teachers to revisit their original intentions for teaching and learning. Together they can share documentation of the unit that might include photographs of the work process, student exit slips, artifacts of student writing, artwork, and assessments of student learning. Arts-integrated learning always reveals unexpected outcomes. Teachers and artists often express delight at the ways in which students have exceeded their expectations.

Shared reflection and discussion provides partners the opportunity to understand the impact of their teaching and to fine-tune lessons for future use. The curriculum process is an art in itself. Project AIM has long-term partnerships that allow teachers and artists to work together for more than one year. Consecutive partnership opportunities always allow teachers and artists the opportunity to spiral back on their own learning and to go deeper with their work.

Educators across all disciplines face the challenge of creating strong assessment instruments to measure complex student learning beyond the standardized test. The creation of meaningful assessment tools is an art form still in formation within the arts integration field. Project AIM looks forward to developing new assessment tools and learning from arts partnerships across the country who have developed their own meaningful measures of student learning.

The learning spiral mirrors the artistic process—ask any artist who takes their work seriously and they will most likely relate to each of these steps in the never ending spiral of art-making. We know that these steps don't always follow this exact order. The same way that art can be fine-tuned, there is also a kind of fine-tuning in the teaching process—and arts Integration is about the work of surprise.

Arts Integration: the rigor of preparation, the willingness to plan for the unexpected, and our disposition to be pleased by students' responses that surpass expectations.

"To know and to grow—

Everything yet to see."

— **Paolo Freire**
Teachers as Cultural Workers:
Letters to Those Who Dare Teach

TEACHERS AND ARTISTS
DISCUSS THEIR SCRIPTS
IN ORDER TO DISCOVER
NEW INTENTIONS.
PHOTO BY JOEL WANEK.

TEACHERS CLOSELY
OBSERVE THEIR DANCE-
MAKING PROCESS.
PHOTO BY JOEL WANEK.

CHAPTER ONE
Bibliography

Burnaford, Gail, Arnold Aprill, and Cynthia Weiss. Eds. *Renaissance in the Classroom: Arts Integration and Meaningful Learning.* New York, NY: Taylor & Francis Group, LLC (formerly Lawrence Erlbaum), 2001.

Clyde, Jean Anne. *Stepping Inside the Story World: The Subtext Strategy—A Tool for Connecting and Comprehending. International Reading Association (2003).* Beyond Reading and Writing: Inquiry, Curriculum, and Multiple Ways of Knowing, (2000).

Eisner, Elliot, *The Kinds of Schools We Need-Personal Essays.* Heinemann, Portsmouth, NH, (1998).

Freire, Paolo. *Teachers as Cultural Workers: Letters to Those Who Dare to Teach.* Westview Press, (1998).

Friere, Paolo, *Pedagogy of the Oppressed.* Translated by Myra Bergman Ramos. Continuum, New York (1998/1970).

Livingston, Jane. *The Art of Richard Diebenkorn,* Whitney Museum of Art, in association with University of California Press, Berkeley, Los Angeles, London (1997).

CHAPTER TWO

Diverse Portraits
of Classroom Life

Diverse Portraits

of Classroom Life

Cynthia Weiss and
Amanda Leigh Lichtenstein

We sing, we write, we film, we bind, we frame, we stitch, we question, we teach, we wonder. This collection of first person essays invites you to step inside arts-integrated classrooms in order to experience diverse portraits of arts-integrated teaching and learning.

In the following essays, you will notice how Project AIM artists and teachers respond to the complex questions and experiences that arise in AIM classrooms. From intense exploration of language and social justice to mentorship and relationships, Project AIM artists capture the essence of arts integration by carefully balancing rigorous inquiry with tender and compelling stories about arts and learning.

Each essay addresses the immense wonder and complexity of arts integration and never shies away from the generative questions that arise. Every Project AIM artist recognizes the power of relationships as the central force in all collaborative work in schools. These essays illuminate the ways in which teachers, students and artists ignite infinite connections with one another and, consequently, nurture the process of art-making otherwise neglected in public schools.

This collection of essays begins with broad observations on the changing shape of arts-integrated classrooms. Writer Emmy Bright, Project AIM Observation Specialist, unearths the spatial and emotional configurations in the teaching of three artistic disciplines. Poet Jenn Morea surprises her students (and herself) with unexpected relationships found between math, poetry, and music in the classroom. Poet Tricia Hersey encourages teachers and artists to "make their classrooms breathe with words," instilling a love of language and poetry across the curriculum. Writer Lisa Redmond calls for a new creative writing pedagogy that views all language as art and specifically addresses African-American English (AAE). Photographer Deborah Guzmán-Meyer addresses the language of photography as seen through the eyes of a young ESL student.

Writer Julie A. Downey encourages us to closely observe the world in an essay on expecting the unexpected in the classroom. Spoken word artist avery r. young writes in his own poetic vernacular about a crucial moment he coins "the do-over," the opportunity to ask for and give second chances. avery's teaching partner, photographer Cecil McDonald, Jr., traces the development of their project from the spark of an idea he got in a record store in the south of France. Photographer Joel Wanek's photo essay details a thematic photography unit that leads to "The Emptiness Project," while visual artist and teacher Mathias "Spider" Schergen explores the evolution of "Friday Boys," with filmmaker Crystal Griffith and a group of rambunctious sixth-grade boys. And finally, high school humanities teacher Meg Arbeiter speaks passionately about self-discovery through the visual arts in a residency with painter Guillermo Delgado. Each of these essays told in such diverse styles affirms Project AIM's commitment to nurturing the uniqueness and value of each individual voice within a collective.

Arts integration practice prepares for the teachable moment, an opportunity for transformation, when after careful planning, one is asked to think on one's feet and respond to the unexpected. Each essay documents those moments of change and the insights that follow. The rigor and intention of planning, coupled with creative process, makes space for discovery. A light bulb goes off for a student. Teachers and artists become aware of core principles. A student teaches and a teacher learns. This paradigm shift is more apt to happen in classrooms where the arts are present.

Finally, these essays illustrate the importance of reflective practice. We hope that our readers will recognize similar moments in their own teaching lives and share them with colleagues and friends. It is in the act of reflecting and writing where key ideas are crystallized, moments remembered, stories retold.

The Changing Shape of Learning

Emmy Bright

ARTS EDUCATOR
PROJECT AIM OBSERVATION SPECIALIST

Like fingerprints, each classroom is unique—bearing the marks of the teacher and the students, the accoutrements and tools that are or are not available to the school. But also like fingerprints, there is a standard form. When asked to imagine a fingerprint—we know what to expect—an oval shape with swirls and bends and ridges. So too with a classroom. The structure is so familiar we often don't notice it. The form is so well known as to be overlooked.

What is the ordinary form of the classroom and how does this translate to its function? The shape of classroom space is common and understood by our society, having stayed more or less the same for a hundred years. How do we understand the traditional function of the classroom in order to explore what else might be possible? Even an empty classroom has its particular personality.

As the Observation Specialist for Project AIM, I visited classrooms to observe, interpret, and document the qualitative outcomes articulated in our FIPSE grant proposal. I looked at student/teacher engagement and artist/teacher partnership dynamics. What I observed about arts integration exceeded many of our expectations.

I began to understand the "ordinary" classroom when I started to observe "extraordinary" ones. I watched teaching artists take the form and materials of the classroom and twist, change, reinterpret, and break down these traditional forms. Thinking of forms, I was reminded of my high school biology teacher who told us, "Form follows function… if you remember that, you'll go far." She was describing phototropism, the way the plants bends towards the light. Plants literally change their shape to serve their purpose.

I saw artists building new structures and finding new spaces—in hallways, play yards, corridors and classrooms. In these new forms and structures, I saw students and

teachers bending toward a new and different light. I saw them connect with one another more equally and actively than in other classrooms. Students took risks, delved inside for ideas and reflections, and supported each other in their work.

I saw multiple and rich departures from my old understanding of how classrooms look and function. I observed that indeed, form does follow function. Each different arts discipline illuminates new forms and possibilities for learning—ones that are spatial, intellectual and personal.

Setting the Stage: Theater

Teaching artist Khanisha Foster worked with one classroom to adapt novels into plays and performances. In a classroom cluttered with 28 desks, students, and backpacks, this was no easy feat. The space presented an obstacle for art-making, but her charge was to problem solve ways to make the space work.

Khanisha's entrance alone signaled a change, and the students and teacher responded accordingly. With the clap of the teacher's hands, students knew to shove the desks and chairs to the perimeter—yielding an empty center. Everyone circled up shoulder to shoulder in the center of the room to warm up.

In this circular arrangement, the students had to make eye contact with their peers. They played a theater game where, through gesture and eye contact, the focus was passed across and around the circle. Unlike sitting at a desk, this game required each student to be aware of and present to the whole group. They had to be ready to give and receive. The circle taught an awareness of the self as an equal and important part of a larger whole.

Then the hollow in the center of the circle widened and became a rectangular stage. Small groups of students took turns performing silent tableaus of their stories. The audience members watched attentively and applauded prior to giving feedback. The performers were learning to add physicality to their story, choose clear visual symbols and practice moving in unusual ways to express the narrative arc. The audience supported their fellow classmates' work and provided a critique to help them develop their piece. The groups switched, all audience members performed, and all performers eventually served as audience. Khanisha's spatial choices were grounded in her intentions of community building among the students, personal engagement, collaborative creation and active reading and response to art.

Outside the Frame: Photography

How a photography class, or any visual arts class, "should" look is perhaps less clear-cut than one based on physical movement like theater or dance. Cameras do not, by themselves, tell us how to move the desks or how the students' bodies might be positioned. The form of Teaching Artist Joel Wanek's photography class was driven by his assignments.

Joel entered the classroom and asked the students to swivel their desks to the front. Joel flashed images of portrait photographer Dawoud Bey's photos and asked the class, "What do you notice? What do you think about the girl in this picture? What else do you see? What do you not see?" The students responded verbally and sketched in their journals. The darkened room and looming images helped the students enter, study, and remember photographic images. Joel repeatedly pointed out the frame and asked the students to consider what was inside the frame and to imagine what was outside of it.

Joel turned on the lights and told the students that the next step was to walk around inside the school and "frame" emptiness with their cameras. The students broke into teams and became explorers in their own school, finding vacant hallways, corners and empty staircases. They examined and captured where doors met walls and a boundary turned into an opening, where spaces changed and transformed into others.

There were, of course, sporadic shouts and laughter, but it was manageable and negotiated together by the teacher and artist. They were willing to venture outside of the traditional boundaries of the classroom in order to give the students the space and freedom, coupled with the purpose and understanding, to approach their image-making. By venturing outside of the classroom with their new tools, students became decision makers and image takers. They began to realize and communicate more expansive concepts in their lives that are not always best expressed in language.

A Space of One's Own: Writing

Writing, of all of the arts disciplines, can look the most like traditional schoolwork, and, it might be assumed, linked to traditional thinking and learning. In writing, the artful teacher helps her students understand writing as an expressive and crafted discipline instead of simply as a vehicle for the transfer of information.

Writing is most often considered a solitary process, but many creative writers encourage group warm-ups, writing from images, physical games, or collaborative writing exercises to enliven the writing experience. These active approaches distinguish creative writing from the traditional report or the essay; they encourage students to draw inspiration from various sources, to experiment and to move beyond the fear of "getting it wrong."

Writing requires an understanding of form and structure and then space for inward reflection. Poet Jenn Morea meets a young writer in the midst of his or her own solitude.

In a particular Project AIM classroom, she begins with a presentation of two model poems. Then, from the front of the room, Jenn leads the students through a series of prompts and questions. Students take notes that will be used as fodder for their writing. The students then lean over their pages and start writing.

Then the space changed. The students and their desks did not move but Jenn began to walk around the room. Some students were eager for her attention and she crouched by them for eye-to-eye conversation. Their bodies were hunched so closely that it looked like a deep conversation between intimate friends. Jenn was able to create a concentrated personal space within a public one. She became their temporary partner in this solitary work. Serving more as a mentor than instructor, Jenn's advice to her students was most often in the form of questions. She did not sit by every student, but instead seemed to check in, in some way, with each of them. In this classroom, it was the interpersonal space between the adult and student that changed. The reinvented classroom allowed each student to be productive and alone but never lost.

Expanding Classroom Walls

Like the plant which bends towards the light, it is our responsibility to change our spaces and shapes to best fit the learning of our students. The classroom needs a brave and intentional leader, one who is willing to forgo the traditional rows of desks in order to make room for the new and the unexpected.

As I watched teachers in the Project AIM classrooms, I often saw them mirroring, in order to learn, the teaching artists' use of space. I watched one teacher lay down on the floor with her students as they all peacefully wrote in their "reflection journals." She whispered to me, "They never are this focused when we're writing at our desks. I'm going to try this." I saw teachers crouching down next to students as they wrote, playing improvisation games in a circle, or setting up stations to facilitate different activities.

Through the arts, the teachers were permitted to trespass traditional and habitual spatial arrangements. They experienced and created more equal and fruitful relationships with their students. It is our charge as arts educators to discover and explore a variety of forms and functions in which our students can grow vibrant and strong. The classroom can be made both bigger and more intimate than the walls around it might imply.

TEACHING ARTIST, KHANISHA FOSTER
LEADS THEATRE GAMES AT ROBERT HEALY
ELEMENTARY SCHOOL. PHOTO BY JOEL WANEK.

The Oooh's and Ahhh's

BETWEEN POETRY, MUSIC, ART AND MATHEMATICS

Jenn Morea
POET, TEACHING ARTIST

During the 2005–2006 school year, I worked with fifth & sixth-grade classes at Casimir Pulaski Fine Arts Academy. This poetry-based residency was focused on the following essential question: Where are relationships found? At the beginning of the residency, students wrote lists of all of the places they could think of in which relationships were located—as well as their own definitions of relationship. The majority of their responses referred to relationships strictly in a human context—relationships between friends and family—or in a few cases, between humans and their pets. Since then, students have examined relationships in language, sound, visual art and mathematics, as well as relationships between Chicago and the primarily Latin American countries where they, or their parents, were born.

When I was younger, math—from basic multiplication and division in elementary school, to the algebra, geometry, and physics classes I was required to take in high school—was consistently a nerve-wracking experience. Even with all of the lunch-time recesses spent with my math teacher and a deck of multiplication flashcards, and all the before and after school tutoring from various members of the National Honor Society, my feelings of dread in relation to math seemed to increase with each school year. But in my adult life, through a growing interest in architecture, I connected with math in a different way. I became fascinated with math as a language, respectful of its precise nature, and intrigued by its similarities to poetry.

The first day I walked into the sixth-grade classroom, I noticed a series of beautiful artworks on the back wall. I asked the teacher about them, and she said the students had been studying tessellation in math class. She went on to explain that each student was responsible for making their own tessellation pattern and that later on the patterns would become part of a collective quilt. A week later, I attended a Project AIM meeting at the school that was held in the art teacher's classroom. There were notes about

tessellation on her chalkboard, and I asked her about them. It turned out that my fifth-grade students had been studying tessellation with her in their art class.

I thought it would be perfect to introduce pantoums, a traditional poetic form from Malaysia written in quatrains wherein lines are repeated throughout in a precise and hypnotic pattern, alongside tessellation. The art teacher was kind enough to let me borrow a transparency of a 6000-year-old mosaic tile pattern from Mesopotamia (now Iraq). I projected the tile pattern and asked the students to say anything they noticed about it. They mentioned colors: red, blue, yellow, white, black; shapes and shape-related terms: stars, flowers, hearts, crosses, congruent, polygons; and concepts: symmetry, reflection, repetition, rhythm.

Then we read a model poem of a pantoum and looked together at a blank structure of the form. Again, I asked the students to say anything they noticed about the poem or its form. They used the same conceptual words they had used to describe the mosaic tile pattern to describe the pantoum form: symmetry, reflection, repetition and rhythm. There were some oooh's and ahhh's around the room as some of the students made the connection between the similar qualities in the patterns. Next, I asked the students to write pantoums about their own tessellation patterns, about the mosaic tile pattern we looked at together, or about tessellation in general.

At the conclusion of the residency I again asked the students to write their own definitions of relationship and to write responses to the question: Where are relationships found? My hope was that, in opening the residency with an inquiry, which was then explored within the context of bringing two or more seemingly discrete and disparate elements together each week, that the student's sense of what a relationship was, and where it might be found, would increase considerably. When I asked the students to again write lists of the places relationships were found, responses such as between two pictures, metaphor, structures, rainforest, soccer field, complemented initial responses like in a family, pen pals, husband/wife.

I designed the residency around this central question for a number of reasons. I liked the idea of thinking with my students about where relationships can be found because relationships signify connections. The more connections that can be made between things, then the more things have a belonging. Also, I am mindful of how painful it became for me to even hear the word "math" when I was younger, and so I approach my students knowing that some of them may have similar feelings towards writing, reading and thinking about poetry. Connecting poetry to math, music and visual arts allows and invites students, who may not be comfortable with poetry on its own, to experience it in a different, less intimidating way.

Arts integration is essentially a field that specializes in relationships. There is the relationship between the classroom teacher and the teaching artist, the relationship between the teacher's curriculum and the teaching artist's area of expertise, and the relationship between the students, the teacher and the teaching artist to the subject matter and art forms. Even though I am a writer, my favorite art form is music—closely followed by the visual arts. My work is influenced by both of these forms, and I am deeply interested in the processes by which both are made, and what I can learn about writing by studying them. Arts integration allows me the freedom to teach what I am most curious about and to engage in a dialogue with my students that furthers this curiosity in compelling ways. Essentially, arts integration gives me the opportunity to go beyond merely introducing poetry fundamentals.

I brought in musician Charles Barbera to assist the students in setting to music the sound-poems they wrote. In response to this experience, sixth-grader Luz stated, "It was really interesting to work with music and poetry at the same time. It really makes sense like if it was a pattern." One fifth-grader wrote, "What I noticed about the words and the music is they both had a part of onomatopoeia. They also had the same rhythm. The music went with the sound of the poem. They had a relationship. The music sounded like the poem and the poem sounded like the music." I

also asked the students what they noticed between when they first wrote their poems and when they transformed them into calligrams (a poem whose shape relates to its subject) with visual artist Cynthia Weiss. Another fifth-grader wrote, "What I noticed was that when it was just a poem on notebook paper [was that] it was just like doing a daily routine like getting up, brushing your teeth, etc. When I turned it into a calligram it was no daily routine, it was like a journey to a new land, it gave it more life." And I am right there with the students in this sense of wonder at where relationships are found and at seeing how bringing two things together can increase the possibilities of each.

Shapes

The yellow hexagon
            Tessellating around
with the triangles
            All the different colors

Tessellating around
            Like in math
All the different colors
            With all the symmetry

Like in math
            And the squares
With all the symmetry
            All around me

And the squares
            With their vertex
All around me
            Like the sky

With their vertex
            Also the sides
Like the sky
            In space

– Felipe, Sixth-grade

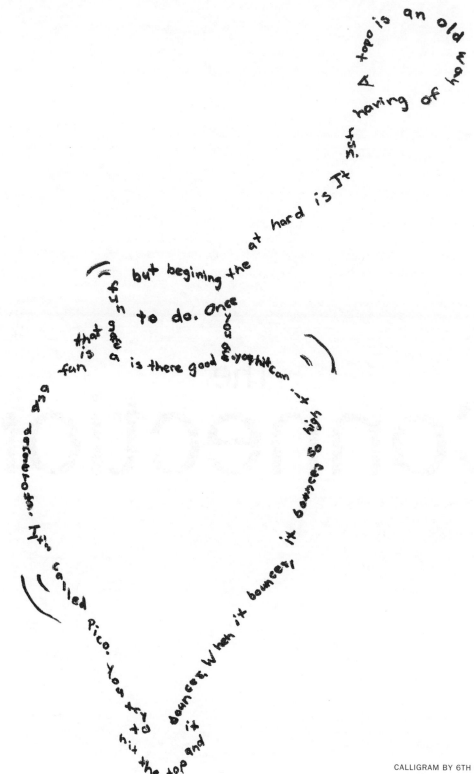

A top is an old way of having of fun. It is not hard at but begining the fun to do. Once that is is there good a it can so high bounces it bounces. When it bounces, and it to try You Pico. called It's deterorote. are a fun you

The
Connection

Tricia Hersey
WRITER, TEACHING ARTIST

Today, at Crown Community Academy on the West Side of Chicago, Ms. Wilson's fifth-graders are writing poems about dreams. I resist the urge to tell them what kind of dreams. Alicia raises her hand and wants to know if these are dreams that they have when sleeping or dreams of what they want to be when they grow up. I tell her I don't know, and as a writer you have to make decisions on what you want to share and write about. She liked this idea. I am not surprised that she questioned me about it. She is a leader and thinker. Then there is Arielle. Another clear example of a naturally creative child with an ear for words. Arielle writes the following poem about dreams that day:

Dreaming

Music going through my head like hip hop
The softness of my pillow and clouds in the sky
On a cloud rapping with Chingy
What does it feel like to be a butterfly in the sky?

I want to get across to them that writing a poem and creating art is a precious thing. Every word chosen should be well thought-out. During the first two poetry writing sessions they all rushed and panicked to be the first one done, to proudly show me their work. Today, I tell them to sit and take time to think and compose something beautiful, slowly, slowly... and they did. I resist the urge to walk around when students are writing and engaged in a deliberate creative moment. I usually give the writing prompt and drift into the background. I am always open to answering questions and wait to get called over to

a young poet's desk. When they call I come and guide. I don't show or tell them what to write. I facilitate the existing connection and creative spark that already exists in children, in humans. I believe everyone's brain has a place that holds immense artistic and creative potential. My mission is to get them to connect; to be led to that place through writing lessons and a teaching model that believes children come to the table with a wealth of unique creative abilities.

We don't need anymore jazzy, fun lessons that can be marketed in all-knowing manuals to solve the challenge of our children not being able to write. I hear from teachers in classrooms all over the city of Chicago, "My students don't know how to express their thoughts on paper." I believe that in order to begin addressing our literacy issues, we should adopt a teaching model that supports the process of writing. Our goal is to connect creative spaces that support children's voices in whatever form they come.

I believe writing teachers have to begin to give equal credit and exposure to all forms of writing. This means that writing becomes a part of your classroom not just a book report or essay on a topic you have chosen to assign to students. Storytelling, poetry, essays, newspapers, lyrics to the latest hip hop songs, love notes, magazines, photographs, maps, fiction, children's books, food labels, recipes & comic books all become opportunities to teach writing. Make your classroom breathe words. While working as a teaching artist at Columbia College Chicago, I attempt to model this when working with teachers in their classrooms.

There is a span of silent energy that starts when I give the writing prompt until I get the first raised hand or holler summoning me with questions. This moment has buried heads, intense faces, and moving pencils. During this three to five minute span of time you are witnessing connection. I take a great amount of time explaining and trying to make connections from the previous week's lessons. During week 1 at Crown Community Academy, in a fifth-grade classroom, I passed out this simple fill-in-the-blank writing prompt:

I AM

I am ____
Otherwise known as ____
Who sometimes likes to ____
I am ____(animal)
I am ____(color)
I am the number ____
I am not ____
I am ____

The children loved the approachable form of the prompt. I love to give it the first day. It eases the intimidation of writing a poem and everyone can do it. This is the hook. I add to the connection in this lesson by always having children read their poems aloud. We start from day one. If they have never written a poem before they will have the opportunity to write their first and debut it in a poetry reading that takes place at the end of all of my poetry writing lessons. On this day at Crown all the children wrote and read their poems.

TRICIA HERSEY AND TONE STOCKENSTRÖM MAKE WORDS COME TO LIFE WITH THEIR POPE SCHOOL STUDENTS DURING A FIELD TRIP TO THE BEVERLY ARTS CENTER. PHOTO BY CYNTHIA WEISS.

An example of leading children to their natural creative writing space occurs when I give the exact writing prompt to the same children 13 weeks later, on my last day of the project at Crown Community Academy. My hope is that through my weekly time with these students I have guided them through lessons that show the magic and spirit of writing. The core to my curriculum is on details. I drive each lesson with ideas on recognizing and expressing details in writing. To the right are before and after writing samples from two students.

These poems show something has happened to the way these children have connected to words and language. The second set of poems are fuller, richer and open. There is life in the words. I see details, metaphors, colorful words, imagery and complete voices. I see children who have began the journey of having the tools and confidence to become excellent writers, not just creative writers but lovers of words. Literacy. The spark has been lit. The connection affirmed.

Self Portrait #1

I am Demetrius
Otherwise known as Poohy
Who sometimes likes to dance
Who sometimes likes to bowl
I am an eagle
I am brown and white
I am the number 29
I am not an animal
I am a boy

Self Portrait #2

I am the blue sky above
Otherwise known as meechie who likes
        to eat meat
Who sometimes likes to play outside
        in the grass
I am a hawk that is in the sky looking
        for prey
I am the color green like grass
I am the number 55
I am not who you think I am
I am the sky above

Demetrius
FIFTH-GRADE, CROWN COMMUNITY ACADEMY

Self Portrait #1

I am Porsha
Otherwise known as Monique
Who sometimes like to jump rope
I am a bird
I am pink
I am the number 13
I am not quiet
I am a person who likes to do math

Self Portrait #2

I am Porsha Monique
With black eyes, long hair and smooth skin
Otherwise known as a beautiful, black,
        powerful diva
Who sometimes likes to run like a cat, chasing
        her prey on a sunny day
I am a cat with long whiskers and strong
I am sitting on the living room rug
I am the color pink that just got painted on
        your room wall
I am the number 1 because I am the first
        person in my life
I am not ugly or weak
I am a happy song that plays when you are sad

Porsha
FIFTH-GRADE, CROWN COMMUNITY ACADEMY

The Language vs. Dialect Debate

Lisa Redmond
WRITER, TEACHING ARTIST

*"To open your mouth in England is
(if I may use Black English) to "put
your business in the street:" You
have confessed your parents, your
youth, your school, your salary, your
self-esteem and, alas, your future."*

– James Baldwin
  The Real Ebonics Debate

I am torn, always torn. Language is art. But then, in the classroom, it seems to become something less. The more Standard English becomes a ticket to a successful life, a ticket that allows its users safe passage through a capitalistic land, while the dialect is perceived as just the opposite. It becomes clear to me that in this country, speaking your own language, no matter how artful, is not supposed to lead to a life of success.

I am torn between the beauty of the language and the constant reinforcements throughout my education and throughout this country that said, and still say, that African American English (AAE) is something defective that must be fixed. Though most linguists agree that AAE is a unique language system, and that its grammar is systematic and rule governed, there was no room for this second language (or language system) in the classroom. We were taught to conform to the more standard diction of white America.

I can say that I loved each of my elementary school teachers. Every one of them brought something new to my experience and my education. But each of them also, as if on a mission, attempted to erase the inherent "Black-ness" from my voice.

They prepared me for a world that was much broader than the one I currently lived in. So I don't damn my teachers because—for many reasons—it had to be done. And surely, with the educated tongue that now rests inside my head, I have benefited from their efforts. I only wish that language had not been 'an either/or proposition.' As Aristotle said, "What we need is a mixed diction." There is a place for the language and the language system in and out of the classroom.

Maybe it was the advent of MTV that allowed free passage back and forth over the cultural divide, but you hear African American English in the media now more than ever before.

Whether it's the Boost Mobile commercial that asks the question, "Where you at?" Or the Verizon Wireless commercial that depicts an African American woman saying, "Sir, you in a hardware store." (Note that the verb "are" is missing, or what linguists call the zero copula rule). Or Nate Birkus, Oprah's favorite interior decorator, saying things like, "Thanks for having my back." No matter how small or subtle it may be, there seems to be some kind of unofficial movement happening.

But officially this country has not made room for AAE, certainly not in the classroom. In the same way that China seeks to move English out of Hong Kong, and Francophone Canadians object to the marginalization of French in Quebec by insisting on new and interesting ways to honor the French language in a mostly English-speaking country, America has also declared war against any language that strays too far from Standard English. In the essay "The Real Ebonics Debate," Baldwin writes, "[a] child cannot be taught by anyone whose demand, essentially, is that the child repudiate his experience, and all that gives him sustenance, and enter a limbo in which he will no longer be Black, and in which he knows that he can never become white. Black people have lost too many children that way."

I recently enrolled in a Spanish class and what I found interesting about the pedagogy of teaching a second language was that students are not only taught the language itself, they also learn the culture of the people who speak the language. Sometimes foods from the culture are brought into the classroom, and the music of the culture (which of course includes the language of the culture) is also played. It was a clear example of the parallel relationship between language and culture. And it made me wonder why AAE could not be honored in the classroom in the same way.

I believe that one of the reasons that AAE cannot be so easily eradicated is because it is a part of the African American culture. It is not a dead language, but a language that students likely hear from their peers, in their homes, and to the extent that popular media has picked up on its value, right on their television sets. In *Language in the Inner City: Studies in the Black English Vernacular,* William Labov writes, "[i]t seems natural to look at any education problem in terms of the particular type of ignorance

which is to be overcome. [There are] two opposing and complementary types: Ignorance of Standard English rules on the part of speakers of nonstandard English, [and] Ignorance of nonstandard English rules on the part of teachers and text writers."

I delivered a lesson to fifth and sixth-graders at Crown Community Academy during the 2005-2006 school year. Essentially, I had one learning goal for the lesson: that the students come away with a broader understanding of language, and language as culture.

I brought several videos about language and/or culture to class: 1) *Do You Speak American,* 2) *American Tongues,* and 3) *The Story of English.* The excerpts that I chose ranged from topics including African American English, American east coast dialects, southern English dialect speakers, and Scottish English (or the Muvver Tongue). We watched and examined the way people speak English across this country and in Scotland. During the first part of this lesson I wanted to place African American English in its proper place—alongside other dialects.

Next I went to the chalkboard and had students help me list the things that make up African American culture. This included the food (i.e. collard greens, macaroni and cheese, fried chicken, chitlins, etc); the music (i.e. Hip-Hop, Rap, The Blues, Jazz, R&B) and other traditions of the African American culture. And then, I included our language as a part of this list. To illustrate this point I played one example of the music of our culture, "Touch the Sky," by Kanye West. We only worked with the tag-line:

> I gotta testify, come up in the spot lookin' extra fly.
> Fo' the day I die, I'mma touch the sky.

We had to rewind the CD a few times to transcribe a portion of the lyrics onto the chalkboard. We dissected it, translated it to Standard English and back again, then considered which version worked best in this genre. Then I simply stated, "It should only follow that the language of the culture is found in the music of the culture."

As the discussion continued one student commented that her uncle tells her that she is turning into "a little white girl" because her speech is leaning more towards that of

Standard English. Another student said that every time her great-aunt comes to visit she always says, "You is gettin' big!" Hearing this it was clear that we run the risk, as educators, of sending the message that anyone who does not speak standard English is stupid, uneducated, and has very little to offer the child, which in turn can begin to further erode the African American family. That great-aunt may hold all the family wisdom, but her language poses a contradiction to the child about language and education, "proper" speech and "broken" English.

At the end of the session one of the teachers remarked that she had been grading papers and making repeated corrections in her students' writing, but the same grammatical "errors" kept coming back. She said that she never knew that AAE was rule governed, and didn't know that the grammatical "errors" she had been correcting were features of AAE.

My last session at Crown that school year was on the very last day of school. Summer break was dripping from everyone and everything. It was already hot outside that day, and as I stood with Cynthia Weiss and basked in the afterglow of another school year gone by, two little boys marched past us. The first little brown boy was eating from a box of candy, the second little brown boy followed right at his heels, tears streaming, crying for a piece of the candy. Then without provocation, the first boy yelled, "You ugly!" And there was that language again, alive and well, living outside of the school building.

What we need is an effective writing pedagogy that honors the child, honors their voice, and honors their culture. The writing classroom should be a place for liberation, not a dark graveyard, or what writer Randall Albers calls the "killing floor," where a language that is alive and well goes to be slaughtered.

Albers, Randall K. "No More Lip Service. Voice as Empowerment in a Story Workshop Composition Class," NCTE Presentation, Charleston, S.C., 1989.

Labov, William, "Language in the Inner City: Studies In the Black English Vernacular." Philadelphia: University of Pennsylvania Press, 1972.

Perry, Theresa and Delpit, Lisa D. "The Real Ebonics Debate: Power, Language, and the Education of African American Children." Boston, MA, Beacon Press, 1998.

English Out Loud

Deborah Guzmán-Meyer
PHOTOGRAPHER, TEACHING ARTIST

There's a whirlwind of voices around me. I have twenty children. They all clamor to get my attention, saying, "Hello, where have you been? What are we doing today? Are we taking pictures?"—so many questions are fired at once I'm glad I'm not on trial. I'm in a fifth-grade classroom; which is equipped with miniature judges, defense lawyers, and prosecution teams, or at least it seems like that sometimes.

After outlining plans for the day and setting the kids to work, I notice an addition to the courtroom: a new student. I walk over and introduce myself, and quickly Rosa, the girl sitting next to the new girl, explains that Yamitza is from Puerto Rico, just enrolled in school, and speaks no English. I quickly recover and address her in Spanish. She understands my instructions but in her nod of response I detect an extreme introverted-ness.

That was me fifteen years ago.

When I was fifteen, a sophomore in high school, my mother decided that returning to the country where we were born after more than a decade was a good idea so we could attend college here. My sisters and I migrated to the U.S. from the Dominican Republic and were quickly enrolled in the English as a Second Language program in our new Bronx, New York high school.

There I tried to disappear. Withdrawn could not begin to explain what I was in those days and in the terrified eyes of Yamitza I saw the girl I once was. Yamitza didn't make a dent in the assignment for the day, which was writing. My guess is that since most of the discussion happened in English and my Spanish explanation gave her unwanted attention, she got frazzled.

Sometimes I am asked whether I chose a visual art form because of my difficulties speaking English as a teenager. I don't think so. Photography didn't feel like a new language but an exit road. I went off on my own and explored the world, made mute sense of it and made it come to life in the stillness of the darkroom. It's not a substitution for language but a way to interact with the world without saying a word.

A few weeks after meeting Yamitza, it was time to photograph. I handed out the cameras, paired the kids up and gave the assignment. They were to photograph something in the room on a solid piece of paper in three different ways. Whenever there's a photographic assignment, the kids usually run up to me, get assistance and show me their efforts—probably seeking some positive reinforcement. In the chaos of children running, laughing, photographing, Yamitza came to me and showed me what she had just photographed. That she came to me did not surprise me, because I had been speaking in Spanish to her every time I was in the classroom. But what she showed me in the little rectangular screen of her digital camera did.

Not only did she understand the assignment well, she actually had the best picture in the classroom. The following week she came over, tapped me on my shoulder and handed me her re-done written assignment from her first class with a teaching artist. She wrote a whole page. I guess I wasn't as lucky as Yamitza. Being comfortable in a new school and a new language is a priceless gift and I'm glad that I was able to aid her through the first leg of the difficult journey in acculturation. My shyness followed me to college, where I eventually had the courage to speak English out loud.

Letting Snow Fall in the Classroom

THE ARTIST AS OBSERVER

Julie A. Downey
WRITER, TEACHING ARTIST

What happens when we look closely at nature?

To get closer to the subject, a photographer can move in with her body or select a longer camera lens. She can bring her subject closer to the camera or wait for it to move closer to her. The process is similar for poets and writers. To get closer to a scent, smell, taste or texture, shape, line or color, I must know it well enough to convey its likeness with words. As a teaching artist, I want to demonstrate the ways an artist and subject can become acquainted. This means being prepared for spontaneity, and that can include bringing the unexpected into the classroom.

During a text and image residency in three fifth-grade classrooms at Albert R. Sabin Magnet School, my co-teaching partner, Deborah Guzmán-Meyer, along with partner teachers Ms. Escobar, Ms. Torres, and Ms. Alcantara and I, decided to follow a science unit on plant life, including lessons on inherited traits, reproduction, and photosynthesis. Together we developed a curriculum that explored the theme of "parts and wholes" in science, photography and writing.

Deborah and I moved back and forth between teaching photography and writing lessons. One residency day, the students were viewing photographer Terry Evans' aerial views of Chicago. I peered out a wall of windows facing the skyline and was amazed to see snow falling. Right then I had an idea. "Alright," I said. "It's my responsibility as an artist to teach you that when something spontaneous happens, it's your job to go check it out!" Being an artist is about making observation a priority. I want my students to know it's okay to divert from a plan if something in real-time is taking our immediate attention.

I asked the students to get a blank sheet of paper and a pencil and go to the window. Some of the kids knew exactly what to do and some of them were less sure of what to notice. I made sure to help those students move toward a better view and talked them through it. What do you see? As I overheard other kids talking, I asked new questions: Where did those snowflakes come from? Which one are you going to look at? I was asking them questions so that they could generate their own. One student noticed how "snow loves to play… [and] is scared to crash!"

You have the text book about snow, you have the photograph of snow, and then you have real snow falling— the chance to watch it in motion. Watching the snowfall in the context of a regular school day invited my students to consider the value of looking closely at what was happening around them beyond the walls of the classroom.

We literally left the classroom one day on a field trip to Garfield Park Conservatory in Chicago, where Deborah, the teachers and I continued to encourage close observation. We circulated between three different rooms which were divided by climate and type of plant. While in each room, students focused on a single plant, looking closely at its details throughout three encounters with it: photography, writing and scientific research. Deborah taught them how to take photographs, and my job was to help them write what they observed. I told them, "You are all explorers, this is your mission." They were given questions to stir their senses, memories and associations.

As an explorer myself this year, my job was not to recreate a standard lesson but to present an extended, creative approach to that lesson. By looking more closely at the required text, we showed respect to our teachers for the work they do with their students. Just as we asked the kids to get closer to their subjects, my work as a teaching artist brought me closer to my colleagues. Spending more time with fellow teachers and sharing the classroom with another teaching artist also allowed me more one on one time with my students. Looking more closely at the world actually brings us closer to one another. What I hope is that my students don't stay in "tunnel-vision land"—but instead look outside their comfort zones and routines.

I hope my students will have the courage to break away from the everyday so that their curiosities become greater than their fears.

STUDENTS AT ALBERT R. SABIN
MAGNET SCHOOL LEARN TO LOOK
CLOSELY. PHOTO BY DEBORAH
GUZMÁN-MEYER.

Prickly Pear

Family: Cactaceae
Genus: Puntia
Species: spp.
Cultivar: none
Category: vegetables ground covers perennials
Height: four to six feet
Sun exposure: full sun
Bloom color: red, bright yellow, purple
Bloom time: late spring/early summer, mid summer
Foliage: grown from foliage evergreen
Other details: drought tolerant; suitable for landscaping this plant is attractive to bees, butterflies, and birds

Thorns, Thorns, Thorns!
Ow! Owie! Oooooouuuuuu! Yikes! Spikes!
Thorns, thorns, thorns!
Take 'em off Pleeeeeaaaassseeee
Thorns, thorns, thorns!
I hate thorns they are hurting me
Thorns, thorns, thorns!
Now I learned to never touch a thorn again
Thorns, thorns, thorns!

photos and poem by Christian

When the World Looks at Me, What Should it See?

Cecil McDonald, Jr.
PHOTOGRAPHER, TEACHING ARTIST

I walked down a narrow street in the province of St. Remy in the South of France observing the visual feast of a foreign land; its people, architecture, cuisine and language. I felt at once privileged and home-sick, after all, this was a long way from the South Side of Chicago—a land also rich with culture, conflict and history; the place where I began my love affair with art, fashion and house music; a music that on that bright, lavender scented day in St. Remy, seemed oddly familiar as French lyrics caressed the beats that emanated from tiny passing cars and century old, storefront doorways. Feeling both nostalgic and contemporaneous, I stepped into a record store to find a sample of this hybrid, French House, to celebrate the moment and commemorate my trip.

Once in the store I was met with the ominous stare of the rap/hip-hop artist 50 Cent, immortalized in the form of a very large, very glossy promotional poster. Had it not been for the clerk cooing, "Bonjour Monsieur, peux je vous aide," I would have sworn I was in Coop's or George's Music Room, (major music retail institutions on Chicago's South and West Sides, respectfully). As I searched through bins of French and English titles, I was amazed at the number of genres of music created by Americans of African descent. Countless academic papers, essays and novels have been dedicated to the influence of Black Americans on the United States and the world, but as the saying goes, "Seeing is believing." I made my way back to the streets of St. Remy, and while I was still in search of a French House recording, what I had found was the genesis of what would become my next project as a teaching artist.

On my return flight I began formulating a planning session for the approaching fall season. I spoke at length with a fellow artist, collaborator and dear friend, avery r. young, about my experience abroad, and how this experience could be channeled into a photography and literacy residency. As it turned out, avery had had similar experiences during a

poetry residency with black youth in London and was eager to relay that experience in the residency as well.

My most urgent concern: how do I, a black artist, educator and mentor, convey both the significance and the influence that a steady barrage of unfiltered imagery has on the mind? More importantly: how to most effectively convey this notion to young, black, boys and girls, whom for the most part are allowed—often encouraged—to consume many more images than they would ever produce or distribute. Children, who during their commute to and from school, church, stores and parks, regularly encounter the following: seductively lit and posed, black men represented as virile players with black women as vacant, oversexed playmates as adornments; or models of color cast as stars in liquor and cigarette billboard advertisements that saturate the urban landscape of every major city in the country. If we included the BET/MTV version of what it means to be hip and desirable, it becomes evident that our children need the tools to critically engage and respond to what has become a media waste visited on the poor and young.

"When The World Looks At Me What Should It See?" This was the line of inquiry that began our Project AIM fall residency at Theodore Herzl Elementary School in Chicago's Lawndale community. With this question we hoped that the students would come to realize that they could, to a degree, control the manner in which the image, their image, could be seen by the world. We explained that their image was in fact projected into the far corners of the world, further than their comparatively tiny world had led them to believe.

avery and I proposed the idea of a billboard project, an advertisement campaign that would portray these children as they truly were: citizens of the world, with all the potential for greatness, and, more importantly, ordinariness, without conditions or labels. We began by giving the children existing art and commercial imagery in order to begin to build a level of critical engagement with the image, and, at times, the accompanying text. We posed a simple question: "What is the image saying? What do you see? Who is the image made for? What does the image want you to do? Is the image attractive?" We then asked the children to change the text, or add text to an image that had none. This would encourage the student to exert control over the image, to re-read the image for a new meaning, or reveal that which was once hidden.

The children were then given cameras to photograph their neighborhoods, themselves, friends and family—the very things that made them ordinary folk, or, as the project became to be known: REGULO. We then had the children make lists of essential words that described the image. This was a process created by fellow Project AIM artist Jenn Morea. Once the list was pared down to three essential words (which become the copy for that image), these images were then enlarged to 30x40 inches. The photographs were displayed in the school as art conceived within the conceptual framework of critical engagement with the self as a reflection—or as in this case a deflection—of the larger society.

Although REGULO was conceived as a billboard project, avery and I were more concerned with the function of the billboard as a tool within a larger capitalist construct. We wanted to know how we could use that tool to reconstruct a fresh, if not entirely new, reality for our students. However, an actual billboard, given its size, visibility and perceived authority, would have given the students the real world experience and authenticity educators are continually seeking to complement the safety of the classroom.

It does not escape me that, despite our best efforts as teaching artists, many of our students may never experience the actuality of international travel. Many may be unable to will themselves from the severity of an urban existence. But for sixteen weeks on the West Side of Chicago, two artists brought a tool kit containing a camera, pen, and mirror; a camera to capture a new reality, a pen to write a new reality, and a mirror to see the beauty of their reality.

(See *Regulo* images on inside back cover.)

TEACHING ARTIST, CECIL MCDONALD, JR.
WORKS WITH STUDENTS AT THEODORE HERZL
ELEMENTARY SCHOOL. PHOTO BY JOEL WANEK.

do over
do over
do over
do over
do over

avery r. young

SPOKEN-WORD POET, TEACHING ARTIST

somewhere inside a monday mornin i find myself in a box of blkned q-tipped brothers they faces n bodies are a majestic bouquet of cocoa plentiful in shades n scents just-a bouncin bumpin bendin breathin this moment of stillness fo all the seconds it will last inside this here box— a class situated third floor of a lil-big beige schoolhouse harborin a corner of an urban jungle i wish abc world news tonight would document then plaster across screens of its upside-down-world-wide audience my young men-folk on this reguloishh this normalishh this lil somethin inside this still that connects them to any n erything not a monsterishh or deprived of father figures or threatenin or gangsta or statistics drenched in the curse of james evans sr. inside this monday the world should see what i know these brothers heads miles above water they sit open fo learnin exposed to challenge confronted by change haunted by the fact they be human redeemed cause even they make a difference a difference through words a difference through photographs a difference in the message that words n photographs spit into the eyes n minds of folk who may never feel comfortable drivin in neighborhoods that find them on the corners without assurin all doors are secure

this monday the assignment is to surf through magazine ads n come up with other language fo them   its part of the process to gettin them ready to formulate their own billboards weeks prior to this one they have discussed what the world should see when it sees them theyve also discussed what they perceive of people n situations just by lookin at an image so here myself n photographer Cecil McDonald (partner in crime) are tryin to get them to see how billboards work how they sell say represent the folk of the communities they are propped in we hope they begin to change what the world see by figurin out how to look at themselves

rough beginnings but thats to be expected   we brothers different from what they may see but brothers just the same n we aint goin nowhere which may have boggled a few but we here fo the long haul we have to be more like duty than job cause Gordon Parks and Langston Hughes influenced our futures but never were within arms length and still we here this monday calm n they are lookin at pics Anthony Hamilton whisperin from radio speaker Mrs. Melendez's smile uncut like him voice she (the teacher teachin us artists patience) is requestin the men chirrun to open they mindz as big as they be n not choose pictures that are familiar but choose those pictures that will ask them to stretch

D. scans then selects a picture from a seven dollar magazine its one of three white boys dressed like the men in black but they a rock band a mtv2ish white boy rock band they album comin out D. shows the picture to a cluster of young men who giggle then one goes this the one we gon do

its time to present a couple of folk show they pictures n distinguish whether or not the photo is a portrait landscape or still life they explain what goin on in the pic they read what the picture says then they read what language they would put to the picture n why they talkin all quiet n stuff they heads down unsure D. gets up shows the picture of the mtvish white boy band in the men in black fits with the black boy rocker words plastered above they heads d. mumbles it's a portrait they think it don't go with ah-num-min-nuh whah whah

i'm like huh i go wait a minute you all are men young blk men with a lot to say you do yourselves n the world a disservice when you don't speak so that other folk can hear you Mrs. Melendez cosigns a woman dont want a man who cant speak up

TEACHING ARTIST, AVERY R. YOUNG COACHES A YOUNG
WRITER AT THEODORE HERZL ELEMENTARY SCHOOL.
PHOTO BY JOEL WANEK.

D's chest swells his heads tilts a bit tward sunlight he
raises his hand n asks if he can go again i look at Mrs.
Melendez she looks back at me we bofe go huh with our
shoulders i grant the lil brother him wish

n D. is articulate n mighty the words flippin from his tongue
be fresh n sharp n precise intentional solid i cant be any
prouder of a student than i am right then n there   Mrs.
Melendez has a mt. everest smile nowhere near leavin her
face she is impressed n now a believer that art works i'm
clappin my hands screamin boy! i aint yo daddy but if i
was i would go "that's my boy!" oooo weee that right
there is what i'm talkin bout the rest of the class laughin at
me n my glee

n this monday is glowin now no weapon formed against it
shall prosper the next young warrior gets up n repeats the
performance of D. so does the next student then the next
one n the next one after that eventually the bell rings n i
tell em all i will see em next week D. asks if Cecil will be
there I testified yes then give D. a thumbs up

dont think my feet ever touched a stair its like i floated
outside to the parkin lot i call the Mcdonald (Cecil) n tell
him bout the goin ons of this monday him smile heard
through him language i feel you brother i bear witness to
the door that opened in my heart openin the opportunity
to D. to prove to me himself n the rest of anyone who
may ever get to hear him speak that words most definitely
sound power him strength will always be in his ability to
communicate what he sees hears n feels inside this
monday him got to find out what i found out a-many-a-moon
ago speakin can be a brother's most efficient weapon
cause voice cuts voice informs voice represents n voice
ring that you think so therefore you are.

Déjà Vu

MENTORSHIP ALL OVER AGAIN

Luis Crespo
ACTOR, TEACHING ARTIST

Mentorship happens when you're not looking—and half the time, you don't even know when it's happening. As a youth, I had no idea how the impact and influence of my mentors would lead me to succeed in what they seemed to do so naturally.

At Thurgood Marshall Middle School, Casey Goldenberg, my fifth-grade teacher, was an early mentor of mine. He was one of the only teachers I remember from my grammar school experience because he made school interesting for me. I remember the way he interacted with us, and in retrospect, I want to shape myself as instructor like him—he is a wonderful model for how I want to interact with young people.

Ralph Flores, the Art Director for Association House in Chicago, was another mentor in my life. I started working there when I was fourteen-years-old. The year before I'd been a janitor at my high school and when I went back to try to get that job again, they made me take a test. Because my math scores were so low on that test, the only job available was at Association House. Ralph interviewed me for the *Voces* Theater Project—and from then on theater was something I loved doing. We would work to write and perform our own play. I did it for five summers in a row and Ralph was a great mentor—just the way he cared about us and really wanted to make a difference. I was able to feel very close to him and rely on him to talk to him about anything. He was a guiding force in allowing me to feel a part of it, pretty good at it, and getting better at it all the time. When I think back to how he handled things, the way he did things, I use him as a template for what I'm doing now.

From Bryn Magnus and Ron Bieganski at Free Street Theatre to Brian Shaw at Columbia College Chicago, countless others have mentored me and, at this point in my life, I feel I have developed into a mentor myself, an equal with my peers. This work has led me full circle back to the places where I was inspired and it's actually a great privilege to have started at Association House and to now actually run the *Voces* Program and to return to Marshall Middle School where my fifth-grade teacher can actually see that a kid there could make it. It makes me really proud to be able to talk to Ralph about the work I am now doing in the community. He's seen me through a lot of my growth and he's known me enough to where I can tell him about my accomplishments and concerns. He gives me support in hanging on during the really tough times that this work can throw at you. The hardships are made worthwhile by the quality of the work and the young people with whom I work.

One project that comes to mind is the mask making project—it's an idea that was actually presented to me by my mentor Ralph at a *Voces* Program. The experience of casting a mask of my own face was so memorable and challenging that I decided to initiate a mask-making project at Marshall. Students would be able to use the theme of spirit animals (a curriculum that was initiated by Columbia College Chicago professor George Bailey and his senior students) to create the masks and at the same time be able to experiment with their creativity and imagination in designing the masks.

TEACHING ARTIST LUIS CRESPO LEADS A
THEATER EXERCISE AT THURGOOD MARSHALL
MIDDLE SCHOOL. PHOTO BY JOEL WANEK.

For the most part, the initial fear is that in a day and age when image and coolness is at the forefront of these kids' minds, it's hard to get into the initial step of mask making—which is to get greasy Vaseline on their faces. Students had to rub that stuff in and get messy—it was inevitable! I thought that it was going to be a concern but in reality, it was surprisingly easy. They all participated and even the coolest kids who didn't want to get sullied up ended up doing it and having fun with it. There was not one student who didn't want a casting of their face. Over the course of fourteen weeks, everyone created a spirit animal mask. They created appendages like bird beaks, horse muzzles and bulb eyes for frogs. They also painted and decorated to where each individual mask was unique and infused with their own personalities.

Each student was totally engaged and had his/her own subtle breakthroughs throughout the process. But there was one student who was considered the "troubled" kid in the class and apparently never finished his work. He did finish his mask and put a lot of effort and thought into it. It turned out to be a wonderful mask. He chose a harder animal to do—a frog—he had to form a frog mouth, and really bulbous eyes, and a tongue that he added an additional fly onto. That kind of detail was probably not expected of him so it kind of gave him the power and pride he needed to take control of something and at the end feel very proud of his work. It was good to give him the opportunity to succeed and to give him an immediate sense of satisfaction to what he was doing—it was right there in front of him and the impact was immediate.

The way I see it, I know what the impact of art-making had on me, so all I can do is present these really great projects in fun, meaningful ways and hopefully the same inspiration I felt will transfer to my students. I feel more like a guide than a teacher. I present this stuff to them and then it's really up to them to take it upon themselves to shape it. But I try to be there to consider other options, to really encourage the imagination, and to use their imaginations to create. It kind of goes back to the advice I was given by Ralph, who said that you never know how what you say or do is going to impact someone's life. That's what mentorship is really about for me—to be a positive influence in young people's development and to help them find their own potential.

This work all comes back full circle. From me returning to Thurgood Marshall Middle School as a teaching artist, using a project that inspired me as a youngin' as a way to inspire a new generation of youth, I found that mentorship is something that continues to happen and it's really something that should happen. As teachers and instructors, our job is to guide and inspire youth—we're mentoring without it being obvious.

Thinking in Pictures

PROCESS AND PRODUCT

Joel Wanek
PHOTOGRAPHER, TEACHING ARTIST

Philosophy

Visual images dominate young people's lives. It's essential for students to be critical of the images that they encounter everyday. Knowing how to decode and decipher what they see on television and magazines, video games and elsewhere is a good first step toward understanding how to use images instead of being used by them.

Just as the English language is taught, I feel visual language should be taught. Students should study the grammar and syntax of images alongside the written word: composition, framing, focus, sequence, narrative, perspective, point-of-view all have meanings within photography. Just as a writer composes a text by assembling words on a sheet of paper, a photographer, too, creates a composition by arranging objects within an empty, rectangular area. The shared language provides a more concrete way to introduce photographic and visual concepts.

One goal of my residencies is for the students to be able to think in pictures—to be able to preconceive and visualize their photographs before making them. This is a key technique in becoming fluent in any artistic medium. It shows that the artist knows her equipment and knows what she wants to accomplish once the tools are in her hands. This also helps to slow the picture making process down, which I believe results in photographs of much higher imagination and quality.

Process

I begin my residencies with an in-depth study of framing and composition. We start the project by looking at a wide variety of photographic works with the intention of broadening the students' sense of photography's possibilities. Exposing the students to a diversity of photographic forms and content allows them to find their own way into the medium and develop a personal connection to it.

We also pay attention to and discuss how the photographers frame their subjects. Do they frame things from close-up or far away? Do they center the subject in the middle of the frame or cut things off with the edges? To be critical consumers and makers of images, students must be aware of everything that is in an image, particularly when it's their own.

Students then work on a series of exercises that have them creating their own compositions from other photographers' works.

PHOTO 1
AS A CLASS, STUDENTS ARE INTRODUCED TO THE DIGITAL CAMERAS AND GIVEN A BRIEF LESSON ON HOW TO PROPERLY FOCUS AND TAKE A PICTURE. USING SOME OF THE FRAMING CONCEPTS, STUDENTS TAKE A SERIES OF PICTURES BASED ON A SHOT LIST PROVIDED BY THE ARTIST.

PHOTO 2
FILLING AN EMPTY FRAME, STUDENTS CAREFULLY COMPOSE A SELF-PORTRAIT.

PHOTO 3
STUDENTS TAKE A MOMENT
TO REVIEW SOME OF THE
PHOTOGRAPHS THEY'VE MADE.
PEERS GIVE EACH OTHER
POSITIVE CRITICAL FEEDBACK
TO HELP DETERMINE THE
STRONGEST IMAGES.

PHOTO 4
DEVELOPING TEXT FROM IMAGES:
STUDENTS POOL THEIR IMAGES
WITH THOSE OF THEIR PARTNERS
AND ARRANGE THEM TO COMPOSE
A NEW STORY.

The impetus for our final project came from a conversation I overheard between Albert R. Sabin Magnet School teacher Iris De Jesus and her students. Ms. De Jesus believed that the kids were not very connected to the school because very few still live in the neighborhood. Students responded by saying that there was nothing in the school that they felt connected to beyond the murals and displays of artwork on the walls. I wondered how we could visually represent this feeling of disconnection and sought out a way to interpret and represent those students' feelings through a final photo project.

For the Emptiness Project, I developed and then gave the students some guidelines on what to seek out in the school. There were just a few rules. I asked them to find the empty places in the building which were underused, unused or unnoticed. I asked them to keep people out of their pictures.

After students took their pictures, we looked at them as a group and each student picked one final picture to feature. Visiting poet Amanda Leigh Lichtenstein led a writing workshop in which students wrote poems in response to their selected photograph. First she asked them to imagine a space and listen for sounds, look for actions; to notice the light and how the body feels in this space. Then she asked students to imagine this space empty. Students wrote freely for ten minutes on these ideas. Then they picked a single word based on their photograph and were asked to "go inside" the word they chose by free writing thoughts and feelings associated with that word. The following week she returned to help them shape and edit their free writes into poetic forms using stanzas, line breaks, repetition, and rhythm.

The results of the work were beyond my expectations. Students were now able to look at an image and think about it in more than one way. They understood the aesthetic, emotional, and technical points of view. Knowing how to be a critical maker and consumer of images was empowering. They had the experience of producing, critiquing, revising, and analyzing their work. When young people are given the right tools and guidance they are capable of creating artwork that is as nuanced, complex and profound as anyone.

Text and images from *The Emptiness Project*

Gone

When you're gone
    it's like you were
    never here.
It's like you just disappeard
    in thin air.
When you're gone
    you're gone. You might not come
    back. It's like something
    just went crack.
Cause you know you're
    not coming back.
So you're gone
    just like that.

POEM AND PHOTO BY Tyteanna
ALBERT R. SABIN MAGNET SCHOOL SIXTH-GRADE STUDENT

Which Way?

I am at the point where I can't decide
Which way?

Right or left, left or right
Which way?

Shortcut, longway, longway, shortcut
Which way?

It's too hard to decide.

This side, that side
Which way?

I'm losing my patience
Please help me decide!
Which way?

POEM AND PHOTO BY Rocio
ALBERT R. SABIN MAGNET SCHOOL SIXTH-GRADE STUDENT

The Joy of Critique

**LOOKING AT
STUDENTS' WORK
FROM START TO FINISH**

Leah Mayers
BOOK & PAPER ARTIST, TEACHING ARTIST

A few years ago, I learned a method of formally critiquing works of art in progress called Critical Response that changed my life as both an artist and as a teacher. Liz Lerman, choreographer and founder of Liz Lerman Dance Exchange, MacArthur "Genius Grant" recipient and writer, developed Critical Response out of her own frustration with art critique. She felt increasingly troubled by her own unsatisfying experiences as a critic. Lerman believed that comments were more often about others' biases and outlook than about the motivations of the artist.

I also felt that my experiences with critique in art schools and editing sessions in classrooms were less than inspiring. Too often critique leaves artists either without any useful and constructive feedback or with only negative comments about their art, often justified as tough love. Lerman wanted critique to make artists joyfully and immediately return to work. Critical Response is all about paying attention and asking questions rather than stating opinions.

As teaching artists, we often have dual goals: one is to integrate our art form into our students' literacy learning, and the second is to help our students make aesthetically captivating art work. I don't want kids to make books only to house their poems or make them more apt to seek out new novels, though I do want both of those things to occur. I also want my students to learn the vocabulary of book making, to master complicated stitches and structures, formal and creative book layout and beautiful, professional looking art objects.

When we open up our art-making process for affirmation and response from our peers we become accountable for our work and enter into a dialogue between artist and audience. If students think no one will see their work, they are less invested in making it. More constructive feedback obtained during the writing and art-making journey translates into higher quality, more compelling artwork; we learn how what we are attempting to communicate is being received. Lerman has stated in her writing that, "It is important that we want this artist to make excellent work. I think sometimes, for a host of reasons, people looking at work don't want the artist to succeed, especially on his or her own terms." (www.communityarts.net/readingroom)

Critical Response: A Method for Critique

Critical Response as laid out by Lerman includes three roles and four steps.

The three roles are:

- Artist
- Responders
- Facilitator

And the four steps are:

- Statements of Meaning (Affirmation and Observation)
- Artist as Questioner
- Responders Ask the Questions
- Opinion Time with a discussion of Next Steps

I have modified Lerman's Critical Response with the same roles but the four steps have expanded to five:

- Listening to Read-Aloud
- Recall
- Writer/Artist as Questioner
- Responders Ask the Questions
- Facilitator asks Writer/Artist about Next Steps

TEACHING ARTIST, LEAH MAYERS
RESPONDS TO A STUDENT'S IDEAS
AT THURGOOD MARSHALL MIDDLE
SCHOOL. PHOTO BY JOEL WANEK.

During my second residency year at Thurgood Marshall Middle School, I worked in collaboration with fellow teaching artist and actor, Luis Crespo, four teachers, and nearly 90 eighth-graders. This year's assignment included drama exercises designed to focus attention—an example of this is having the students move their bodies comfortably in space to tell stories, thus bonding them to the group. We asked the students to write a story for a younger child or a peer and create a one-of-a-kind artist's book to enter into the Citywide Young Authors Competition. The students could write about anything they felt was important. Most of them chose to write stories with a message or a warning to other teens.

We began the residency with a pre-writing exercise: a stream of consciousness letter to be written to a trusted friend sharing their story ideas. Once these letters were complete, we began our modified Critical Response process. We first modeled the process several times with the whole class, working through each step as long as it took to understand and practice the method. The students received a handout that outlined Liz Lerman's three roles: author/artist; facilitator (a teaching artist or another adult); responders (the rest of the class) and the five steps I modified to use with writing groups: read; recall; question the responders; question the author; and, finally, next steps. Once students had a rough draft of their stories, we broke into small groups—each of which was facilitated by an adult.

Over the following five weeks, the students engaged in two phases of critique. The first phase was for developing story ideas and completing a full draft. The second phase involved taking three scenes, from the beginning, middle and end of each story, and transferring them from the page to the stage. Through tableau acted out by their classmates, writers became directors who could literally see their words in three dimensions.

During the writing phase, we initially asked a brave volunteer to stand in front of the class and read aloud the first page of their story. Once the student was finished reading, we asked the class to engage in recall—to tell us what they remembered from what they heard. At first this was met with blank stares. They didn't think they'd be asked to remember anything; most of them probably hadn't been listening. I love this part because we can discuss presentation, performance, and read-aloud proficiency and maturity. When kids know they will be asked to reiterate what they've heard, they try harder to pay attention and really listen for appealing or memorable moments.

Recall helps focus the attention for the group and teaches the writer to be more intentional about what they write. During recall, the responders may only mention positive or interesting things that stood out to them. As the students tell the author what they remember, the author takes notes—keeping in mind that what is recalled by the audience usually represents the strongest parts of the work. The third stage allows the writer to ask the responders any questions. Most of the students ask if everyone liked their story, but as they move into their third and fourth drafts, the writers begin to ask more sophisticated and specific questions of their audience.

The fourth step gives the responders a chance to ask the writer informational and non-judgmental questions. At first, students want to give suggestions as to what they would do or how they would write the story. This is a good time to discuss Lerman's own fourth step, Opinion Time, but I rarely use her suggestion of asking the writer if they want to hear a specific opinion by a responder. Young people in a classroom setting have less time to devote to their composition projects and may be insecure about their writing skills. They tend to take such pointed opinions or suggestions to be criticisms or indicators that their present ideas are not good enough. As Lerman said in our Project AIM Teaching Artists' workshop, "Most opinions are questions disguised." The time for responders to ask questions usually gives writers ample material from which to continue creating unimpeded. Finally, the facilitator asks the author about next steps with the work. It is important to allow students to get back to their stories and revise as soon as possible after a Critical Response session when the motivation is high and the memory clear.

Critical Response from Page to Stage

After the students complete full drafts of their stories, we take them to the stage. Another fearless volunteer picks a few scenes from their story and becomes the director. This is best achieved after students have some experience with drama games and tableau. The author will read or recount a scene from her story and pick out the main characters and any important objects. She then directs several of her peers on where to stand, sit or lie down in character. Once the students have assembled in the scene according to the writer's direction, they freeze in tableau. We ask the writer if what she sees on the stage mirrors what she saw in her mind as she composed the story. The non-actors become the responders, asking questions and making links between what they see and what they heard during the read aloud.

Through tableau-making, the author has another chance to translate her thoughts. She gets a chance to see her words in action. Gaps in continuity or descriptions of characters are more visible than they were on the page. Once the actors have a chance to move within the story, and the responders are familiar with both the written words and also the gestures and action, everyone becomes more excited and interested in the success of the story. After the writer has received feedback in the form of questions, she takes her notes and returns to the page to rewrite or augment the story to make it clearer and richer.

Youth Respond to Critical Response

Before we used Critical Response at Thurgood Marshall Middle School, students usually did not answer the Exit Question, "What did you like in someone else's work?" More often than not they didn't have an opportunity to be involved with another's process. There never seems to be enough time to look at students' work during a residency. If Critical Response was not built into the schedule, students probably would not read each others' work at all. Some examples of this year's responses to the Exit Question included:

> "I liked Star's whole story because it was based on a true life story and Brittany's story because how the characters spoke and acted."

> "Jairo's project was great. I liked his beginning and the middle part had good detail."

> "I liked Elisha's work because she really talked about things that could and still do happen in teens' lives. In her story instead of her having the teenager run off doing drugs, the teenager did good things."

Other students responded to the questions regarding what they liked most about this project and what they learned from the residency:

> "How we got to get advice from our peers about our story."

> "I like helping others and giving them advice about their school work."

> "That we got to share our stories with our friends and got ideas from them. Even the teacher proofread it a few times, that's what I liked."

> "The games that we played, more specific is that we acted out and created scenes from our story to get a better in-depth thought at the outcome of the story."

I am thrilled by Critical Response and convinced that presenting this formal method of looking at and discussing work in progress free of judgment and competition inspires students to be excited about what they create. Today's schools seem to be more concerned with cramming as much information into students with as little depth as possible in order to pass state exams.

Teaching artists can facilitate project oriented lessons that more closely resemble how we really learn about the world, not in isolation but with collaborators who work together to make meaning and seamless connections between disciplines. And though it is desirable to focus on finishing the play or a painting or artist's book, it is equally important to teach young people to value process, to slow down and become more fully engaged with their work from start to finish.

After using Critical Response, I have watched 25-year-olds, 14-year-olds, and 20-year teaching veterans, be they seasoned extroverts or reluctant writers, actors, or artists, feel safe and encouraged enough to leave their comfort zones, to uncover hidden talents in writing, illustrating, sharing, and using their bodies to tell stories.

Seeking Inner Truth

Meg Arbeiter

HUMANITIES TEACHER
ACADEMY OF COMMUNICATIONS AND TECHNOLOGY
(A.C.T.) CHARTER SCHOOL

Go home and write

a page tonight.

And let that page come out of you—

Then, it will be true.

— **Langston Hughes**

For our twelfth-grade humanities class, I begin the year with Langston Hughes's poem, "Theme from English B," and I invite students to consider personal truth. The exploration and expression of inner truth is an important journey for all students, but it is particularly relevant for seniors as they prepare to embark on their journeys beyond high school. This is what makes teaching seniors at A.C.T. Charter School so exciting and challenging. Every day I carefully consider how to help students cross the bridge to graduation and, subsequently, life beyond high school. I always ask, is this lesson relevant? How do I connect this material to their lives and encourage them to stretch beyond what they already know? I encourage them to consider other perspectives, expand their own worldview and express their inner truth.

Effective arts integration not only empowers students to find their creative voice but also to develop critical consciousness and become aware of the inextricable connection between the classroom and the world—of the interplay between curriculum and lived experience. I want students to articulate and question the way the world is—as they perceive it to be. The transformative power of critical consciousness, as educator Deborah Stern explains, lies in teaching students "to imagine and experience the world that does not yet exist... [and] to confront inequities in their own lives."

Artist Guillermo Delgado and I strategically chose works of literature and art to spark ideas and encourage students to engage in difficult discussions, beginning with their experience. Does wearing a mask make you more powerful, less powerful, or both? My students and I wrestled with the question together as we read Paul Laurence Dunbar's poem "The Mask" ("We wear the mask that grins and lies...") and the Fugees' lyrics for "The Mask" ("Put the mask upon the face just to make the next day...I walk the streets and camouflage my identity...").

We also raised the issue of judging other people's masks and their power as we read Amiri Baraka's play *The Dutchman*. Angel, one of my students, asked me if I wore a mask and how I felt about removing it. Her question provoked an intense and honest discussion. It also opened the door for me to ask, "Is it easier for me, as a white woman, to remove my mask? Do I have more opportunities than you to choose whether or not to wear it?"

Using historical case studies, we challenged each other to dig deep and go beyond identity hinged on pop culture clichés. We examined human rights through the eyes and experiences of a young Muslim woman during the rise of the Taliban; as we read her memoir, *My Forbidden Face,* we confronted our misconceptions about Muslims. Students then chose one of several international human rights case-studies to explore through the Transitional Justice online module developed by *Facing History and Ourselves* (www.facinghistory.org). As we questioned, discussed and defined human rights and justice, we explored the power of art and murals. Guillermo elicited the students' observations and interpretations of Picasso's Guernica, which they found to be a potent expression of humanity and violence. In order to continue the discussion of the purpose of art and provide an authentic experience outside of the classroom, Guillermo and I organized a field trip to see and study several murals, taking students out of their neighborhood on Chicago's West Side to the South Side Mexican American community of Pilsen. As students shared their interpretations of the murals, they began to question common misconceptions of Mexican immigrants, consider the immigrants' perspective and discuss immigrants' struggles and rights.

This process of discovering and expressing their views of the world equipped students to grapple with their own individual situations, fears and dreams. Students want independence—they are excited to leave their homes, schools and neighborhoods—yet they are afraid of being on their own, earning and managing their own money. "I won't be buying Jordans anymore," acknowledged Dominique. They are on the brink of realizing their dreams or admitting defeat, and this is frightening. "Teachers need to understand that we are young adults because we're preparing to face the world, which is kind of scary and exciting at the same time because nobody wants to fail and run back to [their] parents," commented Aaron.

In Dominique's self-portrait of inner truth, two dollar bills cross his throat, almost strangling him. The memoir that he wrote to accompany his portrait explores this theme further as it begins with an imagined future scene of him arriving home from work. In this scene he describes his dream and his successful career as a video producer. He talks to his mother about a new artist he has just signed, and he is proud and grateful for his success. Then the story shifts to an actual day last year when he brought home his first paycheck and handed it over to his mom. He is filled with pride that he can help take care of his family, frustrated that it isn't enough, and torn by his desire to keep the money for himself.

For many students, visual art allows them to express feelings and experiences they have difficulty putting into words. "By using objects and pictures, I was able to express myself in a way that I wouldn't normally," explained Aaron. He became open to sharing feelings about his brother. "I don't like talking about it but I can find images and objects that remind me of him without getting broken up inside." Using assemblage, Aaron transformed a cigar box into a loving tribute to his older brother, who was shot and killed three years ago.

The process of creating visual art empowers students to create powerful metaphors for their experiences. An empty medicine bottle in Lonnette's identity box becomes a symbol which she says represents "the time me and my daddy got in an accident and my head hit the steering wheel and messed up my teeth. I was shaken… and feeling insecure about my mouth, but people didn't know because I still acted like smiling, fun-loving Lonnette." Dominique explained that abstraction and collage allows us to express our inner truth without others knowing and judging us. "I included before-and-after pictures of the actress Regina King—the picture of King from 'before' shows my insecurities, while the 'after' picture represents success and confidence. I hope to be famous and successful someday."

Throughout this project, we challenged our students to play with juxtapositions and dance with metaphors. We enjoyed watching it all unfold. A.C.T. graduate Latanja learned that, "like reading between the lines, you're reading the art. Like when Guillermo showed his paintings and asked us what we saw, I gave my opinion on what I thought the story

EXAMPLES OF INNER TRUTH SELF-PORTRAITS, LED BY
TEACHING ARTIST, GUILLERMO DELGADO AND MEG ARBEITER
AT A.C.T. CHARTER SCHOOL. PHOTOS BY BOB KUSEL.

was behind the painting, and he listened. The girl with the map—what did he want to use this map [in his painting] to represent? I thought she was dreaming... It turned out she liked to travel. Even though my story wasn't the true story, it still fit the painting. Everybody has their own story, and no one knows the real truth except the artist."

Arts integration, when done well, empowers students and teachers to consider inner-truth. Working with visual artist Guillermo Delgado allowed my students to explore and express identity and inner-truth through the creation of self-portraits. Whether they chose to create art that was realistic or abstract, the goal was to let what was on their minds and in their hearts to pour out of them.

As a humanities teacher, I used to be afraid of engaging students in creating works of visual art. Not all students see themselves as visual artists, and I have never seen myself as an artist, either. If I feel insecure about my own artistic talents, how could I possibly expect my students, who do not see themselves as artists, to be confident and willing to create visual art? But I learned new techniques from Guillermo and tried and created alongside my students. In turn, my students commented that they saw me as open to new things, and that encouraged them to

have an open mind. Guillermo and I engaged the students in a number of activities and provided them a buffet of materials to discover the art forms they preferred. Reluctant artists took chances with assemblage and collage to find their creative voice. Watching skeptical students pay close attention to detail and declare, "This is really cool, not what I thought we'd be doing," was worth every bit of anxiety I felt and extra time spent planning. Now I enjoy creating art with my students.

Senior year is a storm. Many of my students will be the first in their families to go to college and pursue a college degree. Sometimes the storm is turbulent as students face what feels like insurmountable obstacles in the way of graduation. Sometimes the storm is glorious when my students gain a better understanding of themselves and feel stronger for having endured. Through this project of self-discovery, Guillermo led us to a clearing in the storm of senior year.

You know more surely who you are on a strong bright day after a storm when the smallest falling leaf is stabbed with self-awaremenss.

– **Don Delillo,** *The Body Artist*

It is our charge as arts educators to discover and explore a variety of forms and functions in which our students can grow vibrant and strong. The classroom can be made both bigger and more intimate than the walls around it might imply.

—EMMY BRIGHT, PROJECT AIM OBSERVATION SPECIALIST—

CHAPTER TWO

Diverse Portraits
of Classroom Life

ESSENTIAL LESSONS LEARNED

- Teach your passion. Fall in love with your curriculum.

- Remember what it was like to be a student and write your curriculum with a student's perspective in mind.

- Let your curriculum emerge as you connect with your students and their questions.

- Closely examine what you are doing in your own practice as an artist and teacher.

- Ask teachers and students what they are interested in learning.

- Strive to create an original curriculum. Each class is different.

- Embrace an element of risk in your curricular visions.

CHAPTER THREE

Professional Development as Reflective Practice

Professional Development as Reflective Practice

Cynthia Weiss and
Amanda Leigh Lichtenstein

*The best [staff development] activities provide a
mirror in which teachers see themselves in new
ways. They draw on teachers' prior knowledge and
abilities, and help them construct new approaches
of their own. They renew peoples' enjoyment of
their own learning. And they provide space to re-
conceptualize what learning and teaching can be.*

— **Zemelman, Daniels, Hyde**
Best Practice Today's Standards for
Teaching and Learning in America's Schools.
*Heinemann. Portsmouth, New Hampshire,
2005 (p. 283).*

The image of a mirror is a fitting metaphor for the kind
of reflective professional development that Project AIM
designs. Throughout the school year and into the summer
months, we provide teachers and artists with the time
and space to look at their own practice and expand their
capacity to imagine what their practice may become.

We are interested in creating structures and opportunities
that inspire a renewed sense of purpose, passion and joy
for teaching. We do that by inviting participants to explore
arts-integrated learning as *students themselves*. In nearly
every Project AIM professional development session,
teachers and artists have the chance to: share personal
stories, engage a work of art, create and share their
artwork, take risks, laugh, experiment, revise, reflect, and
bring new strategies and ideas back to their classrooms.
The learning that takes place mirrors student learning in
the classroom; participants are often surprised by their
own and their colleagues' creativity. Teachers and artists
come together to share in both the theory and practice of
the work through hands-on experiences in the arts.

TEACHERS FROM ALBERT R. SABIN
MAGNET SCHOOL GET CURRICULAR
IDEAS FROM AN EXHIBIT AT THE
CHICAGO HISTORY MUSEUM.
PHOTO BY JULIO FLORES.

Our professional development is guided by a common set of goals and principles that contribute to meaningful learning. These goals include our intention to:

- Create a respectful community of learners
- Provide a safe and joyful learning environment
- Celebrate the diverse cultural heritage of our students, teachers and artists
- Access prior knowledge and personal experience
- Offer inquiry-based teaching strategies
- Pay close attention to the details of the practice
- Provide interdisciplinary hands-on arts experiences
- Create opportunities for discussion and reflection
- Work across the parallel processes in Literacy and the Arts
- Develop the leadership capacity of teachers and teaching artists
- Guide teachers and artists through the Arts Integration Learning Spiral
- Demonstrate and disseminate the Project AIM model

Project AIM has developed various structures and occasions for professional development where our partners can learn together as peers.

Through these structures, we have learned so much about the value of reflective practice in all aspects of this work. We recognize that reflective practice is about examining our intentions and effectiveness. It allows us to step away from our day-to-day teaching to refine, rethink and try again. Through dialogues between action and reflection—what Brazilian educator Paulo Freire calls praxis, we discover new theories. This, in turn, inspires us to create new strategies to test our theories. This powerful cycle of action, reflection and theory builds upon itself, generating new questions, ideas, curriculum and models.

Continuous evaluation and reflection leads to stronger personal practice as well as a stronger, more responsive program. Project AIM has an extensive external and internal evaluation process that provides a feedback loop for program design and delivery. Teacher and artist surveys, journals and exit slips serve as a mirror to the relevance of our program model. Through on-going evaluation, we become more responsive to our experiences, learning to listen for the stories we will tell even as they unfold.

In this chapter, we provide an overview of each of these structures and invite you to: take a closer look at the Project AIM artist cadre meeting; study the anatomy of planning a summer institute; and hear Kennedy Center consultant, Deborah Brzoska, redefine arts assessment through the lens of reflective practice in her essay, *Spirals and Chills – The Assessment of Arts Learning in AIM*. The chapter closes with specific examples of Arts Integration Strategies, written by Project AIM artists, and offered at professional development workshops throughout the year.

Project AIM Professional Development Opportunities

1. Monthly Teaching Artist Cadre Meetings

From the inception of the Project AIM program, teaching artists have been compensated to gather at monthly artist meetings to discuss and reflect on their work. These meetings, held on the Columbia College Chicago campus, offer an opportunity for a generous exchange of ideas and support. AIM artists report that this commitment to the development of a Teaching Artist Cadre has created a sense of identity and belonging not often provided in other arts education programs. As the field grows and develops, more organizations are recognizing the need to support teaching artists as intellectuals and professionals who are on the front lines of the work. Eric Booth, the founding editor of the *Teaching Artist Journal* (TAJ), and an inspired champion of the teaching artist writes:

> We see how a group of learners, in a safe and charged environment, can boost the growth of all the individuals involved—far beyond what the individuals could do on their own... (Booth, TAJ Volume 2, Number 2, 2004 p. 139).

(Cynthia Weiss explores the safe and charged environment of the Project AIM Artist Cadre meeting in her essay, the *Power of the Chill: Artist Cadre Meetings as Professional Development* reprinted in this chapter, with permission from the *Teaching Artist Journal*).

2. Project AIM Annual Orientation

The Annual Orientation to Project AIM is the opportunity to set collective intentions for teaching and learning across the program for the upcoming year. New and veteran partners relish the opportunity to hear their peers talk first-hand about real life classroom situations. Teachers and artist partners have shared the pitfalls and successes from their own residency work in panel presentations. The presentation of student work, in the form of slides, student-made films or process documentation offers models and inspiration for work to be developed in the coming year. Evaluators and staff discuss the goals for the year with partners and set the tone for the year. This is a chance to put a face to a name celebrate past achievements and create a common sense of purpose across school sites and partnerships.

3. Cross Project Curriculum Share

Project AIM organizes a curriculum fair at the end of the project year. The Curriculum Fair is an opportunity for teachers and artists to exhibit and reflect on their teaching and to engage artifacts of student learning. Taking the form of exhibition, demonstration and formal presentations, teacher/artist teams document and share the processes and the products of their arts-integrated instruction.

The process of writing up a curricular unit, and selecting student work that shows evidence of learning in the art forms and the content area is one of the richest and most demanding forms of professional development for practitioners. These events are both social and informative, taking on a celebratory feel. Teachers and artists gather to eat, drink, share work, ask questions, and think about future possibilities. Sometimes students are present to speak candidly about their artwork. The event usually takes place in the evening, giving it a different feel than school-day professional development sessions.

Currently, Project AIM has shifted the focus from presentation to a Curricular Peer Share. Teachers and artists met in small groups across school sites, to have deep conversations about the student work, with the work in front of them. They were asked to respond to the Questions: *What do you Notice in the Student Work? And What Questions Does this Raise for you?* These facilitated conversations allowed for a respectful and joyful exchange. The student work itself helped to tell narrative of the residency and to instill wonder and new inquiry on the impact of the arts on student learning.

4. Summer Institute at Columbia College

(See *Anatomy of a Summer Institute* later in this chapter)

5. Cross-school Workshops at Museums and Cultural Institutions

Project AIM engages the vast resources of Chicago's cultural institutions and museum exhibitions as sites for project-wide professional development. Project AIM artists have led workshops at the Garfield Park Conservatory, the Museum of Contemporary Art, the Chicago History Museum, South Shore Cultural Center and the National Museum of Mexican Fine Arts. The beauty of leading professional development at museum sites is that teachers are introduced to resources that they can bring back to the classroom. Curriculum developed for exhibitions can also become the access point for arts-integrated curricular learning. These sites become resources for future residency work. For example, the ecology at the Garfield Park Conservatory became the site and subject for the Looking Closely project at Albert R. Sabin Magnet School with Deb Guzmán-Meyer, Julie A. Downey and the fifth-grade team of teachers.

6. Arts Integration Workshops at Individual Schools

Project AIM offers a whole school arts integration workshop during a teacher institute day at each project school. A leadership steering committee, which includes the principal, reading and arts specialists, teachers and artists, work with Project AIM staff to create workshops that meet the needs of the school. The workshops are designed to connect the arts to literacy issues. For example, at Casimir Pulaski Fine Arts Academy reading specialist Luz Jorges identified that students needed support with learning how to make inferences while reading. A professional development session on *The Arts as an Inference Tool* was developed with the steering committee.

School workshops have also served to highlight instruction around Big Ideas and school-wide themes; represent ideas from young adult literature through the arts; or showcase arts integration projects from school teams of teachers and artists. Veteran teachers are invited to co-present strategies alongside artists. One of the most gratifying experiences at school workshops is to see teachers fully engaged in the creation and presentation of their artwork. Teachers always express delight at seeing their colleagues in a new and creative light. Artists get a chance to see their strategies in action with adult learners. These experiences, outside of the classroom, are a key component in building solid workshop partnerships between teachers and artists and support the development of teacher leaders who champion the cause of arts integration in their schools.

7. Classroom Residencies with Artist/Teacher Partners

Within the laboratory of the classroom, teachers and artists engage in the most immediate and compelling professional development. In this setting, they have the opportunity to observe, borrow and expand on each other's teaching strategies. Artists learn about content area curriculum and classroom management, and effective rituals of classroom management. They get the chance to catch glimpses of their students' lives through watching the relationships between the teacher and students. Teachers often observe their most reluctant students respond in new ways and shine forth in new ways in response to an art form and the presence of an artist in the classroom.

The classroom residency provides the ultimate performance assessment for a teacher and artist. Teaching partners can ask themselves: *did we reach the students as we intended?*

They can collect and document evidence of this learning and reflect on the impact of arts instruction to engage and deepen student learning.

FILMMAKER SUREE TOWFIGHNIA, EXPLORES
DESIGN AT A PROJECT AIM PROFESSIONAL
DEVELOPMENT WORKSHOP AT THE MUSEUM OF
CONTEMPORARY ART. PHOTO BY JULIO FLORES.

THURGOOD MARSHALL MIDDLE SCHOOL TEACHERS,
"DREAMCATCHERS TEAM." PHOTO BY JOEL WANEK.

The Language of Story

**THE PROJECT AIM SUMMER INSTITUTE:
AN ESSAY IN MULTIPLE VOICES**

Cynthia Weiss

I am grateful to have had the privilege to take part in such a creative community. I plan to use everything in my classroom. ...I am left with a feeling of rejuvenation and anticipation.

This was a fabulous summer institute enabling all of us to learn how to take risks, make mistakes and succeed all at the same time.

The community that was created over the three days was phenomenal.

Being put in a student's role really helped me understand the intent of the activities as well as what it feels like as a student.

— **AIM teachers'** exit slip comments
    in response to the AIM Summer Institute

Project AIM was excited to see what would happen if we set aside three days in the summer, away from our hectic schedules for real conversation and art-making that would push our limits and beliefs about what we thought would be possible arts-integrated practice. Project AIM training workshops have traditionally taken place on designated Chicago Public School professional development days during the school year. These days have always been rewarding, but left participants wanting more time and space to engage the ideas and work presented. By gathering in our state-of-the-art Columbia College Chicago Film Row, with all the amenities of an arts college, teachers and artists finally had the chance to immerse themselves in arts-integrated praxis.

We were inspired by reading current research on professional development, as sited by Elizabeth Lindsley, in her article, *Teaching Artist as Teacher Trainer* in the Teaching Artist Journal. (Volume 4, number 1, 2006) that reported:

> *Summer intensives in the arts were unanimously proclaimed by teachers to be the most transformative professional development that they had ever experienced...The summer intensives allowed teachers to step outside of their area of expertise and feel comfortable taking risks; to learn by doing.*

On the strength of this research, the needs of our project, and knowledge of other successful summer training models across the country, we resolved to organize and facilitate our summer institute around the goals we share for all our professional development events.

Building a Leadership Team through Intentional Planning

After setting these goals, we widened our leadership team. Deborah Brzoska, arts integration consultant from the Kennedy Center in Washington, DC, with whom we had previously worked, was hired to facilitate the institute. She brought a national perspective and was brilliant at tapping into the shared knowledge base of the Project AIM team. In early spring, Deb came to Chicago to facilitate a meeting with the Project AIM staff and a veteran team of teaching artists.

These artists, Jenn Morea, Amanda Leigh Lichtenstein, Sadira Muhammad, Archie Roper, Jeff Spitz, Luis Crespo, avery r. young, Lisa Redmond, Deborah Guzmán-Meyer, Cecil Mcdonald Jr., and Leah Mayers, were invited to make up the institute's arts faculty representing the artistic disciplines of writing, poetry, photography, theatre, film, dance and the book and paper arts. Matthais "Spider" Schergen, Fine Arts Specialist from Edward Jenner Academy of the Arts, and Luz Jorges, Literacy Specialist from Casimir Pulaski Fine Arts Academy, brought insights to the table from the teachers' perspective. Along with School Partnerships/Project AIM staff, Joanne Vena, Cynthia Weiss, Sadira Muhammad, and coordinators, Shawn Renee Lent, Liz Parrott, and Emmy Bright, the group convened to hatch summer plans. A communal excitement spread as we shared ideas and shaped our agenda.

Developing Big Ideas and the Narrative Shape of the Institute

Project AIM often uses written texts as an entry point to arts-integrated practice and professional development sessions. We like to select writing from young adult literature reflective of the cultures and interests of our students. For this institute we asked the leadership team to select a text from their own reading interests.

The selection of text led to a very generative discussion. Emmy Bright offered a favorite passage from the non-fiction book, *Wanderlust: A History of Walking* by Rebecca Solnit.

The theme of walking, beautifully elaborated by Solnit, was abstract and deceptively simple. Yet every artist at the table found a personal connection to the idea of walking as an innately human and universally-shared experience.

Sadira Muhammad associated the theme with the legendary dancer Katherine Dunham's "walk" and decided to honor the recently deceased dancer's memory in her workshop. Leah Mayers and Jenn Morea connected walking, mapping and memory for their book-making and poetry workshop. Archie Roper and Jeff Spitz planned to create on-site video documenting stories of walking. Cecil McDonald, Jr. and Deborah Guzmán-Meyer, photographers, and Lisa Redmond, writer, planned to combine digital photography and creative non-fiction writing in their workshop session.

Cross cultural curriculum can come from all sides and in surprising ways. There was an openness to engage curriculum with a cross cultural point of view that emerged from the conversation around the table. Performance poet, avery r. young, found that connection when he expanded the scope of walking from a solitary activity to the collective walking and marching in the civil rights movement.

Educator and mentor Steve Seidel has spoken eloquently about the need to find big ideas worth teaching. We wanted to model those big ideas by devoting a whole summer institute to meditations on walking. Our charge was to make sure these big ideas and questions would be unearthed through conversation and that the educators themselves would be excited about these ideas.

Arts and Literacy Learning —Parallel Processes Across Art Forms

On the first day of the institute, texts by Rebecca Solnit, Alice Walker and Joanne Hindley were introduced. We had decided to add the two other writing passages to connect the big ideas back to classroom practice and to larger social issues. The group was asked to read the passages out loud and listen to the rich variety of voices in the room. The discussion that followed provided a common context among all the participants and prepared them for the range of artistic responses cultivated in each workshop. When the teacher participants read the three passages at the summer institute and were asked to find their own connections between the three pieces, one teacher made the lovely observation that all three pieces dealt with *living with intention,* and how important intentionality is for teaching and learning.

Cynthia Weiss shared with the group Project AIM's approach of working across parallel processes in art-making, reading and writing. She explained how working back and forth between an art-making process and a literacy process can develop greater reading comprehension skills, expressive responses and activate higher order thinking in their students. The language of the arts is a vehicle for students to construct, represent and extend new meaning from ideas on the page.

Teachers expressed their new understanding of the value and impact of moving between expressive languages:

> *The experience of collaborating to tell a story through movement and then revising that story with an assigned theme showed vividly the similar thought processes required for language-based and arts-based activities.*

> *I understand better now the concept of the arts as a language.*

> *As an art teacher—the institute bent my mind to look for ways to add writing and texts into the arts, not only to improve writing and reading, but to improve the artworks as well. I think it will now be easier for me to ask teachers what they want to reinforce through my art class and just bridge the concepts from the texts themselves.*

The Shape and Structure of the Institute Days

The structure for the institute came from the well-crafted and highly successful Walloon Institute, an intensive summer professional development institute for teachers, developed by Smokey Daniels, Steve Zemelman and Marilyn Bizar with the Center for City Schools at National Louis University. Like the Walloon Institute we wanted to offer a morning plenary session each day that got the group started on common ground. We then provided lunch and time for conversation, followed by self-selected interdisciplinary art workshops in the afternoons. The values of voice and choice, hands-on learning and the creation of a community of learners were built into every part of each day.

Deborah Brzoska led each morning's plenary sessions by infusing her teaching with dance and movement to teach principles of partnership building, arts and literacy learning and assessment practice. Her sessions were highly interactive, reflective and deeply engaging. Participants said:

> *I learned how any artist in any art form can point out commonalities between the art mediums. Deb, in her presentation, showed how to use dance elements in building community and trust.*

> *My understanding of arts integration was enhanced by Deb's exercises where she took us in a specific direction with her activities. This put me in the place of a student and will help me give better directions when I return to my classroom.*

Teachers then selected an interdisciplinary arts workshop to stay with throughout the three days. These afternoon sessions offered an introduction to the language of the art form, and a chance to brainstorm, develop ideas, revise and refine work, exhibit and perform in a culminating event, and respond and reflect on their learning.

The three-day institute gave us an opportunity to lead participants through the full art-making learning cycle from beginning to end. The Project AIM Arts Integration Learning Spiral fit nicely with the Kennedy Center's arts education cycle of Creating, Performing/Exhibiting, and Responding. Each day built on the other and the teachers understood the value of creating a work of art through to its completion and public showing.

> *I was very impressed by the final documentation; we could see how we all evolved from drafts, to critiques to final presentations.*

> *The culminating event was so helpful to see how the different disciplines worked to resolve the same issues and ideas. It was the evidence of the work that we had been doing all week.*

Lessons Learned—
Impact in our Schools
and Studios

The summer institute was an alchemy of creativity, good will and energy. Something very special happened in those three days. Teachers loved the opportunity to become students/artists themselves and to activate their own creativity. Artists felt renewed and inspired to return to their studio practice. Everyone felt the excitement working under Deborah Brzoska's magical leadership. There was a collective spirit and a great sense of generosity. We walked away with renewed feelings of love for the work, for each other's commitment, and to a broadening sense of community to help us through the struggles that emerge in taking new risks.

The lessons learned include:

- The importance of creating a leadership team to develop shared values and intentions from the beginning meeting.
- A skilled facilitator, expert practitioners, and dedicated staff with plenty of positive energy to take care of the details are essential for success.
- A commitment to teach authentic art-making processes tied to big ideas that really matter.

The transformative process of these three days has carried over throughout the summer months and the start of the school year. The time and space made for exploration and discovery was well worth the effort. Teachers will begin the school year with a passion to share their own learning with their students and each of us is immeasurably richer for the experience.

I feel fed as a creative spirit.

What worked best is not only talking about the things we can do in the classroom, but actually performing them ourselves.

I plan to steal a lot of the activities that we observed and participated in. And I plan to restructure the way I work to put art at the center...to find away to make the integration whole rather than it being viewed as a special activity.

TEACHERS EXPLORE COUNTER-
BALANCE AND STABILITY AT
THE AIM SUMMER INSTITUTE.
PHOTO BY JOEL WANEK.

TEACHERS AND ARTISTS
EXPERIENCE THE JOY OF
WATCHING THEIR COLLEAGUES
LEARN THROUGH THE ARTS.
PHOTO BY JOEL WANEK.

The Power of the Chill

**ARTIST CADRE MEETINGS
AS PROFESSIONAL DEVELOPMENT**

Cynthia Weiss

On a wintry Chicago morning, Daniel Lopez, teaching artist and percussionist, begins his lesson. It is Friday, and his weary students have worked a long week. Daniel knows he has to focus their scattered thoughts. He introduces an engaging exercise that will connect percussion and writing.

Today, we will work with the idea of opposites in percussion. I am going to ask you to create opposing rhythms using your left and right hand. But first, to get you into the idea of opposites, please write down five sentences about your morning so far. And... please describe the opposite of what actually happened to you this morning, using your opposite hand to write.

Daniel's visceral and playful assignment pulls everyone in. His students pick up their pencils with their non-dominant hands. They laugh at their chicken-scratch writing and descriptions of their inverted morning routines.

Daniel's students are indeed eager, but they are not in a school setting. Rather, they are a roomful of teaching artists, coming together to share strategies and challenges, theory and practice, at a monthly Arts Integration Mentorship (AIM) project meeting of the Center for Community Arts Partnerships (CCAP) at Columbia College Chicago.

The group laughs in recognition when they read aloud morning routines that are common to teaching artists everywhere:

> *This morning, I did NOT push the snooze button on my clock radio.*
> *This morning, I was NOT running late.*
> *This morning, I felt secure to see the HUGE balance in my checking account.*
> *This morning, I was NOT delighted to be here, doing this exercise with all of you.*

Daniel asks the group to connect the written phrases to drumming patterns and perform for each other. Some of the teaching artists who are not performers are a bit reluctant to share their work but the cadre meetings provide a safe atmosphere for taking risks and everyone gives it a try. Then the artists have a chance to debrief. They ask Daniel questions about the structure and goals of his lesson. Their questions have the nuanced specificity of practitioners— wishing to learn and adapt new strategies in their own teaching practice.

Teaching Artist Cadres: Stories from the Field

This opportunity for peer sharing takes place at the Project AIM Teaching Artist Cadre meetings held the first Friday of each month. Artist attendance is expected, and meeting time is compensated. Beyond routine staff meetings, these monthly gatherings have evolved to meet a common need for support, guidance, and shared reflective practice. While not fancy, there is always food and coffee. Breaking bread together on a regular basis has become a metaphoric and literal opportunity for collaboration. The richest time is often the round-the-table sharing of classroom challenges and successes.

Amanda Leigh Lichtenstein, Project AIM arts educator and poet, describes what she receives from the monthly meetings:

> *The exchange of teaching ideas and front line stories— failures, success, surprising moments—has made an indelible impact on my teaching. I leave these meetings energized, ready to reflect on, and revise my teaching strategies and curricula, and make my time in the classroom more meaningful and real to both myself and my students. Project AIM meetings give me the chance to let my guard down, take a deep breath, and speak openly about the frustrations and joys of being a teaching artist.*

Learning-Centered, Constructivist Classrooms

What has emerged from the Project AIM artist meetings is a learning community that bears a strong resemblance to a constructivist classroom where participants are active, motivated learners co-creating knowledge with each another. By sharing experiences across disciplines and schools, teaching artists raise common issues, including:

- dealing with classroom and time management;
- building partnerships with teachers;
- understanding the value of culminating events;
- learning how to best critique student work;
- working with shy students;
- building trust in the classroom;
- developing curriculum from inquiry questions; and
- making breakthrough connections between arts and literacy learning.

Most importantly, the process of discussion and reflection helps to build a *theory of practice* that will in turn deepen the quality and impact of our work.

Cross-Disciplinary Conversations and Curriculum

Project AIM's common curricular goal is to energize the reading and writing process through the power and imagination of the art-making process. Project AIM artists are fiction writers, poets, spoken word performers, actors, dancers, percussionists, photographers, video and filmmakers, bookmakers and visual artists; they come from many Columbia College Chicago departments as well as community-based arts organizations. They bring their multiple art forms and a passion for their craft to the classrooms. Artists are encouraged to access the dual languages of *text & image* to help students make deeper connections to reading and writing.

Photographer Joel Wanek works with students at Albert R. Sabin Magnet School in Chicago; they are studying the portraiture work of famous photographers. Students learn to develop a critical eye for composition, framing, and finding a compelling image through the viewfinder.

Joel directs his students to compose portraits of one another, and shows them how to use the strong light and dramatic architecture of their majestic school building as a background. The students create arresting portraits that in turn inspire narrative writing filled with visual detail, persona, and the mystery of place.

At the same school, Daniel Lopez extends the ideas developed at the artist meeting to create teaching strategies to connect rhythm, percussion and reading fluency. Daniel works with fifth-grade students to record a straightforward reading of original folktale stories. He then coaches them to create a beat, rhythm and tempo that match the dramatic qualities of their writing and to read their stories with a layered, musical expression. The students reflect on how the meaning of their stories has been enhanced by this music-making process.

There is much to learn about the impact of these interdisciplinary connections in both our project and the field of arts and education. Project AIM staff is working with the teaching artists to articulate and create curriculum that utilizes these *parallel processes* strategies. Collection and dissemination of work will culminate with an end-of-the-year curriculum showcase. While assessment of student, teacher and artist learning is an on-going process, exciting outcomes are already reported. Teachers routinely talk about the ways that the artists and art processes engage their marginalized students, students talk and write about their own learning in both content learning and arts skills, and samples of student work show growth in students' abilities.

Making Deeper Artist/Teacher Connections

Project AIM teaching artists have formed strong professional and social bonds with each other over the past three years. The strength of this artist-to-artist connection highlights the need to build more opportunities for artists and partnering teachers to make deeper connections. Teaching artists and classroom teachers work in very different contexts. An on-going challenge is to find ways to bring teachers and artists together to work out the delicate dynamic of team teaching and clear understanding of the gifts that each person brings to the partnership.

Professional development workshops are an ideal time for teachers and artists to get to know each other as fellow students outside of the school setting. Project AIM Teacher Development workshops follow the same model and spirit as the artist cadre meetings. The workshops have been set in Chicago museums (Mexican Fine Arts Center Museum, Chicago Historical Society and Garfield Park Conservatory) to access the city as a resource.

avery r. young, a spoken-word poet with Young Chicago Authors (YCA) and a Project AIM teaching artist, embodies the very nature of community building. His kinetic energy and passion for poetry, spectacle and student voice can energize a room of teachers, artists or students, anywhere. avery, along with all the artist cadre members, leads workshops at project-wide professional development sessions. Teachers have the chance to experience the same lessons that their students will be taught. They return from these sessions laughing and ready to perform for one another. The best practices that engage students and artists also engage teachers: working with a sense of joy, taking the time to build community, providing hands-on activities, encouraging teachers' creativity, and facilitating dialogue and group reflection.

Power of the Chill

Most teaching artists live fragmented lives, working as independent contractors for multiple organizations. They travel from school to school, working their magic, but often don't have peer groups with whom to share their concerns. Paul Teruel, friend, colleague, and Director of Community Partnerships at the Center for Community Arts Partnerships (CCAP), talks about the *power of the chill.* He is talking about the power of serendipitous connections made in the downtime of work, over lunch, a beer, or an open space found in a hectic schedule. The Project AIM monthly meetings, and the Urban Missions partnerships meetings that Paul directs, are an enforced slowing down and coming together; they are an incubator for the *power of the chill.* Arts education programs need to create these open studio environments in order to support teaching artists to refine and revise their craft. Regular, paid artist meetings, facilitated with the intention to create a shared sense of purpose and vision, will surely lead to the formation of stronger learning communities and advance the work of arts integration.

PROJECT AIM TEACHING ARTIST CADRE AND STAFF 2007. PHOTO BY JEHAN ABON.

(LEFT TO RIGHT) **ROW 1:** DANA LOGIUDICE, SHAWN RENEE LENT, LUIS CRESPO, LEAH MAYERS **ROW 2:** SADIRA MUHAMMAD, QWEEN WICKS, JULIE A. DOWNEY, CYNTHIA WEISS, GUILLERMO DELGADO, LISA REDMOND, AVERY R. YOUNG **ROW 3:** JOHN LYONS, MARTEZ "MISTER" RUCKER, TONY SANCHO, KHANISHA FOSTER, AI LENE CHOR, RON PAJAK, JENN MOREA, BARLOW **ROW 4:** CYNTHIUM JOHNSON-WOODFOLK, DEBORAH GUZMÁN-MEYER, AMANDA LEIGH LICHTENSTEIN, ARCHIE ROPER, JOEL WANEK, CECIL MCDONALD, JR., DAN GODSTON

Project AIM artist meetings represent a legitimate chance to take a break with colleagues and friends. It provides us with a chance to exchange ideas, to be challenged, and to re-engergize. These meetings carry over into all aspects of my life. I learn everything from nuts-and-bolts classroom strategies to inspirations for making a new piece of work and new ways of working as a photographer. These meetings give me a chance to discuss my life's work.

–CECIL MCDONALD, JR., PHOTOGRAPHER, AIM TEACHING ARTIST–

Spirals and Chills

THE ASSESSMENT OF
LEARNING IN PROJECT AIM

Deborah Brzoska

ARTS EDUCATION CONSULTANT
KENNEDY CENTER FOR THE ARTS

I spend a lot of my time working with folks around the country on the notion of assessment in the arts—a dubious career, but gratifying, nonetheless. Some of my most gratifying moments have occurred in Chicago with the talented staff and teaching artists of Project AIM, crowded into an energy-filled meeting room at an urban youth hostel, surrounded by images and artifacts of children's art-making. Between donuts and sandwiches, we re-enact Project AIM lessons, easily becoming children, and then transforming ourselves back into teaching artists reflecting on learning. Here in Chicago, this is assessment in action.

Cynthia Weiss, Project AIM's director, calls these sessions, "The Chill," and like a wise mother bear, she fiercely protects and preserves these reflective opportunities that are the very soul of Project AIM. Taking the time to build a learning community, to share and reflect—and paying teaching artists to do it—places assessment at the heart of Project AIM. And I am honored to be a part of it.

Like good teachers and teaching artists everywhere, we first needed to challenge and sort out our pre-conceptions of the assessment vocabulary: critique, evaluation, rubric, judgment, criticism, and that most onerous term of all, *"grading."* We made a few agreements: first, we agreed that when we talked about assessment in Project AIM, we would be talking about the assessment of **student learning.** Second, we agreed to define "assessment" in Project AIM as the **process** of giving **feedback** to students about their work. Finally, we agreed that although we would create rubrics—**rich descriptions of quality**—we would create these along with classroom teachers and with kids—a process infinitely more meaningful than traditional "grading."

Arts Assessment—
It's About Student Learning

One of the advantages of Project AIM is that classroom teachers have reinforcements. The teaching artists lead students through arts-integrated lessons while their partners—the classroom teachers—are able to take part and to observe for student learning. Each teaching team collects a variety of evidence of learning, not only student art products, but journals, unit plans, quotes and comments along the way—little case studies. These are the stories of the impact of arts integration that Project AIM will be able to tell the world.

More importantly to the AIM Arts Integration Learning Spiral, these stories and artifacts become the source of ongoing reflective practice for the teachers and artists—formative assessment—that allows them to grapple with challenges and re-shape instruction. Many of my sessions with the Project AIM teaching artists have been centered on these reflective conversations and the only requirement is that student work be on the table. With the artifacts in front of us—images, poems, paintings, and films—we are able to collectively attend to student work, giving it the careful attention to detail that it deserves, and mine the work for evidence of learning.

We examine difficult questions of quality; "What does a quality fifth-grade film look like?" "Can we agree that this is a powerful image?" and "What makes it so?" Armed with new insights that come from these reflective discussions, Project AIM teaching artists are better able to give students the information they secretly desire: HOW to create satisfying, quality work in the arts.

Arts Assessment—
Reflective Feedback from Beginning to End

Education expert Grant Wiggens defines "feedback" as "information." He points out that it is not praise or blame, but information that students can use. Like jazz artists, Project AIM teaching artists practice together regularly: informational conversations, descriptions of what they see in student work, and through practice, they collectively improve their "feedback chops." They graciously allow me to play the role of the "describe police," making sure that we describe what "our eyes see" in the artwork of students rather than interpretations from the mind's eye.

This process of describing student work—giving students information they can use—has its payoff in Chicago classrooms, where Project AIM teaching artists work to carve out the time necessary for reflective conversations with students about their ongoing work.

Assessment happens on most points of the AIM Arts Integration Learning Spiral and the work of artists and teachers is to highlight assessment each step of the way. When creating a safe community of learners, artists and teachers assess whether a space has been established where each person and their work is honored and attended to. When artists, teachers, and students revise and share, everyone commits to an ongoing investigation into their own learning. When the time comes to perform and exhibit, the ultimate performance assessment, process and product are indispensably linked. By the time teachers, artists, and students arrive at a space to reflect and assess, when everyone compares final products with original intentions, each has the opportunity to assess the ways in which they have grown throughout the process.

Arts Assessment—
Creating Rich, Descriptive Rubrics

Rubric. In my nearly twenty years of leading professional development in arts education from Portland to Pago Pago, I have found no other word that instantly garners more fear and resentment than *Rubric.* I have tried to disguise it with various other terms: "scoring guide" (too much like the Olympics), "descriptions of quality" (true, but once you put it onto a chart that looks like a rubric, no one is fooled). So I tried definitions. The dictionary has many—and often conflicting—definitions which are perhaps one source of educators' instinctive distaste for the word:

2. "a title or heading of a statute or chapter in a code of law"
3. "a name for a class or category"
5. "any brief, authoritative rule or direction"
7. "from the Latin rubrike, 'red earth'
   – 'anything written in red.'"

"Law," "Class," "Authoritative rule," "Anything written in red"—it's no wonder the term "rubric" fares badly in Democratic classrooms.

I encourage the teachers and teaching artists in Project AIM to think of rubrics as journeys, rather than endpoints—road maps, if you will, that describe work at varying stages of quality and allow students to chart their own progress. When students are involved in the assessment process, they take greater interest in their own learning. Some of the best rubrics I have seen—and written—are those that were designed along with students, using the students' own descriptive vocabulary.

Every day, the teaching artists in Project AIM model for students that art-making is a process—an often messy one—filled with thoughtful reflection and ongoing revision. It is a process that will serve students far beyond the arts classroom, preparing them for a future where creative solutions are required. We must educate whole children for the future they will face. The children in Chicago have a healthy start, thanks to Project AIM.

TEACHERS AT THE AIM SUMMER
INSTITUTE TAKE A MOMENT TO
FRAME AND REFLECT MID-PROCESS.
PHOTO BY JOEL WANEK.

*Every day, the teaching artists in
Project AIM model for students that
art-making is a process—an often
messy one—filled with thoughtful
reflection and ongoing revision.*

–DEBORAH BRZOSKA–

12
Strategies

For Teaching In And Through The Arts

Cynthia Weiss and
Amanda Leigh Lichtenstein

What exactly happens in an arts-integrated classroom? How does arts integration look and feel? In most of our professional development sessions, we work with artists and teachers to develop and practice arts strategies that we can transfer to our classrooms. We share activities, questions, exercises that inspire new experiments. While we recognize that each residency, like an artwork, is unique to its contributors, we want to share techniques and methods that others can adapt.

Project AIM artists "aim" in on specific arts strategies in their medium that never seem to fail to engage a wide variety of learners. Project AIM artists and teachers think of "strategies" as readily applicable exercises, games and artistic experiments that can be used interchangeably to meet myriad interests. The specificity of these strategies makes them more immediately accessible and sparks experimentation across disciplines. It is through specificity of a strategy that artists and teachers feel that they can borrow and apply these exercises in multiple contexts.

At professional development sessions, teachers have an opportunity to explore, discuss and adapt these "tools of the trade." We generously share with each other and with you, the reader. We welcome you to use these strategies the very next day in your classroom!

The first strategy, "Responding to Text Through the Arts," is a distinctive process used in Project AIM professional development workshops to engage text and image. Each of the following strategies echo the value we place on reading and responding to texts of all sorts through the arts. (With a special thanks to Jackie Murphy and the Arts at the Center team from Chicago Teachers' Center who first inspired us in this process.)

Poet Jenn Morea and visual artist Cynthia Weiss explain a multi-phased writing exercise that uses photography to help writers "get to the essence" of an idea. Visual artist Barlow tells us how he teaches gesture and line in the classroom. Another great exercise is Guillermo Delgado's "The Seven Minute Shoe Drawing" which invites learners to draw without thinking. Filmmaker Bryan Litt gives us a hint on how to prepare students for "test interviews" in a documentary film workshop, and filmmaker Ai Lene Chor explores the links between filmmaking and storytelling in "Composition Mission." In "The Listening Exercise," writer Cynthium Johnson-Woodfolk writes on the power of listening and describes a focusing exercise for the classroom. Amanda Leigh Lichtenstein offers a way to connect writing and photography in her haiku workshop, "Capturing the Moment." Book and paper artist Jamie Lou Thome explains one of her favorite writing exercises called "Found Poetry," and Khanisha Foster offers one of many fantastic theater exercises in her strategy "Steal the Focus." Dancer and choreographer Shawn Renee Lent explains a movement exercise used to create confident movement through an exploration of stability and extremes. Finally, dancer Sadira Muhammad offers a way into teaching culture through intensive studies of ethnic Afro-Caribbean dance.

Arts Integration Strategies

Try It Now.

Index

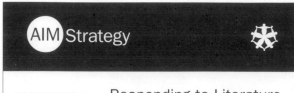

PROJECT TITLE	Responding to Literature through the Arts
ARTIST	Project AIM Cadre and Cynthia Weiss
ART FORM	Interdisciplinary Arts

Context

Reading research has shown that proficient readers are able to visualize images in their mind while reading, and in the words of educator Jeffrey Wilhelm, "to enter the story world." The arts can offer powerful strategies to deepen reading comprehension and support students' capacities to visualize, make inferences, discover main ideas, and make personal connections to texts.

The cycle of activities described below has been used as the foundation of many Project AIM teacher professional development workshops. The sequence of events can be offered to both adult and student learners to respond to both fiction and non-fiction texts.

Description

- Select a story or text relevant to your students' interests and lives.
- Lead a front-loading discussion that helps everyone to make a personal connection to the text and access prior knowledge before they begin to read.
- Read the text out loud, allowing students to read in the order that they wish.
- This reading serves to build a sense of community and create a shared experience for the audience.
- Create a sensory web with the group; soliciting images from the five senses.

- Discuss the big ideas implied in the images and write down the concepts and main ideas. (For example, decide if the story is about displacement, freedom, coming-of-age, etc.)
- Offer break-out workshops in at least 3 different art forms to respond to the ideas of the text.
- Return to whole group to share art products.
- Reflect on how the different artistic responses contribute to new understandings of the story.

Challenges

The main challenge of this strategy is to find and bring together a group of artists, art specialists, and/or classroom teachers with expertise in different art processes. They will need to construct lessons that use the elements, principles or processes of the different art forms in order to express an aesthetic response.

This workshop cycle works the best when at least 3.5 hours can be devoted to the process.

A good break-out of time is: 1) Introduction of Text and Discussion, 0.5 hour; 2) Break-out art-making workshops – 1.5 hours; 3) Sharing of Art Products – 0.5 hour; 4) Reflection on the experience – 0.5 hour.

Variations

The very strength of this workshop is found in the variation of response to a single text. Each of the art forms will offer students a different language of expression. For example, Visual Arts: Collage Compositions to express abstract ideas; Video: Storyboards to reinforce sequencing, close-ups and long shots to express point of view; Dance: Levels and qualities of movement to express the emotional tone of the text; Drama: Voice and gesture to express character's point of view, and Tableau to visualize relationships between characters; Spoken Word Performance: Repetition and musicality of words to capture emotion; Poetry: Use of syntax and line breaks to get to the essential ideas; Creative Writing: First person narratives to explore a character's inner dialogue.

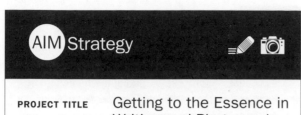

AIM Strategy	
PROJECT TITLE	Getting to the Essence in Writing and Photography
ARTIST	Jenn Morea, Poet Cynthia Weiss, Visual Artist
ART FORM	Writing and Photography

Context

This text and image exercise allows participants to move back and forth between words and pictures in order to make editing choices and arrive at essential ideas. This lesson provides structures that help students move from the literal to the abstract in both writing and visual image making.

The power of this interdisciplinary lesson comes from the reinforcement of parallel concepts in two different mediums. It offers participants *a-ha* moments where insights in one art form may illuminate an idea in another.

This a great first-day lesson for both writing and photography units of study.

Description

Framing Warm-up Activity

Each participant is given a small cardboard viewfinder. They are asked to look through the frame, to move it back and forth in front of one eye, and to notice what changes when they hold it closer or farther away. They are then invited to frame a detail in the room that captures their attention. These framed views are shared with partners. The framing activity and viewfinder are great focusing tools to encourage careful observation.

Looking at Photographs through the Artist's Natural Frame

A collection of Xeroxed photographs by professional photographers is laid out on a table (see resources).

Participants are invited to choose one of the photographs and examine the natural frame composed by the photographer. Each participant tells the group what caught their attention in their photos.

Writing the Story with 24 Words

Participants are then asked to write the story of their photographs in exactly 24 words. They are instructed to write in sentences, as opposed to writing a list of words. Participants can write in 1st, 2nd or 3rd person—whichever they feel will help them tell their story the best, and are encouraged to notice the possible narratives of the wide views, as well as the narratives in the smaller, more subtle details.

Phase Two

Cropping the Photographic Image

Participants are then given a viewfinder with a smaller opening (4" x 5"). They are asked to re-see and re-frame their photograph by moving their frame over the photograph and creating a new composition with the frame.

Writing with 12 Words

Following this, participants return to their writing. They are asked to skip a line, and to pull 12 words from their original 24 to write the story of their photograph again. They are allowed to rearrange the order of their words, but not allowed to add any new words, or to change the words in any way.

Phase Three

Closer Views

Participants are given viewfinders with smaller openings (2" x 2.5"), and asked to re-see and re-frame their photograph once again.

Writing with 6 Words

From there, they return to their writing. This time they can only look at their previous 12 words and select 6, following the same rules.

Phase Four

Closing in on an Essence

Finally, participants return to the small viewfinder that they used in the warm-up with a 1" x 1.25" opening. They are asked to place their frame on their photograph and move it around—up and down and across—until settling on a perfect fit. Many of the images at this point, in such small frames, with so much context excluded, take on lives of their own. These very abstracted images may tell entirely different stories.

Writing the Essence with 3 Words

Finally, participants pull 3 words from their 6. They are asked to hold up their photographs and read their poems, beginning with 24 words and ending with 3.

Reflection and Discussion

The workshop concludes with a discussion on how images and stories change when the work is pared down to its essence. Participants discuss the relationship between the process of cropping photographs and editing words, as well as how the reduction of an image to its details, and a story to 3 essential words, leads to abstraction, and therefore the expansion of an idea. Teacher workshops conclude with a discussion on specific ways this lesson can connect to subjects and concepts being taught in the classroom.

Challenges

Participants state that in Phase 3 and 4, as the viewfinder gets smaller, it is difficult to continue writing with the same words because the process of moving the frame to a new area changes the story. They are encouraged to focus on the writing as separate from their current frame, and reminded that both the details they have chosen to frame, and their 6 words, both have their origin in the photograph as a whole.

When Essentialization is taught as a stand-alone writing exercise, students sometimes insist they can't tell their story in just 24 words, and want to be able to add new words as they go through the next steps of the process. But, when they are encouraged to find a solution within these rules, they feel the lesson to be a very engaging experience.

Variations

Essentialization Autobiography

Jenn Morea often begins her writing residencies with the Essentialization exercise without using the photographic component. She asks her students to write their autobiography, the story of themselves in 24 words, then asks them to make edits to 12, 6, and 3 words following the same directions given above.

Abstracting the Still Life

Cynthia uses the frame as a visual and conceptual organizing tool for a variety of lessons. One application is the frame as a compositional device in observational drawing. Students frame close-cropped views of sections of a still life to set up in the room. This lesson encourages different abstracted perspectives and variations from each member of the classroom.

Photographic Images Used
- Graciela Iturbide, Images of the Spirit, Aperture.
- Flor Garduno, Witnesses of Time, Aperture.

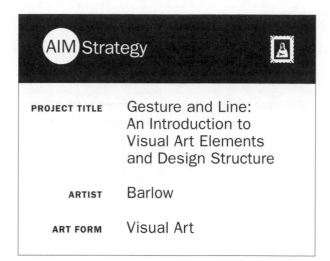

PROJECT TITLE Gesture and Line:
An Introduction to
Visual Art Elements
and Design Structure

ARTIST Barlow

ART FORM Visual Art

Context

This exercise is designed to be an introduction to the visual arts elements (line, shape/form, value, texture, color and space) and to the principles of design structure (balance, contrast, emphasis, repetition and unity). Ideally, this exercise would occur during the first session of a residency in a middle or high school setting.

The following is an interactive drawing activity that focuses on the importance of line as the primary visual structure used to produce graphic representation. The focus is on gesture line drawing (quick sketching emphasizing the essence of form, not rendering) using the human figure as the model.

Description

Because most students are familiar with the 'stick figure' as an easy representation of the human form, the instructor first demonstrates this through drawing. Students can begin to understand the structure of the human form (e.g., head is connected to the neck, the neck connected to the thorax, the arms are connected to the thorax).

The instructor should demonstrate by conducting a series of short poses for the students to capture in 'stick figures' quickly with pencil and/or charcoal sticks. The instructor's poses should be gestural in nature and should communicate mood, action, and/or expression so that students make the connection that the gesture line drawing is used to communicate as well as produce graphic representation.

Students then participate by taking turns posing for one another, trying their best to capture poses that communicate mood or action. The instructor uses this opportunity to observe students' drawing skill levels.

Challenges

This exercise may require various adaptations for physically challenged students. Students younger than 6 years-of-age may not be able to handle this exercise as described above.

Variations

This activity can be expanded further by adding the techniques of 3-dimensional form (mass and volume) as it relates to the human figure. Drawing through the form is a term used to suggest and encourage the investigation of the shapes such as cylinders, ovals, circle and triangles. Again, the instructor should lead off the modeling demonstration so the students have a visual representation of the potential outcome of this technique. This activity can further be expanded by adding hatching and/or cross-hatching to emphasize the "play of light" value.

AIM Strategy

PROJECT TITLE	The Seven-Minute Show Drawing
ARTIST	Guillermo Delgado
ART FORM	Visual Art

Context

This activity creates a positive sense of tension and excitement for artists at any level. There is no time for the artist to think about drawing or to feel that they will fail. The process of the Seven-Minute Shoe Drawing forces artists to be careful observers–to pay attention to detail, and get up off their seats. Usually this activity is done at the beginning of a residency to engage artists, and is then revisited at the end in order to evaluate growth.

Description

Artists are asked to draw the "best" shoe drawing of their life, without erasing, and using only one sheet of drawing paper. Students partner together and take turns modeling for each other. Models carefully stand on the desk in front of their artist partner and pose their shoe (profile/side position). Students start and end together, wait for teacher to say "Go!" and "Stop." The artist must draw for the entire seven minutes; the model must keep their foot still until the time is up. No talking is allowed during this exercise. Periodically, the teacher calls out the remaining time. Artists are asked to sign their pieces and title them, "(My Name)'s First Shoe Drawing."

Challenges

The teaching artists may be challenged by getting the students to draw for the entire seven minutes, denying them to erase, and allowing them only one sheet of paper.

Variations

Ask the student to write a letter to the shoe in the drawing and to also write a response from the shoe. Students take turns reading their letters aloud to the class.

PROJECT TITLE   Test Interview

ARTIST   Bryan Litt

ART FORM   Film

Context

Before students shoot longer films, they work with their entire crews to shoot test interviews. This is done to simulate the experience of shooting their films in a safe environment where students feel free to experiment while also gaining a better understanding of the equipment, the crew dynamic, and how to think on their feet.

Description

A crew of six students have the following roles: Producer, Director, Camera Operator, Assistant Camera Operator, Sound Mixer, and Boom Operator. The Producer must find a subject from the class for the director to interview. While the producer finds a subject, the director reviews his/her interview questions or goals. The camera operator prepares the location for shooting with the help of the camera assistant. When the subject is brought into place for the interview, the sound mixer and boom operator must get into position for optimal sound recording. During the interview, the producer and director take notes on the subject's responses. Immediately following the interview, the director and producer find appropriate b-roll (complementary) footage. For example, one interview subject talked about how much she enjoys jumping rope. That crew then located a jump rope and shot footage of the subject jumping rope with friends.

Challenges

Challenges to this exercise can include getting students to work together in crews; clear communication of ideas throughout the crews; effective soliciting of information from subjects; finding an appropriate balance between aesthetic preferences, time and location restraints, and clarity of content; introducing multiple new concepts at one time; as well as problem-solving in a group within time constraints.

Variations

One variation is to simplify the exercise by not using the mixer and boom pole operator. This is effective if the students seem overwhelmed.

PROJECT TITLE Composition Mission

ARTIST Ai Lene Chor

ART FORM Film/Photography and Writing

Context

By combining photographic composition and free writing, students produce short stories/writings that show depth, even when the nature of the project doesn't call for a final writing project.

Materials needed: Assortment of full-sized photos (color photocopies of travel photos from foreign countries from *The Lonely Planet*), pre-cut paper frames (sheets of paper with a rectangle that mimic the viewfinder of a camera), glue, scissors, pencils, and students' journals.

Description

This activity starts out with the students holding up pre-cut paper frames and looking through them to see their environment, as if framing-up photos with actual cameras. The concept of zooming in and out is introduced as students can move the frames closer or farther away from themselves. The compositions within the frames change, as with a zoom lens.

Each student places his or her frame over a large photo (students each pick one photo that interests them). Students are instructed to stencil out a framed composition using the paper frame. They cut out the compositions and glue them into their journals. The idea of how a photo is "worth a thousand words" is explored. The class discusses the elements that caught their interest in terms of composition and content. Students then write a creative story based on the photos. They label their compositions, reinforcing their understanding of labeling shots and shot scales such as CU (Close Up), MS (Medium Shot), etc.

Challenges

This exercise requires a certain amount of time and assumes that there have been prior lessons introducing film/video/photography, shot scales, storytelling and writing techniques, etc. This exercise also requires a certain degree of literary competency (e.g., spelling, grammar, command of the language of choice). Allow much more time if the students have yet to develop such competencies.

Variations

Students' stories could be told in different languages to encourage personalized creative freedom, particularly since this exercise is generally more useful early in a residency. Students could also do a "Walk and Talk" where they get up and, similar to attending a gallery exhibit, view their classmates' choices and compare how others may have had a completely different viewpoint of the exact photos they chose. Students' stories could also be shared aloud in class.

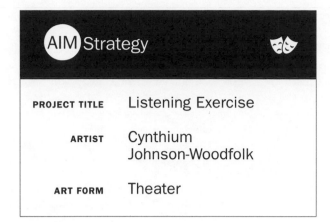

PROJECT TITLE Listening Exercise

ARTIST Cynthium Johnson-Woodfolk

ART FORM Theater

Context

The Listening Exercise produces abstract thinking and utilizes seeing-in-the-mind. It is designed to open creative space and it guides students into a deeper realm of listening. Their awareness becomes keener and they follow the rhythms of the sound. Images of shapes are formed and connections are made, causing them to see a gestural image for the sound. The rhythms become, as in writing, the patterns sought after in voice and the natural rhythms of the language. The gestural images or shapes seen for the sound becomes the physical vehicle used to project the telling. It allows students the opportunity to get in-tune with their physical self, combining consciousness with kinesthetic awareness.

Description

In the Listening Exercise, the teacher coaches a student to:

- Listen. Listen to the sounds in the room, send your listening through all of its spaces, every corner, to the ceiling and the walls. Listen. See what's taking your attention. It can be a real sound or an imagined sound…but listen.

- Listen as the sounds begin to separate one from the other, following the directions of the sounds. What's there? See it and follow the sounds from beginning to end. Let them begin to separate, picking up another sound while at the same time listening to the spaces between the sounds. Without dropping your sound, keeping your listening in the room, expand and send your listening out into the hall, down the stairs, and onto the street, picking up another sound. It can be a real sound or an imagined sound, but listen. See what it gives you to see.

- Trace the sound in your mind's eye. See the gestural shape of the sound. What does it remind you of? Get your best sense of it. What does it give you to see? When you've got it and can see it clearly—even feeling and tasting the texture of it—tell it out here in this space and tell it as if it's being told for the first time, keeping your eye right on it, see it, making the image with both your body and your voice, drawing it with your hands, tell it out here in so that we can see it, giving it to the semi-circle.

- Keep making that gesture. See what that gesture reminds you of. See what the motion gives you to see. What is it like?

- Drop your hands. Do the gesture again. What else does it give you to see? Search deeper, push past the gesture that's making the sound and take it from the hand. See it as something else. Go for something more abstract; make it a moment of history.

Challenges

It is important that you keep timing in mind because it is of the utmost importance. Speeding through the exercise can affect the students' seeing, while droning can also have an adverse effect. Pacing is the key. Become an active participant in the exercise yourself, and use your sense of seeing as the meter.

For your first time trying this exercise with a group, things may not go as smoothly as planned. These students are new to this. They won't understand what you're pushing for and they definitely won't understand why they're listening to the sounds in the room. They'll think it's a silly exercise and that you've lost your mind. This is the case even with adults. Make it interesting to them and push them to test their abilities. If need be, stack the deck. Pick one student to experiment on and coach him to try, praising his attempt, pointing out the parts of the exercise that were successful. Also, question the student that made the attempt on his experience after having tried the exercise. Let his responses do your selling. The rest will conform and join in. Surprise and off-balance moments are good for seeing. It adds to the sense of discovery.

Variations

To further stimulate your students, explore and see what happens if you make them stick to the gesture, forbidding it to change.

Detailed in *Writing from Start to Finish: Teacher's Manual* by John Schlutz.

AIM Strategy

PROJECT TITLE	Capturing the Moment: Writing Haiku in Reponse to Photographs
ARTIST	Amanda Leigh Lichtenstein
ART FORM	Poetry/Photography

Context

How can you capture and express a single moment in time through poetry? How can a photograph inspire tone and word choice in poetry? How can writing poetry allow for deeper meaning and connection with a photograph?

The following is a great exercise for writers and artists of all ages. This is also an excellent activity for professional development with teachers and educators interested in developing and understanding arts-integrated curriculum. The length of this particular activity is approximately 60 minutes but can be expanded to cover several sessions.

Description

In this workshop, participants learn about Japanese poetic forms and then write within these forms in response to photographs. First, look at a photograph and brainstorm words, phrases and thoughts associated with that photograph. Discuss the mood and feeling of the photograph. Next, look at and read model haiku poems. Talk about these poems as "snapshots"—or as a single moment in time. Using a frame (cut simply out of paper) narrow in on a single aspect of the photograph and write a haiku that captures that image with words. Choose three moments within a single photo to "frame" and then create a haiku for each. Read poems out loud to someone sitting next to you. Experiment with a collage of photo and poem to present to the class.

Challenges

Participants should have a working basic knowledge of poetry, poetic language, and poetry elements. Photos should evoke strong emotion and feeling and participants should be able to choose the photograph they want to respond to poetically. Using Model poems are definitely helpful. I like to combine Langston Hughes' haiku with Gordan Parks' photographs. A general understanding of the following vocabulary words are helpful: mood, tone, haiku, image, gesture, line break, syllable, sensory details.

Variations

Participants can learn not just about haiku but related forms like Renga and Senyru. Participants can create a book of their poems and photographs. They can take their own photographs and respond poetically to create a text/image series.

AIM Strategy

PROJECT TITLE	Found Poetry
ARTIST	Jamie Lou Thome
ART FORM	Poetry

Context

This exercise can be used to provide students with an "in" to a piece of literature that the instructor believes the students may find difficult to access or understand. This activity may also be used as a quick writing exercise within a longer project.

Description

Students read a short, age-appropriate text aloud in class. Students then think of the main idea or theme of the piece, discussing the most poignant imagery and what resonated with each of them. The students are asked to take out their scissors and literally cut up the text, in 1-3 word phrases that resonate with them in some way. Students are given about 5 or 10 minutes for this part of the process.

After the time limit for cutting is reached, students arrange the cut phrases into a found poem. There is a given time limit for this activity as well. After approximately half of the time limit has passed, a challenge is thrown in. Students must take one of the words/phrases that the students haven't yet placed into their poem and trade with another student. Then they must use that new word/phrase in their poem. Staff can choose to do this challenge more than once; after you have used this exercise a few times, the students come to expect the challenge, so mix it up. When the time limit is up, have the students volunteer to read their poems aloud.

Challenges

Students may feel self-conscious while creating poems, so having them 'arrange' the words and phrases they chose rather than 'write' may help them lose that self-consciousness. Once the class has done this exercise a few times (or if the students are older), the instructor should avoid assigning the next reader. Students will eventually jump in and this process will help inspire spontaneity in the rest of the exercise.

Variations

Students can be encouraged to paint the journey of their texts onto a long thin paper. Then, after folding the paper accordion style, students can paste their poems into these books they have created. Watercolor is an ideal technique for this process. Students could also use text from fiction, non-fiction, history textbooks, etc.

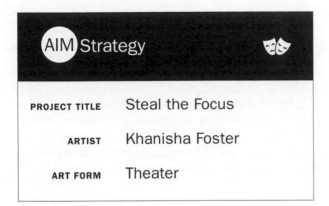

AIM Strategy

PROJECT TITLE	Steal the Focus
ARTIST	Khanisha Foster
ART FORM	Theater

Context

This game is derived from "Theater of the Oppressed" by Augusto Boal. The activity works well during the beginning of a session or residency in a middle school setting. By the end of the game, student vocabulary has usually increased and the class is encouraging each other to make bold decisions.

Description

The class creates an audience on one side of the room and a bare stage space on the opposite side. In the center of the stage space, there is a single chair.

Students are asked to add chairs one-by-one. The trick is that as each student has to steal the focus of the audience, his/her chair has to dominate the picture. Students on stage are not allowed to speak; they are only to make bold and creative choices.

Each time a student places his/her chair, the audience must discuss whether or not the chair has succeeded in stealing the focus. If the answer is yes, the class discusses why this is so before the next student takes a turn. If the answer is no, the class discusses why this is so and the student tries again until the class is in agreement.

Challenges

Facilitators should encourage the students to let others make their own choices about where to put the chairs. Try to acknowledge everything, even the choices that seem disrespectful; often these students actually have an incredible artistic eye.

Variations

After the students have tried this activity with chairs, encourage them to try it with their bodies. Rather than placing chairs, students freeze in positions that steal focus. In addition, feel free to discuss the relationships being created on stage. After all, if an inanimate object can create a relationship, then it should be a breeze for the students.

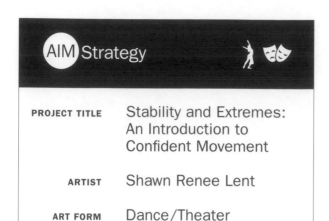

AIMStrategy

PROJECT TITLE	Stability and Extremes: An Introduction to Confident Movement
ARTIST	Shawn Renee Lent
ART FORM	Dance/Theater

Context

This exercise asks participants to explore balance, coordination and confidence; it is most appropriate for grade 6 through adult. The activity serves as a great warm-up for a workshop, rehearsal or performance. With further expansion of this exercise, poses and gestures can be extracted for the development of movement and choreography based on a theme.

Description

Standing in a circle, the facilitator asks everyone in the group to each find his/her own center of gravity, where weight is precisely equal on both sides, as well as front-to-back. Each participant is to imagine themselves as trees with deep roots and branches out to the sky, in all directions—sending energy and breath out through his/her chest, back, ears and eyes. Each person is to find a point where (s)he is at their most stable, first on two legs and then on only one. Other images to explore during this initial standing activity include: cotton candy (with a solid core and a sweet, active outside), saboteur (growing wings out your back and four legs like a deer).

Participants are then asked to explore the room; walk around...walk alone...walk in a pattern as if you had paintbrushes for feet...walk a grid...follow someone...walk alone but observe what is happening around you. Whenever the facilitator calls out the word "stable," participants

return to their stable positions. Each time they are asked to create even more extreme variations of stable positions (extremely low, extremely tiny, extremely tall, extremely fast, extremely wide, etc.)

The activity progresses to include running and jumping into position, then balancing on one foot or in a counterbalance position with a partner (either convergent or divergent energy). Each round of this exercise expects participants to find more extreme poses and movements.

Challenges

Space is the biggest challenge. Ideally, this activity is done in an open, safe environment with no obstacles and proper flooring. Watch out for dusty or dangerous flooring, sharp objects, etc. If the space is not ideal, those challenges and considerations could be incorporated into the exercise. Boundaries, proper attire, and speed limits may have to be determined and clarified. The exercise can be done with students in wheelchairs with little to no adaptation.

Variations

These "stable" moments can be expanded to include gestures or shapes associated with thematic concepts and terms such as time, boundaries, (in)dependence, searching, etc. Extremes could include extremely low, extremely large, extremely tiny, extremely robotic, extremely dependent, etc. This exercise is a great method for students to explore settings or maps; putting themselves physically inside a story or place increases literacy and comprehension of geography. Students can transfer an imaginary or real place to the classroom. While traveling around these settings or maps, the facilitator can call out directions such as "Go to a place that feels like home; Go to a place that feels foreign; Go to a place with a unique smell; Go to a place that looks amazing; Go to a place where you are in control; Go to a place with conflict; Go to a place that's fast-paced; Go to a place that's laid back, etc." Naturally, these directions guide the participants to physicalize these settings, adding gestures and actions to these places. Each student can then take a partner on a tour of his/her setting or map, with each partner reporting back on where they've been.

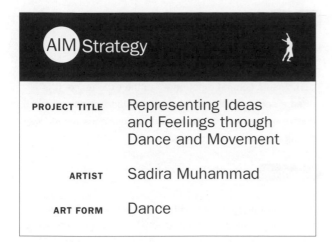

AIM Strategy

PROJECT TITLE	Representing Ideas and Feelings through Dance and Movement
ARTIST	Sadira Muhammad
ART FORM	Dance

Context

This dance lesson will help teachers and students to kinesthetically represent the ideas and meanings of a text through movement. The lesson will offer ways for students to express their inner feelings and emotions outwardly which allows for self expression and encourages awareness of the body and the language that it can speak. I have found that when students physically engage in the language of stories they gain enlightened knowledge around core ideas. Often, my goal is to use the kind of texts that have the potential of bringing out ideas with strong, emotionally charged human values, such as sisterhood and empowerment, longing, or remembrance; or use texts with cultural themes, to focus on one element of that particular culture.

Artist Statement of Belief

When I dance to the rhythm of drums, the drum propels my body forward in an effort to catch up with my soul which has been dancin' all along. When I dance to the rhythm of the drums, moving to set choreography or an 8-count beat become meaningless; I experience the emotional outpouring that is my nature.

I think of the ritual and tradition of my ancestral beginnings. Every time I move in this spirit, I am granted confidence and a pure sense of self.

I believe that this is what my students get when they dance to the rhythm of the drums. There is definitely a healing element at the psychological root of African dance. When a student is charged with learning about their roots, and engaged in a physical activity that is indigenous to those very roots, a powerful method of gaining knowledge is at play. The result for our students is a renewed sense of self-understanding and worth, and awareness and appreciation of the body as a vehicle for rich and meaningful expression.

Simply stated, dance is a universal language and engagement in it opens up a whole new world of critical and conceptual thinking and vocabularies.

Description

Reading the Text

Participants will read a chosen piece of text, (both fiction and non-fiction texts will work for this exercise) out loud. Participants will discuss the main ideas in the text and look for action words and sensory-based details that support those main ideas. Students will be asked to pick sentences in the text that have a personal meaning to them, and discuss why these ideas are important.

Breathing and Movement Warm-up

Participants will be led through breathing meditation exercises; they will be asked to raise their hands upwards, as in a prayer or praise dance, breathing in with upward hands, and out when lowering their arms.

They will then be asked to follow the facilitator through a stretching routine in order to loosen muscles for injury prevention and preparedness for movement.

Matching Movements to Ideas

Participants will be given a rhythm either by way of live percussion, and will walk around the room trying out simple movements that in some way represent the ideas from the text—specifically the part(s) of the text that opened up something personal for each person. They will be coached to either make direct translations of movements and words, or to create more abstract movements that are their own personal reactions to the words.

Sharing Movements within the Group

Once participants have decided on some initial movements they will share these and get feedback from a partner in the group.

The dancer/facilitator will work with the group to shape the individual movements into a narrative sequence, so that the movements will flow with each other, the music and the sequence of the text. The dancer/facilitator will coach participants to enlarge and stylize their movements to make sure that they portray an emotional connection to the ideas and to the music.

Presenting the Dance to an Audience

The participants will present their sequenced and choreographed movements to an audience of peers, and ask for some response about how the dance served to communicate new ideas about the written texts.

Reflection

Participants will be asked to reflect on how the translation of ideas into movements in their body helped them to make new connections about the work. They will also be asked to reflect on the experience of dancing and to talk about their comfort level with performing ideas.

Challenges

It is important to select texts and ideas that are relevant and interesting to the participants, and that the participants commit emotionally to the experience. It is often a special challenge to reach adolescent boys through dance; a focus of the rhythm and percussion is a good way to engage boys in the process.

Variations

An element of the lives of African people, either from a historical perspective or a traditional one, can also become the entry point and subject for a dance. For example, choreography can be created based on the Haitian revolutionary war to focus on a significant event in African history. A folkloric dance theater piece might be created based on Caribbean people selling their wares in the marketplace and focus on core lessons about the Caribbean economy, geography, hand-crafts and cultural expression.

CULTURAL DANCE EDUCATOR, SADIRA MUHAMMAD
SETS THE CONTEXT FOR A COMMUNITY DANCE
PERFORMANCE AT THE AIM SUMMER INSTITUTE.
PHOTO BY JOEL WANEK.

Professional Development As Reflective Practice

- Value and set aside ample time for professional development and make sure participants are compensated for their contributions.

- Food and humor is a must.

- Create and nurture a community of learners by organizing non-competitive, non-hostile group experiences in the arts.

- Be willing to be a teacher and student at the same time.

- Offer a variety of professional development opportunities and curate them as artfully as possible.

- Create a space at the table for everyone.

- Create an intellectual atmosphere where people's ideas and thoughts are respected.

- Make sure teachers and artists can take away something from the experience that is immediately meaningful in their classrooms.

- Recognize the need to make art as part of our development as arts educators.

- Create rubrics with your students.

- Provide opportunities for reflection at all professional development sessions.

The Art of Partnerships

The Art of Partnerships

Cynthia Weiss

The people I love the best

jump into work head first

without dallying in the shallows

and swim off with sure strokes

almost out of sight.

– Marge Piercy
From her poem "To Be of Use"

Arts Integration partnerships are complex systems that support complex work. The need for strong coordination and leadership at the organizational *and* interpersonal level is essential. The contribution of an anchor organization and its program staff to the success of a strong partnership cannot be overstated. A strong anchor provides fiscal management, grant development, marketing, human resources, program coordination, professional development, and evaluation. More intangibly, a lead arts agency offers leadership to directly support the continuity and sustainability of a program.

A good match between the mission of an anchor organization and the school program partners is paramount. All partners need to be sensitive to each others' rituals, rhythms and cultures to cultivate and imagine a shared vision. Project AIM is a program of the Center for Community Arts Partnerships (CCAP), which serves as an anchor organization and bridge between Columbia College Chicago and our partner schools. Anchor organizations like CCAP provide crucial external support and outside resources to overtaxed schools. The role of facilitation is often invisible, but attention to tasks like scheduling and coordinating meetings provides essential structural support to develop and grow successful programs.

At the Center for Community Arts Partnership and at Project AIM, program staff brings an artist/educator sensibility to the direction of the work. The values that guide Project AIM classroom practice also define our administrative approach. On our best days we work hard as a staff to create a spirit of camaraderie at all levels of the program.

In this chapter you will hear contributors speak to the Art of Partnerships, and the importance of open communication in sustaining long-term relationships.

- Joanne Vena, CCAP Director of School Partnerships, and Barbara A. Holland, Project AIM/FIPSE Program Evaluator, write about the value of *reciprocity* in college/community/school partnerships.
- Columbia College Chicago English professor, George Bailey, speaks about the *fellowship* formed when he and Thurgood Marshall Middle School teachers created a meaningful learning exchange that led to a vibrant, long-term partnership.
- Principals Leonor Karl from Casimir Pulaski Fine Arts Academy, and Dr. Betty J. Allen-Green, from Theodore Herzl Elementary School speak to the importance of the arts in their quest for positive school change.
- Good partnerships are often built on good chemistry. Edward Jenner Academy of the Arts' art teacher, Mathias "Spider" Schergen, and Project AIM filmmaker, Crystal Griffith felt an affinity and connection with one another from day one. Their mutual respect became a model and inspiration for the Friday Boys film crew who blossomed under their co-direction and co-teaching.
- This Chapter on the Art of Partnerships ends with the artful and honest voices of seventh-graders at Thurgood Marshall Middle School. Amanda Leigh Lichtenstein interviews her students who speak uninhibitedly about their desire for adults to take them and their ideas seriously.

With these varied voices, we see the mutual benefits for all partners. Here we speak to the dynamic between Project AIM, our school partners, CCAP and Columbia College Chicago, and yet across the country similar partnerships inspire:

- teaching artists to develop richer teaching lives;
- public school children to gain a broader sense of possibility;
- public school teachers and principals to have an extended professional community beyond school walls; and
- institutions of higher learning to have a dynamic relationship with their communities.

The parting words of Thurgood Marshall Middle School students remind us that the ultimate intention behind meaningful partnerships is to give voice and opportunity to the hopes and dreams of young people.

THE CENTER FOR COMMUNITY ARTS PARTNERSHIPS (CCAP)
IS LOCATED AT COLUMBIA COLLEGE CHICAGO'S SOUTH
LOOP CAMPUS. PHOTO BY NOLAN WELLS.

Building
and Sustaining
Sucessful Partnerships

Barbara A. Holland, Ph.D.
FIPSE PROJECT AIM EVALUATOR

Joanne Vena
DIRECTOR OF SCHOOL PARTNERSHIPS
CENTER FOR COMUNITY ARTS PATNERSHIPS

Many colleges and universities link their services to local educational institutions, community-based organizations, or citizen groups. They do this based on the assumption that their attention constitutes a sustainable partnership. However, building and sustaining an arts/education partnership requires greater intentions than a series of random or episodic interactions. We have seen many schools engage in "checkbook diplomacy"—this refers to keeping partners connected as long as both are compensated for their time. Unfortunately, there is no true link to learning or the development of skills—both by the educators involved or by the students who receive these services.

A partnership is built on a true relationship that ensures reciprocity and mutual benefit. This requires the development of long-term goals that demonstrate sustainability beyond the immediate project or event. In order to create a successful partnership, several questions must be asked: What are the connections to the overall school improvement plan? How do teachers and artists that have worked together discuss their outcomes with their peers? Are there innovative teaching strategies that can be learned by others? What are the recommendations of the partnership that can be shared within the school as well as within the district and, beyond that, nationally?

When a school joins forces with an arts organization/institution to build a partnership, they must function like a group of architects—by this we mean that each may have his or her own unique sense of style as to approaching the design phase. Then, through much conversation, they must collaborate to take on the actual construction. In addition, each partner organization or individual has specific strengths and limitations that help define their role and capacity to contribute to the partnership. Most of them will join the circle to be part of a local group experience, but they all have a specific idea of what they want. At the "partnership table" are educators, artists and administrators who have varied interests. Some are glowing with enthusiasm for the creation of something new while others in the group want a more classic form to take shape, while still other participants are there to support the mechanics of the construction phase.

Effective partnerships exhibit particular characteristics that are strongly associated with success and sustainability. The following factors represent values and strategies that support positive relationships, shared decision-making and mutual benefit:

- Joint exploration of goals and interests
- Creation of a mutually rewarding agenda
- Emphasis on positive consequences for each partner
- Identification of opportunities for early successes
- Focus on knowledge exchange, shared learning and capacity-building
- Attention to communication, cultivation of trust
- Commitment to continual assessment of the partnership itself, as well as the outcome(s) of the partnership

In the best situation, these factors are able to be seen and felt by all of the participants in the development of the partnership. A prime example of a partnership that grew out of the needs and interests of several educators and the Center for Community Arts Partnerships (CCAP) is the one we created with Crown Community Academy. Four years ago, in a meeting with a staff member of the Chicago Public Schools, concerns were expressed by the fine arts staff that teachers at the school needed to more fully understand how the arts could play a critical role in overall student learning. A core group of teachers came to the CCAP office to discuss the potential of building a partnership that would incorporate the arts specialists in addition to the general classroom teachers. As a result of this meeting, greater input was given by other staff members. This eventually grew to encompass parents as well. The project grew and diversified to encompass both in-school and out-of-school program opportunities for the children and their parents. During this initial year, a relationship was kick-started. That relationship has grown significantly but still maintains its core group of leaders that help to plan and determine programming throughout the year.

Play, Learn, Engage

Whenever you work with a group of diverse and creative thinkers, it is a given that each member of the partnership will have their own interpretations of how the arts can be used as the foundation for effective, engaging learning. There is usually some heavy lifting required by most of the partners throughout the beginning of the planning process in order to conceptualize what is going to happen and when. In an ideal situation, building a partnership means that the weight of the decisions will be equally distributed—but that doesn't always happen without considerable effort. Attention to strategies that ensure good communication and shared decision-making make for the best partnerships. We recommend using a model of leadership that connects people to their strengths as they move forward. This approach will maximize participation while making the experience memorable and rewarding for all participants.

When particular members assume the leadership position, they should be careful to allow the group a sense of direction without being overly controlling—all voices must be heard. Keeping the entire group involved when determining the partnership's next steps will encourage continued investment and energy. As the work evolves, this sense of connection through inclusion of all members will help to cement the foundation that supports the group's commitment to success.

At Casimir Pulaski Fine Arts Academy, Principal Leonor Karl has made it her personal business to keep all of her arts partners engaged in the process of building stronger and more coordinated programming. Doing this ultimately benefits all of the teachers and students. She holds quarterly meetings with all the representatives of the arts organizations that work at Pulaski to share information and plan effective schedules for the school. This helps to maintain a personal connection to everyone who brings services and support to her teachers in the arts and learning.

Trust and Communication

Sustaining a partnership relies on the participants having trust in the leaders of the group that the relationship has created. These leaders must ensure that commitments will be met and that each partner's goals and needs are respected. While the work matures over time, trust develops. Trust is invaluable to the partnership in order to meet the needs and interests of all involved. Respect is one indicator of reciprocity and will ensure that your partnership can weather the difficult times that can emerge in any collaborative effort.

Keeping everyone in the "loop" is critical to being a good partner, as well as bonding the group of participants. Good communication demonstrates and strengthens a sense of inclusion and shared responsibility. This idea of "shared responsibility" includes making time for the group to share their stories, ideas and concerns with others. This is especially important when processing the outcomes or planning the next steps.

Think Strategically

While your partnership framework may be solid, changes in people, organizations, assets and programs almost always occur. There comes a time when you must mend holes or fill gaps. Partnerships, while not always perfect, can be flexible enough to allow the partners to admit their missteps, rework troublesome areas, and then continue to work ahead without fear of losing sight of the overall vision.

Uncertain funding, cutbacks in government spending and rising expectations of educators to meet unfunded mandates in their schools have presented very real challenges to many partnerships. Honest evaluation and open discussion among all partners is the best way to adapt to changing conditions. Focus on previous successes and respond to these challenges without a sense of threat to the partnership. This constructive-reflective practice will support the partnership's work objectively. It will also permit other perspectives on the value of the collaboration.

Celebrate Successes

Frequently celebrating the successful conclusions of the partnership's efforts can remind everyone involved of how important their collective energy is to the whole group. Celebrating success will also demonstrate how far the group has come from their beginning. Culminating events draw attention to the participant's efforts and can also bring in new supporters and partners.

The resources and energy invested in partnerships are greater than the single transaction of service by an artist in order to work with just one classroom. This display of collective action can build momentum as well as greater options for improving student learning and the quality of teaching.

The Project AIM Curriculum Fair is an annual culminating event for all of the schools. The showcase celebrates the cumulative efforts of the educators and teaching artists who have worked together all year. Each partnership is represented by a display of process and product through the digital and hard copy documentation. Actual, authentic pieces of artwork by the students and a visual presentation for the group also serve to recognize and value everyone's efforts. This special night brings all of our schools together. It allows us all to share in the discreet and collective efforts of the Project AIM participants as educators who share common goals and strategies for high quality arts educational experiences.

Sustain Relationships

Partnerships are not just a series of projects or events—they are relationships. The emphasis on clear goals, mutual benefit and shared responsibility means that partnerships are relationships of "exchange." We work together because each of us has our own assets, needs and opportunities that can be leveraged to greater effect through collaboration. As in all relationships, partnerships require maintenance, time and attention. Here are some proven strategies for sustaining partnership relationships:

- Invest the time to build understanding of each partner's organization, culture, assets and limitations—get to know each other!
- Create clear partnership structures with decision-making guidelines
- Articulate substantive and specific roles for all partners
- Meet regularly and often
- Create a timeline for both short and long term goals
- Take time to assess the impact on partner organizations
- Reflect together on the "state of our partnership"

Making Lasting Connections

COLUMBIA COLLEGE FACULTY IN THE COMMUNITY

George Bailey

WRITER, ENGLISH DEPARTMENT FACULTY
COLUMBIA COLLEGE CHICAGO

When individuals and groups of individuals come together to build partnerships and collaborations that foster arts in the schools, templates of inestimable value come forth. The results of such labors provide opportunities for all concerned to participate in *creating something.* In particular, when children engage in processes of *making something,* they are (in essence) building themselves. It is through the guided and spontaneous acts of manipulating materials to a conceptually humanistic purpose that children are brought into the gloriously entangled orbits of calling self into being. These are the grand generalities with which I am left after participating in dynamic, multi-layered arts in the schools initiatives.

I make these unabashed claims based on my experiences and the observations of productive relationships between a broad array of individuals and groups representing Thurgood Marshall Middle School, Columbia College Chicago's Senior Seminar (now defunct), CCAP and respective individuals, too numerous to name. When I use the phrase "arts in the schools," I reference the specific connectives and relationships instigated between the three above stated organizations.

During the spring of 2001, I first met Mary Clare McCarthy (Clare), my liaison at Thurgood Marshall Middle School. I don't remember the exact language of that first phone conversation we had, but after we'd finished talking, we'd launched a partnership and a collaboration that continues between Marshall Middle School and CCAP to this day. Our initiations into our first project grew out of our collective needs to provide purposeful and meaningful learning outcomes and experiences for our respective students. We decided to link our project to the "One Book, One Chicago" community reading of *To Kill a Mockingbird,* the highly celebrated novel written by Harper Lee. For us it was a seminal moment; we inaugurated our project at the critical moment as did Chicago's Mayor Daley, who desired to

"cultivate a culture of reading and discussion in Chicago by bringing our diverse city together around one great book."

We cobbled together a few organizational meetings with Marshall teachers, Julienne Backstrom, Dee Simpson, and Clare, and soon forged ourselves into a highly motivated and organized fellowship. I will always remember these teachers as individuals who came at their work with great power, great delight, with a consummate relish for firing the imaginations of even the most unsuspecting mischief-makers. I was amazed at how they gained the attention of their students, how they were always in each others' rooms, with each others' students, shaping and guiding these middle school children to light-bulb moments by alchemies, wondrous and marvelous to behold.

Over the summer we called each other to reflect on what exactly we'd do in the fall. We decided that we'd create an activity in which Marshall Middle School students would read the novel and extract key scenes from the story that they would then stage and act out. The goal was to collaborate with the Thurgood Marshall Middle School for the purpose of creating an "infomercial" related to the citywide reading of Harper Lee's *To Kill a Mockingbird.* Seniors enrolled in my college seminar, a ready-made work force, provided technical and artistic support by way of taping and post producing the product. The objective was to create a short, entertaining persuasive message to middle school students arguing the benefits of reading the novel. In addition to providing college seniors an immersion experience in using technical skills and equipment, this collaboration made it possible for middle school students to observe the values and the behaviors that the seniors modeled.

As a Senior Seminar instructor, I took the approach that the class should function as a capstone, providing graduating seniors with a space to reflect upon the status of their skills as measuring devices to validate what they had learned. In this highly activated real-time classroom space, college seniors were called to "take stock" of who and what they thought they'd become over the course of their undergraduate careers.

I challenged them to ethically examine and re-examine their skills-base and to declare how such skills could be used to legitimize their roles as artists in the community. I encouraged them to consider that they were real students, with real skills, engaged in doing real activities, in a real situation. In each of my class sections I was amazed by the quality and quantity of "know-how" accumulated in a classroom of graduating Columbia College Chicago seniors. The space emerged as a wonderfully crazy, risky testing ground for students of diverse interests to use the semester-long activity as a kind of simulation for making future projections after graduation.

The culminating activity of the *To Kill a Mockingbird* infomercial project was a screening of the video in the Ferguson Auditorium on the campus of Columbia College Chicago. Columbia College students and Marshall Middle School students sat in the dark, laughing, slapping palms, biting nails. I was also reminded that I am forever the student before I am the teacher, always eager to locate something new in something old. We learned a great deal from that experience. I learned that I had to learn how to delegate more responsibility to my seniors. I learned that I did not have to rent a bus to get students across town to the site of the project, that leaving that problem for students to solve was a great education for those who were uncertain about public transportation and city dwellers alike. I learned that when mounting large scale projects, partners had to have good overall organization and there were students in the seminar who were always itching to show how much of an "A" personality they possessed.

The second—and perhaps the most satisfying project— developed over the course the fall of 2002 and the spring of 2003. Two different groups of graduating seniors participated in the Community Chess project. Once again we were working with the same team of teachers from Thurgood Marshall Middle School. This was truly an extraordinary coming together of energies. The goal of the two-year project was to develop a life-size chess game and perform the game at *Manifest,* a festival of the arts held each

year to showcase Columbia College Chicago's graduating seniors' work. Throughout this project, Columbia College Chicago seniors and Marshall Middle School students demonstrated the highest levels of cooperation, creativity and inventiveness as we researched the game of chess and made other preparations. One of the Marshall classes was doing a unit on the history of heraldry which complemented our project. Marshall Middle School teachers wrote and received a grant from the Oppenheimer Foundation to procure materials to build the board.

We had all learned lessons from earlier projects and we brought those lessons to bear on the chess project. The fall semester teams of seniors wrote proposals, solicited food and contacted college administrators for support. The spring semester team of seniors built the costumes (red and white queens, kings, knights, bishops and pawns), some of which have since been used by Shakespearian players. So many individuals stayed up all night the day before the performance of the chess game to complete the work. A senior named Anna Livermore coordinated the sculpting of the garments. We were all grateful for her fashion savvy and skill with a sewing machine. We were sure that the Manifest chess game performance would never happen, and when it did happen, we could not believe how beautiful it was.

The children from Marshall Middle School arrived, dressed in the costumes and paraded around the building with the shields they'd made out in front. It was a wonderfully promising day in May and there was color and music and well-focused children realizing what we had all accomplished. Champion chess players from Beethoven Elementary School were invited to join us. They invited passersby to play the game. Mr. Oppenheimer came and commented that it was one of the best uses of foundation funds he'd seen in a long time.

The level of participation in response to the excitement generated by this project motivated first semester seniors to return to see the performance. After the culmination of this project, the Senior Seminar curriculum was phased out. But, because such vibrantly alive links had been formed between Columbia College Chicago and Thurgood Marshall Middle School, we established a plan to continue those links between Marshall Middle School and the Center for Community Arts Partnerships. The work goes on today in Project AIM.

DIANE SIMPSON, CARLOS MENDEZ,
AND GEORGE BAILEY AT A PLANNING
MEETING AT MARSHALL MIDDLE
SCHOOL. PHOTO BY CYNTHIA WEISS.

Talkin' Back:
Chicago Youth Respond

A COLLABORATIVE EXHIBITION OF STUDENT PHOTOGRAPHY AND WRITING BETWEEN THE MUSEUM OF CONTEMPORARY PHOTOGRAPHY AND PROJECT AIM/CCAP

Cynthia Weiss

The *Talkin' Back: Chicago Youth Respond* exhibition, now in its fifth year, began as a conversation about text and image among photographers and writers working in programs sponsored by the Museum of Contemporary Photography (MoCP) with the Center for Community Arts Partnerships of Columbia College Chicago. This collaborative partnership, directed by Corinne Rose, Manager of Museum Education at MoCP and Cynthia Weiss, Project AIM, showcases student work that is created at many sites, from schools to community arts centers throughout Chicago.

Collaborative teams of classroom teachers and teaching artists (drawn from Columbia College's photography and fiction writing programs and community-based arts organizations) engage Chicago youth in exploring the power of one art media to inform the other. All of the projects encourage students to go beyond a one-on-one equivalent of word to image, searching for a deeper mode of expression that resides in the tension between the two.

Students from fifth-grade through high school make photographs and write on themes including identity and self, and the documentation and representation of their communities. Students also explore conceptual and experimental uses of photographic processes and writing genres. Teachers, artists and parents are always impressed by the power of photography to motivate even their most reluctant writers.

A centerpiece of the exhibit is the group installation titled, *1000 Words/1000 Images.* Participating students are asked to write in response to a photograph from the museum collection, and to collectively take 1000 pictures in response to a generative word. The installation creates a collaborative vision and voice gathered from all the program workshop sites. This installation was inspired by a series of inquiry questions posed by teachers and artists in the project. Their questions included: *What do words add to images? What do images add to words? Which has more weight or authority? Will an artwork develop differently if the image is made first? if the words are written first? What happens when words and images mean different things? How can an image be used to get beyond literal meanings of words? Is a picture worth a thousand words? Is a word worth a thousand images?*

The high-quality, professional presentation is mounted by dedicated museum staff and demonstrates a respect for students' ideas and efforts. This partnership brings together Columbia College faculty, graduate and undergraduate students, teaching artists, classroom teachers and public school students throughout the city.

This collaboration between the Museum of Contemporary Photography, directed by Rod Slemmons, and the Center for Community Arts Partnerships, directed by David A. Flatley, began through a grant from the Surdna Foundation and continues today with support from the Lloyd A. Fry Foundation, City of Chicago Department of Cultural Affairs/ After School Matters, and other funders.

STUDENTS CREATE ONE THOUSAND WORDS IN RESPONSE TO PHOTOGRAPH BY ABELARDO MORELL,
AND ONE THOUSAND IMAGES FROM THE WORD, *RHYTHM,* FOR THE TALKIN' BACK EXHIBITION AT
THE MUSEUM OF CONTEMPORARY PHOTOGRAPHY. PHOTOGRAPH BY THOMAS NOWAK.

One Thousand Pictures
Rhythm

Leadership Matters

PRINCIPALS WITH A VISION

Cynthia Weiss and
Amanda Leigh Lichtenstein

AN INTERVIEW WITH

Dr. Betty J. Allen-Green
PRINCIPAL OF THEODORE HERZL
ELEMENTARY SCHOOL

AND

Leonor Karl
PRINCIPAL OF CASIMIR PULASKI
FINE ARTS ACADEMY

DR. BETTY J. ALLEN-GREEN,
PRINCIPAL OF THEODORE HERZL
ELEMENTARY SCHOOL.
PHOTO BY JOEL WANEK.

LEONOR KARL,
PRINCIPAL OF CASIMIR PULASKI
FINE ARTS ACADEMY.
PHOTO BY CECIL MCDONALD, JR.

**What is most essential
in building arts partnerships?**

Mrs. Karl: You have to pick your partners carefully if
you want success. You have to make sure that you
can help each other and that your school will be a
cooperative school. I would like to say how fortunate
I feel to have the external partners that we have
at Pulaski. The right people have come to me with
proposals, and I have to be been able to just trust
them and say yes.

Through our Fine Arts specialists, Debbie Sanchez
and Annie O'Malley, we made initial connections
with CCAP and Hubbard Street Dance Chicago. We
had some good history with Cynthia Weiss through
her past work at the Chicago Arts Partnerships in
Education (CAPE) many years ago, and we were
impressed with Kathryn Humphries at Hubbard Street
Dance. I knew I could trust these partners. With
that start, it just mushroomed and more people got
interested in getting involved.

Dr. Green: The essential element in building an arts
partnership is to select a partner who you can trust
and maintain an open line of communication with.
Communication is primary. We need to communicate
about every aspect of the partnership. Our Community
Schools resource coordinator, Rachel Culich, is in
constant communication with Cynthia, the Project AIM
Director, and the artists working with her. However,
Cynthia, Rachel, the artists, the classroom teachers
and I also collaborate regularly about the Fine Arts
Program. This collaboration is the key to the success
of our program. In addition to Cynthia, we are also
fortunate to have talented administrators like Joanne
Vena and April Langworthy leading our Columbia
College partnership. Everyone involved is skilled at

creating developmentally appropriate arts curriculum for elementary school students. In addition, they are able to select artists such as Barlow, Cecil McDonald, Jr., avery r. young, and Cynthium Johnson–Woodfolk who compliment our school culture perfectly and serve as role models for our gender-based classrooms. Together we are able to talk through important issues and formulate goals for our program. This kind of partnership allows us to develop wonderful programs for our children and we definitely see the benefits.

What is your role as a principal to support and sustain arts partnerships?

Mrs. Karl: I need to come out of my office and show that the partnership programs are important to me and the school. It would be easy to say that I was too busy to attend more meetings, but I know that my showing up and being there really sends a supportive message. I have to make the time available for teachers and artists to plan together. It is important for me to check in, because you don't want people pulling in different directions.

Teachers need to be able to self-select and feel comfortable with the artists and art forms, and with sharing a classroom with another teaching partner. It's all in the personnel whether the residencies go well; if there are issues with personalities, if they don't click, it doesn't work.

Dr. Green: We are a Community School. My primary vision is to increase the academic achievement and improve the children's literacy levels by bringing in as many resources as possible. Project AIM fits very well into that vision because everything the program does is designed to increase literacy levels. We see academic performance improving and we see student attendance improving as well. Our children are very expressive because of the confidence they get in all our in-school and after-school programs. They have been involved in dance, photography, and the arts—all designed to bring out these skills. They feel safe. My job is to support these programs.

How do you manage so many external partners working at your school?

Mrs. Karl: We need to bring all the partners together to meet common goals for the school. If a school has many external partners, it's important that all the stars line up. External partners need to know each other and make sure that there is an overall plan so that each group is not stepping on each others' turf. You need to take into account where the resources are going across the school. I want to make it equitable and provide partnerships for all grades. I also need to protect the instructional time for math and reading. There can be a moment (if there are too many special projects) when there is too much.

The principal has to be a good partner, know what outside partners need and provide it to them. When new opportunities come up, you think about your existing partners and invite them to work with you in new initiatives.

One grant has led to another, the Improving Academic Achievement through the Arts grant made one connection, Project AIM and Hubbard Street Dance Chicago led us to two Department of Education grants. Pulaski is designated as a Community School. Our students love the Columbia College community school's after-school arts program; our site coordinators, Lea Pinsky and Liz Parrott, are so popular with the kids that when they go into the classrooms, they get applause. Our community schools partnership has led to a new state grant to develop resources for parent involvement. If I had to do all the grant writing by myself, it wouldn't get done. I really didn't do all that much work. I just said yes to our partners.

Dr. Green: I came to Herzl as a teacher. I've been here over twenty-five years. We've always wanted to be thought of as a community school and a focal point for agencies and activities. We want to make the parents feel comfortable. So we look for programs that embrace the parents. In addition, we started having parent/family nights. We wanted to provide all kinds of activities to encourage parents. For those parents who didn't finish high school, we have GED programs and literacy classes, both those programs are going strong today. We have great coordination from Rachel Culich, our site coordinator; she coordinates a quality program where it's always easy to talk to the administrators and artists about what's going on.

What are the qualities that make this work successful?

Dr. Green: 1) Sensitivity – to the needs of the kids and to those in our communities. There is a great commitment to our kids. We want them to succeed. 2) Positive role models – We need partners that know how to talk positively to our students. They let them know they can achieve whatever they want to. 3) Coordination – we need to make sure that key people are available on staff to coordinate all the various programs at our school.

Also, a primary thing I notice is commitment from the artists. They are not only here for the hour. When they leave, they plan and come back to plan and talk about what they'd like to see happen with those kids. And now those kids have the same kind of commitment to them. Assignments are eagerly finished. Kids come back with photos taken of their bedrooms, their neighborhoods. Every time I walk down the hall they are trying to snap my picture! Project AIM artists motivate those kids, and that is so very important. The first phase of becoming a true independent learner is to become highly motivated. So many children have artistic skills. We have to develop them. Once they develop those skills, they blossom in other areas as well.

One other thing I think is so very important—our sixth, seventh, and eighth-grade classes are divided by gender. The male artists assigned to work with our boys have helped to present positive role models. Cecil and avery feel such a responsibility to be good role models. And the boys really look forward to them coming.

How has Project AIM professional development worked for your teachers?

Mrs. Karl: Teachers look forward to the arts integration professional development. They can experiment with an area and an art form where they might not be that comfortable. The workshops are a safe place to try out an idea or a strategy. The teachers surprise themselves; it lets them experiment just like the kids. It sparks some creative juices and it's different, it is not our usual model of professional development; it lets the teachers go with their strengths.

When you see that the teachers enjoy the professional development; when you know that the quality is good and meeting teachers' needs, and they all come back and say that this is the best workshop they have ever had, then you can support the time required for teachers to participate.

Project AIM also helps us by giving us extra time to talk and opportunities to communicate around the table. We also make sure we are all on the same page in terms of literacy as a bottom line. With Project AIM, I am able to communicate openly and often, and this is important; it is a match made in heaven.

What can you say about the impact of the arts on your students?

Mrs. Karl: Our students love all the Columbia College teaching artists. Theatre artists, Tony Sancho and Khanisha Foster, worked with our students during the school day and after school. Our sixth-grade students worked with Tony and teachers Neeta Agrawal and Eileen Kahana to put on scenes from Shakespeare's *A Midsummer Night's Dream*. Our parents and staff also helped to make costumes and help with the sets. I was totally impressed by the work of the students in every part of the production.

Khanisha Foster and teacher, Judith Diaz, worked with the seventh-grade. This was a group that was not getting a lot of positive reinforcement. Then they got on stage and had great success with their drumming and performances; they got so much positive feedback from the audience. When you see this progress with one of the hardest classes at the school, you realize that the arts provide students a different way to succeed.

There has been a general improvement in the test scores of our students that I attribute to all initiatives in our school. I believe it's a combination of the work of: our classroom teachers and fine arts specialists, the in-school and after-school partnerships with Columbia College Chicago, Hubbard Street Dance, Chicago's work with primary teachers, the Fine and Performing Arts Magnet Cluster, Chicago Arts Partnerships in Education (CAPE) programs, and our Saturday programs. We have received intensive staff development and literacy training from Northeastern Illinois University; many of our staff got their reading endorsement in college classes offered at our school. It is the combination of all these partners that ensures that if we don't reach students in one way, we can reach them in another. It is the mixture of all of this that has made Pulaski special.

Dr. Green: Our children need an avenue to express themselves. Most of our children live in apartments and don't get a chance to run outside, play and release energy. Sometimes it appears that a classroom is in "holy chaos." However, once I enter the class, I realize that the students are just expressing themselves. They may be in a circle shaking their bodies, speaking in unison, singing or even jumping up and down. Right away I realize that in that apparent chaos, there is an order to it all. These activities provide the avenue that allows our children to express themselves and learn valuable skills.

The photography class with Cecil McDonald, Jr. and avery r. young was wonderful. Students took self-portraits and developed beautiful pictures. They learned to write about those photos and express their feelings. Of course, we created a gallery which continues to beautify the school. These students can forever return to the school, see their portraits and remember the experience.

I don't usually cancel morning reading classes. However, this was so important, and generated such an interest in our male specific class, that we held this class at reading time. The boys were so interested in taking photography and I realized that whatever the artists were doing, they were making literacy connections. Whenever they took pictures, the students would write about them. In the art workshops, they are constantly reading and talking about what they have read, which checks their comprehension. The work is *literature rich,* in that there is high-level vocabulary, which increases word knowledge and comprehension. Every activity improves students' writing skills. The teacher collects, grades, publishes and encourages students to share their work. I love the publications, and the children love seeing their writing published. For most, it is their first publication and it's something they have for the rest of their lives.

There is great transference—carry over—from the fine arts classes to the regular education classes. If students can read and comprehend in the arts, they can read and comprehend in any other class. The arts help develop a desire and love for reading. Also, during the regular school day, we teach social skills, how to critique and accept criticism. But if you teach those skills and never practice them, you never really learn them. In the arts, students not only learn the skills, they are provided the opportunity to apply the skills they have learned. This makes all the difference.

I need to come out of my office and show that the partnership programs are important to me and the school. It would be easy to say that I was too busy to attend more meetings, but I know that my showing up and being there really sends a supportive message.

LEONOR KARL, PRINCIPAL
CASIMIR PULASKI FINE ARTS ACADEMY

There is great transference—carry over— from the fine arts classes to the regular education classes. If students can read and comprehend in the arts, they can read and comprehend in any other class. The arts help to develop a desire and love for reading.

DR. BETTY J. ALLEN-GREEN, PRINCIPAL
THEODORE HERZL ELEMENTARY SCHOOL

It Was the Way You Made Us Think

AN INTERVIEW WITH
THURGOOD MARSHALL
MIDDLE SCHOOL
SEVENTH-GRADERS

Amanda Leigh Lichtenstein

"I think as you grow, say, if you're five-years-old,

adults hold on too tight. But when you get

grown, and you get more problems, [they]

start to let go. So I think as you get older,

[they] should hold on tighter. Because say

when you're five, and you fall, they get really

worried, just for a little fall, but then when

you get older, more problems come, and they

just start letting go."

– **Marilyn,** Seventh-grade

Following a 10-week unit called "The Poetics of Time,"
Project AIM artist Amanda Leigh Lichtenstein returned
to Thurgood Marshall Middle School to interview six
students about their experiences with the project. Their
project was a poetry/book and paper arts project, co-
taught with book and paper artist Leah Mayers, in which
students were asked to think about how people describe
and experience time across disciplines. The artists visited
once a week while their classroom teachers created
curriculum that correlated with the theme of "time." Here
is Alejandro, Marilyn, Jeremy, Caitlin, Tavien, and Monica,
talking about their thoughts and feelings on learning in
and through the arts.

When you think back on
your project, "The Poetics of Time,"
what do you remember most?

Jeremy: I think the most I'll remember in my
classroom was when we had a ball of yarn. We started
with a single string and tossed it to someone and
said someone's name and asked a question about
time. And after you ask a question, you had to throw
it again to someone else and you couldn't answer the
question, you just had to ask a new one. Everybody
did that and some of us had more than one but
everybody got a turn and when we were done we made
a big humungous web of string that represented our
questions all around us, we were tangled up in it,
chairs were tangled up in it, that was the funnest part,
I really liked that day.

Alex: The dinosaurs! When our teacher put us in three
different groups, and she gave us cardboard cut-out
dinosaurs, and we had a contest, whoever was the
first group to finish putting together the dinosaur won.
It related to evolution, and evolution relates to time. It
was fun putting it together and working as a team.

What will you remember most about your teaching artists?

Marilyn: Well, in the mornings, we would just have, like, 10 minutes to practice writing whatever you want. And like, sometimes you can't say what you feel, then you can write it on a paper. And like, that's what I liked the most. It's like, your anger comes out or something!

Monica: I also liked how when you would give us the warm up, and like, you know, when you would tell us how to count backwards that really helped us a lot to get out our feelings and stuff and if we had any anger or something, we could get it out, and like, squeeze your fists… It was different.

Caitlin: I liked when the warm-up was over because I wanted to write a lot and I wanted to get to the writing.

Tavien: I liked the fact that when we were talking about time and space I could just, like, look out the window and see what was going on outside.

Monica: I also liked how you, like, brought something out of us, like we—I didn't know that I could write about that kind of way, like *that* and how myself could think about the world in time in a different way because like, before when I thought of time I thought man, it's the next class, oh my god, I can't wait 'til the day's over! But then now, like, man, the time is going by fast…what happened? It was just right there, now it's like, flying away, like the wind…!

Alex: Time *is* going fast. I don't like it because I still want to live my life as a kid and because when I get to high school I'm going to be more responsible and I'm going to have my schedule because right now I'm still busy, I don't get home 'til 6 but later I might not be getting home till like, 8 o' clock. When I'm an adult, when I have my job hopefully I'll be able to relax finally so that all this work finally pays off.

Marilyn: I also liked when we had that hour sheet, like, what would you do with your hour? We would talk about like, each minute, what would we do? What would you like to spend your life doing? And when I did that, I would start to think of every hour as part of my life and then that life is short so, like, you would want to spend it not just sleeping or doing something.

Jeremy: I would spend all my time dancing.

What surprised you most about this kind of learning?

Alex: Ooh, like, whenever you guys were here, like, I never knew that I had so much creation in me that I could make such a good book and now since you guys helped us with this I know that I could be creative, and make a book, in the future, for somebody else. And it's just cool how I put my mind to it and I came up with such a good book.

Caitlin: I think what surprised me the most is that I could write such good poetry. Because I never thought that I could. And also that I could be so creative in making my books.

Tavien: It was the fact that I didn't think I could put so much—all my heart and soul—into something. Like, especially, um, being related to school. Like, I know I put my heart and soul into my sports, like skateboarding and stuff, but if I'm doing homework or something, I'll check it over but I'm done with it. But like, cuz yesterday, I was like sittin' up there, sitting in my living room for like, 2 hours, going through magazines, just clipping out stuff, and I just didn't think I could put that much time into it, that much thought and energy into something like that.

Marilyn: What surprised me was, like, thinking about death. Usually no one asks the real questions, how would you want to die, and then, when you think about death, you think about the rest of your life. And then, how like one little mistake you make could affect, like, your whole life, until the end. It was surprising, to talk about that, but I liked it.

Tavien: It was kind of weird listening to everyone's real thoughts.

Monica: When you guys came, it was like, everybody tried to act all popular and stuff, like, they were all that, but when it came down to the writing? It was like everybody just spoke truthfully, like they were real, like weren't saying, like, oh my god, that's so lame or something. They were actually like, yeah, I like it. Even if it's a person that they don't know, they could still say to that person, that's really good, you know? So I liked it. There was no judging. There was no judging. It was just what you feel and that's that. It was like, if one person speaks their mind, and the other person agrees, then it just falls into place, and everybody just starts agreeing with each other like, you know what, that really is a good piece...

Tavien: I think it's because everybody, once you're writing, and you gotta share it, you're all vulnerable. Like...with that popularity thing? Nobody's on a pedestal. And nobody's lower. Everybody's at the same place...

Jeremy: The experience with you for me has been life changing because now at home I do have my own journal that I write poetry in and I have started a scrapbook and pop-outs and that just takes me to a whole place, I worked for three hours at a time with my mom and my sister on it. Having this experience with you just changed my whole life. My mom's seen a big improvement in me after this and I just want to say thank you to you guys because it just changed me, it changed me a lot.

Tavien: Also the thing that changed me is I found that I spent my time doing things I shouldn't be doing, wasteful, like video games, but now I spend more time collecting things, like pictures from Time Magazine and Sports Illustrated, so like, 80 years from now I can go back and look at what happened, like going to the Super Bowl, the Iraqi war, how that's made me feel, I can look back and remember all those emotions that come back to me when I was a teenager.

How is arts-integrated learning different than other kinds of learning?

Jeremy: You taught us how to do origami folds and just making books that are fantastic.

Monica: You cared about us. It's not that other teachers don't care about us, but you really cared about us. You actually asked us our own opinion and you really thought that we could actually be somebody when actually nobody told you you could be somebody.

Alex: Sometimes it seems like teachers are looking for ways to get us in trouble but you guys were different. Teachers want to get in our business—but you guys, you were—

Tavien: —subtle about it.

Monica: —all *kind* about it.

Caitlin: I think this learning is different because the classes use more creativity than they would with all the other assignments because with the other assignments it's not like you get to make your own book and put like what you want in it, you just like write the answer to stuff so you gave us a chance to express our feelings and opinions how we wanted in our books.

Marilyn: In other classes you're forced.

Monica: You get an F—

Monica: And also this poetry writing is really different than any other writing because, like in reading class, all we do is extended responses—just basically five paragraphs about a story, over and over and over again—that's it! That's it!

Tavien: And every morning we have to do it!

Alex: It's so boring, and so confusing. Everyone in the classroom basically fell asleep.

Marilyn: You can't get it from your own point-of-view— you have to get it from the story's point-of-view.

What did the writing and/or book making teach you about time or yourselves?

Monica: Leah's book making—that was raw.

Jeremy: I could actually relate to and go with time a lot because I think things could happen within years—because actually, I used to have enemies in fourth and fifth-grade, like commando wars, we were just not friends at all, but then over time, for seventh-grade, we're really good friends.

Alex: It wasn't just the writing or the book making, it was really you and Leah, it's what you said, you treated us differently.

Monica: It was the way you made us think.

Alex: Yeah, you talked to us differently. You made us think differently. You guys basically just inspired our lives, you could say.

Jeremy: You guys just came in there without knowing us, treating us like great human beings like you've known us for years and at first we were like what's up with these people!? And now we're just so used to you. Even though we only see you once a week, we were just so used to you guys. And this is like we're one big family, which is really weird.

Tavien: Now we know that's just your nature. You saw us for who we really were.

Alex: And you treated us like human beings.

Jeremy: You didn't even judge us, you got to know us way deep in and you could just tell from our writing how we are, how we acted.

Monica: But you taught us like if we didn't have nothing in life, that we could still write and express our feelings and be like everybody else even if we don't have nothing.

Tavien: Teachers care about our work ethic, but some kids need somebody, a teacher, to look over their shoulder and tell you how to point you in the right direction—it really helped me. Sometimes teachers don't even give you the light of day to point you in the right direction, they just throw work in your face and make 'ya do it and, I mean, a thirty-minute lesson on how to do something is not gonna help.

Jeremy: We like when teachers really interact with you.

Marilyn: I think as you grow, say, if you're five-years-old, adults hold on too tight. But when you get grown, and you get more problems, [they] start to let go. So I think as you get older, [they] should hold on tighter. Because say when you're five, and you fall, they get really worried, just for a little fall, but then when you get older, more problems come, and they just start letting go.

What was the most challenging aspect of this project?

Caitlin: Expressing our feelings. Because sometimes you didn't know, like, how to write it. You know, how to put the words together. You just had to really write what you wanted and didn't really care what other people thought.

Jeremy: One time we were sitting in the classroom next to Monica and I was saying, come on, come on, read the poem, read your poem! And she didn't want to—I was like read it read it read it! And she finally did and I was about ready to cry.

Monica: And I was gonna cry too, I was like, I can't believe I just read that, because it was like, my real feelings.

If the principal came into your class and said that the project was going to be cut for next year, what would you say?

Jeremy: I would be protesting crazy.

Monica: It's not about just coming and doing something straight out of the textbook—this program is not made for you to think hard hard hard about what you think you're going to do in education. It's mainly about how you can be able to express your feelings and helps kids who have really bad problems at home, to help them get it out so that when they come to school they'll have a better personality, better attitude, do their work, and be focused and say their feelings at the same time.

Marilyn: Life isn't just learning about education, it's learning about your life, too.

THURGOOD MARSHALL MIDDLE SCHOOL STUDENTS SHARE POETRY OUT LOUD. PHOTO BY JOEL WANEK.

THURGOOD MARSHALL MIDDLE SCHOOL STUDENTS' BOOKS EXPLORE THE POETICS OF TIME. PHOTO BY JOEL WANEK.

Learning
with the Boys

Mathias "Spider" Schergen
ART SPECIALIST, EDWARD JENNER ACADEMY OF THE ARTS

Friday Boys began as an experiment—a string of questions too intriguing to ignore. Questions like: What would happen if twelve rambunctious middle school boys were invited to form a community of learners that met for two hours each Friday? What would happen if membership in the group was predicated on their ability to maintain their self-control and their resolve to avoid suspension? What would happen if I shared the intent of this experiment with video artist and filmmaker Crystal Griffith in a partnership using video production as a vehicle for learning and self expression? Like every good experiment, these three questions betrayed the complexity of the answers and, in turn, led to even more questions.

When Crystal arrived on the first week, she watched a video that the boys and I had made to introduce her to our group. She responded with smiles that let them know they had won her over. Then, without skipping a beat, she won them over by putting the equipment in their hands and getting them to "work" immediately. Having done this without a lot of prerequisites and undo worry, she established a level of trust in the boys and the process that served both well in the months to come.

Our Roles

Crystal's temperament was very different from mine. She had a quality of deliberate and purposeful intent in her way of speaking and mannerisms, which balanced out my style of spontaneous conjecture and manic energy. Crystal had a way of chiding the boys, gently teasing them into the challenge of trying new techniques with the cameras and sound equipment. She encouraged them to stay on task when they complained about the camera being too heavy or the soundman's job being too boring. Crystal's intuitive understanding of the art form enabled her to identify the

creative gifts each boy brought to the process. We had cameramen, soundmen, directors, story writers, actors and extras who could be called upon to support production activities at all levels. Crystal taught the boys the language of video production and held them to an appropriate level of professional standards that required the boys to stay on task when the tedium of re-shoots and "do-overs" seemed unbearable to them.

During Crystal's weekly visits, my role was to stay attentive and remain present to the boys who were not actively engaged. Essentially, my role was that of a shepherd. I kept the unoccupied boys out of mischief and insured that they did not wander off. My role kept me vigilant of the larger context in which the group functioned both internally and externally. I provided the conceptual/communal space with parameters both physical and psychological. I addressed conflicts as they arose, tempers as they flared, and attitudes as they shifted. All the while, I maintained view of the "big picture" while Crystal worked with smaller, more focused groups.

Crystal and I had a good understanding of our roles while working with the Friday Boys. An interesting dynamic developed when Crystal became the nucleus of the group that left me feeling a bit out-of-the-loop at times. Sometimes I felt that she knew the boys better than I and that they paid more attention to her. The balance of our roles enabled us to establish a studio environment in which knowledge and experience were fused at an intuitive and internalized level. In this space, Crystal modeled her creative process in studio practice. Using models of studio practice in the academic setting is the most effective way to integrate the two domains. Studio practice is a seamless integration of the learning process with the creative process and has much to teach the field of education.

Letting the Story Unfold

Every session began seated in a circle of chairs we called "circle time." The vitality of this community was based on its member's abilities to communicate and share their goals, issues and achievements with one another. After everyone was seated, there was an intuitive reflex that told me it was time to quiet the group and begin. The story for our video emerged from brainstorming during circle time, as well as episodes of script writing in small groups. The boys were certain from the start that the story would involve a fight scene and images that related to school and neighborhood life. They had a visual context for the story without a narrative notion. It so happened that at this same time I had been reading *Green Eggs and Ham,* by Dr. Seuss, on a frequent basis to students in the primary grades. I was beginning to see the story as a metaphor for the experience of conversion, not a specific type of conversion, just the idea that "Sam I am" made it his business to convince his counterpart that green eggs and ham were something of value and if he would only try them, he too, would experience their benefits. I took the book out and introduced this notion to the group. We talked about someone trying to convince someone else of something he/she was not inclined to believe.

One of the boys, Dewantez, jumped in with an idea about a boy who is anxiously awaiting his fourteenth birthday—wondering what his friends were planning to help him celebrate. Dewantez became the main character and narrator. He and Crystal collaborated and came up with the idea to structure the story in chronological sequence by using the days of the week, Monday through Friday. Dewantez became an organizing force throughout the residency. He had the unique capacity to understand the project in its totality and to direct the creative energy toward the group's collaborative product. Dewantez became a creative leader. He was able to synthesize the ideas of others and emulate a disciplined focus on the process/production at hand.

As the story unfolds, the main character's narration takes the viewer on a journey into his day-to-day life, leading up to his birthday. The boy's life is changing and the responsibilities of being "half-gown" and a role-model are a subject of the narration. It becomes apparent that his friends' birthday plans include introducing him to marijuana. The boy thinks they're going to treat him to Sammy's (a favorite local fast food spot). When Friday comes around they take him to a secluded spot where they offer him a joint, which they say will "stimulate his mind" and make him feel better. The boy takes a puff and then realizes it's a mistake. He knocks out one of his friends with a punch and then runs down the street realizing that he's betrayed his mother's best intentions for him and compromised his role as a mentor to the kids in the community tumbling program. The video ends with the boy contemplating his future, reflecting on the pride his mother will have when she sees the success he's made of himself.

Transforming the Mind and Spirit

Thanks to Crystal Griffith's personal dedication to the project and the time she spent editing the video and working on the voice-overs, the Friday Boys' first effort was a remarkable video that projects a media image of their own making. The video was first shared at an event hosted by Project AIM at the Garfield Park Conservatory. Students presented what they learned and produced in their respective residencies. The Friday Boys' contribution was shared last. The lights went out, the shades were drawn and the room fell silent. That silence was broken by the enthusiastic applause of Jenner Academy students. The Friday Boys came to the front of the room to talk about their work and to answer questions from the audience. Many of the parents in the group complimented the boys and praised their efforts. Their fellow students asked questions that the boys answered with a sense of authority that comes with learning through experience. It was a moment filled with revelation for all present; a moment filled with grace and truth.

Finally, I have this to say about Friday Boys: It was fun—the kind of fun you're not supposed to have in school. There were times I felt like a boy, too. I felt caught up in the moment. I felt as though school was miles away and we were in someone's yard playing like there was no tomorrow, no schedules, no bells, no teachers. It was just us figuring things out, making art and learning in ways that transform the mind and teach the spirit.

STUDENTS AT EDWARD JENNER ACADEMY OF THE ARTS MASTER THE ART OF FILMMAKING
WITH ART TEACHER, MATHIAS "SPIDER" SCHERGEN. PHOTOS BY CRYSTAL GRIFFITH

The Learning Arc with Students

Mathias "Spider" Schergen

- Start simple.

- Setting the tone is not a waste of time.

- Draw the students' attention to you—before you begin a lesson.

- Keep the opening of your lessons consistent.

- The organization and prep of materials is crucial.

- Establish a studio environment.

- Do not lay blame; it's hard, but be humble.

- Digression is always an option.

- Lessons that are not "successful" are lessons to be learned.

- Work towards the big idea, but pay attention to the details.

Maintaining Good Partnerships

Mathias "Spider" Schergen

- Teach and serve the students in front of you.

- You are each here to learn.

- Talk to each other about strategies.

- Talk to each other about what is your role, what is their role.

- You have to appreciate interpersonal communication to be effective.

- Try email and phone calls.

- It is easy to forget something in the course of a week.

- If there is a conflict and you take it to someone else, it will not be resolved.

- If it bothers you, don't "get over it."

- If you don't deal with it, it will escalate—the sooner the better.

- Don't underestimate the effect of boredom on behavior.

- Don't get into a power play. Talk to the person on the side privately.

- Honestly assess your role in a situation. Apologize when necessary.

- Respect is earned.

- The work is not always what we think it is.

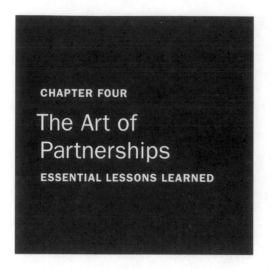

The Art of Partnerships

ESSENTIAL LESSONS LEARNED

- Be flexible, willing to take risks, and willing to try new things.

- Make time to get to know each other as people—it makes working together that much more enjoyable.

- Share the power. Allow for shifts in power throughout the residency.

- Recognize that each of us is a teacher, artist, and student at any given time.

- Create shared meaning from materials in the classroom.

- Strive for continuity—allow your partnerships to deepen over time.

CHAPTER FIVE

The Art of Curriculum

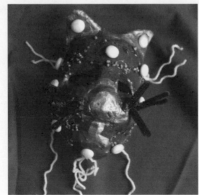

Imagining What's Possible

**THE ART OF WRITING
ARTS-INTEGRATED
CURRICULUM**

Amanda Leigh Lichtenstein

"The role of the imagination is not to resolve, not to point the way, not to improve. It is to awaken, to disclose the ordinarily unseen, unheard, and unexpected."

– Maxine Greene

"For all possibilities reach us through the imagination."

– John Dewey

"Curriculum ceases to be a thing, and it is more than a process. It becomes a verb, an action, a social practice, a private meaning, and a public hope. It is an ongoing, if complicated, conversation.

– Bill Pinar

Curriculum is Everywhere

Curriculum is the clock. Curriculum is your shoelaces. Curriculum is your father. Curriculum is the war in Iraq. Curriculum is star dust. Curriculum is a roaring train. Curriculum is the connection between you and the world— its objects and rhythms, ideas and relationships.

So it's no wonder that educators have a really hard time packaging and binding ideas for mass educational consumption. Passionate teachers often lament watered-down unit plans, condescending test questions that deflate big ideas into disconnected facts, and irrelevant and exclusive course material that has nothing to do with their own or their students' lives. Teachers are expected to "cover" a unit regardless of whether students are truly engaged and students are expected to "receive" information with little understanding of how to *live* their knowledge in real and meaningful ways. How do we conceive of a kind of curriculum that allows us to explore what is *unknown* rather than simply transmitting what is already *known*?

Of course, curriculum is not just content—so much of how we teach and learn has to do with a spirit of inquiry bound up in the relationships we keep and nurture throughout an educational experience. The study of plastic, insects or clouds could be riveting if teachers and students were granted the intellectual freedom to ask expansive questions and make personal connections. The point is that curriculum is ultimately an expression of a culture's ideas about what's worth learning. How do we create curriculum that awakens—instead of lulls—another generation to sleep? How do we create curricular ideas that stir up the *why* in each of us?

The Project AIM Approach

Project AIM artists and teachers co-create original, collaborative curriculum that is both documentation and instruction—a roadmap for the future and a narrative guide through the past. We think about arts-integrated curriculum as a "complicated conversation," recognizing how "[it] changes as we engage it, reflect on it, and act in response to it, toward the realization of our private-and-public ideals and dreams." (Pinar, 187). Together, we continually rework and revisit our plans and ideas just as a painter engages her canvas, or a poet her poem. Freedom to experiment and explore big questions is paramount to the curriculum writing process; artists, teachers, and students encourage one another to think metaphorically and expansively about concepts even as we grapple with a particular skill set. We start with ideas that excite us and spiral through our own learning as we guide our students through the process of arts-integrated learning and reflection.

This multipurpose, multidisciplinary approach to curriculum writing goes beyond "Tylerian" curriculum—named after Ralph Tyler who characterized curriculum design as linear and outcomes-driven. In a post-industrial society, teaching artists and teachers significantly rebuke outdated notions of industrialization as a defining metaphor for American schooling and instead conceive of curriculum as *experience*—inherently interdisciplinary and nested in the power of generative questions to determine shared goals and final showings. The AIM Arts Integration Learning Spiral is our working visual metaphor for addressing specific arts and academic learning objectives. Moving beyond the linear model, we believe that standards and outcomes are continually addressed, revisited, and modified in the course of arts-integrated studies.

The AIM Unit Plan

The AIM Unit Plan form helps artists and teachers do three things:

- **PLAN** and write original curriculum within a given framework
- **DOCUMENT** and back map curricular activities for reflection and clarification at the end of a unit
- **INSTRUCT** and guide other artists and teachers interested in trying a similar project

You'll notice how the AIM Unit Plan form mirrors the AIM Arts Integration Learning Spiral, coaching artists and teachers to think about the ways in which they will:

- Discover intentions for learning
- Create a safe creative space
- Learn in the language of the arts
- Immerse in a conceptual big idea
- Revise and share
- Perform and exhibit
- Reflect and assess
- Discover new intentions for learning

The AIM Unit Plan form is designed to help artists and teachers name and structure their curricular desires. This model promotes project-based learning—defining and naming each step while honoring the emergent and surprising nature of the work. Together, teachers and artists articulate a specific focus and identify questions to guide it. Every week involves a close encounter with text, image and dialogue as students, teachers and artists move toward ideas for final products. We emphasize the pedagogical value of process as much as we appreciate the significance of revised and final artwork—both as objects of celebration and as tools for reflection and critique.

The unit plans included in this chapter document the stories of cross-curricular arts partnerships. Each document addresses a curricular question. How can we get seniors in high school to express their inner truth? Take a look at Meg Arbeiter and visual artist Guillermo Delgado's work with high school students to explore identity and self-portraiture. Have you ever thought about the links between poetry, math and science? Poet Dan

Godston connects with mathematics teacher Theresa Kern and her students to examine the idea of "bridges" through linguistic, mathematical, scientific and architectural lens. Have you ever wondered how to teach the value of looking more closely at the world around you? Photographer Deborah Guzmán-Meyer and writer Julie A. Downey create a photography, writing and botany unit plan that encourages students to closely examine their worlds through their botany studies.

Did you ever think about "relationships" as an organizing metaphor for interdisciplinary studies? Poet Jenn Morea and fifth-grade teachers Melissa Padilla and Margarita Garcia work with their students to deepen their understanding of relationships found in language, poetry, music and visual arts. Have you been wondering how to engage reluctant readers? Take a look at actor Khanisha Foster's unit plan with teachers Michelle Lugo, Judith Diaz, Candace Guevara and Valerie King. Together they bring text and history to life through theater. Did you think it was possible to create relevant documentary videos with fifth-graders? Read the unit plan created by filmmakers Suree Towfighnia and John Lyons with teachers Maria Mertz and Sophia Rempas to engage fifth-graders running for president! Suree's manifesto on developing a short film with fifth-graders demystifies the entire process.

What are the possible connections between book making and narrative storytelling processes? Book and paper artist Jamie Lou Thome connects with teachers Somya Bergman, Michelle Cericola and Rebecca Katsulis to create a unit plan that "houses personal stories" in unique book structures. What can filmmaking teach us about storytelling structures? Filmmaker Ai Lene Chor and Julie Buzza, a language arts teacher, work with their students to create short, animated narrative films that illuminate links between filmmaking and writing processes. Can the production of a Shakespearean play in a sixth-grade classroom ignite students' interests in performing a difficult text? Actor Tony Sancho and teachers Eileen Kahana and Neeta Agrawal help their students form an ensemble to take on this challenging task. Can the infusion of drama and positive feedback strategies change the way students feel about their writing? Book Artist, Leah Mayers, and Theatre Artist, Luis Crespo, work with teachers Mary Clare McCarthy, Julienne Backstrom, Diane Simpson and

Carlos Mendez to invigorate the Young Authors book making process. Every unit plan makes surprising connections in and among disciplines, shuttling between arts and core content learning across the curriculum.

Consciousness. Culture. Communication.

Let's bridge the chasm between book learning and lived experience. Let's make a commitment as teachers and artists to fall in love with what we teach and what we learn with our students. Let's address big ideas and themes often left unspoken in mainstream curricular mandates and agendas. Working with big ideas becomes the organizing principle that gives state learning goals and standards meaning and coherence.

Most of all, let's decide to recognize relationships as a defining metaphor for best practice in teaching and learning through the arts. It is through relationships that our humanity surfaces in all its complexity. We begin to understand ourselves in constant *relation* to the world around us. Relationships account for the cultural, spiritual, political, emotional and social dimensions of teaching and learning so often ignored or denied in mainstream public schooling. They remind us that we are not just teaching the subject, we are teaching the *whole person* about that subject. Relationships remind us that we are equally bound up in the teaching and learning experience. Arts integration is a kind of teaching and learning that reinvents curriculum as a living record of these relationships.

Curriculum is consciousness. Curriculum is culture. Curriculum is communication—a shared conversation between objects, people and ideas. Curriculum—whose root word, "currere" literally means "to run a course,"— should really be about slowing down and letting ideas *course* through us. It does not matter that not every student goes on to become a professional artist; what does matter is that every student believes in their capacity to *think, feel, connect, contribute* and *express* themselves in whatever role they choose to play in life—and that their contributions to this "complicated conversation" are as worthy as any in our collective effort as humans to tell the story of this present moment.

From a Humble Concept to the Big Screen

ADVANCED FILM WORKSHOP
WITH FIFTH-GRADERS
AT CASIMIR PULASKI
FINE ARTS ACADEMY

Suree Towfighnia
FILMMAKER, TEACHING ARTIST

As a Chicago filmmaker, I was initially hesitant to dedicate my time and energy to teaching elementary school children. I thought that my unstable schedule, commitment to my projects, and intimidation at the numbers of students would get in the way of creating a film. However, within five minutes of meeting the class, I changed my mind. Their smiling faces and enthusiasm, as well as their innate knowledge of film as a language, sold me.

Of course, making films with 28 fifth-grade students seems like a daunting task. But with clear intentions, achievable expectations, and weekly deadlines, a short film in fifteen weeks is possible.

Balance an Idea with Ambition

Organization and achievable deadlines clearly laid out at the beginning and ending of each workshop are essential to direct each session. I'm a big believer in establishing the goals of the workshop and then working with the students to ensure that our goals are realized. With the end goal of a finished film, it's important to have clear expectations and achievable tasks that drive the work forward every week.

Allow the Students to Drive the Project

While it's easy to suggest topics, ideas and images and then have students fill in the blanks, it's more interesting to allow them to drive the story. By owning the concept and story, students are vested in it and give it their all. This level of commitment drives the project through the huge amounts of hard work needed to complete the film.

Establish a Set of Filmmakers' Rules with the Class

On Day One of the workshop, we develop a body of rules that begins with the following sentence:

In order to be successful filmmakers, we need to...

For example, "In order to be successful filmmakers, we need to: listen, collaborate, work hard, get along, do our assigned tasks, participate."

By establishing and accepting a set of guidelines, students understand how necessary they are for accomplishing our goals. Students realize, and are reminded weekly, that making a film takes A LOT of work, and that we all need to work together to get this work done. Every person is essential.

Develop a Working Relationship: from Individual Student to Young Filmmaker

Film is such a common medium that it's relatively easy to pull out the vocabulary needed to speak the language of the form. During the first week, students list film terminology. This exercise encourages critical thinking, writing and participation by every student. Some possible first questions include:

- Who works on a film set?
- What are some genres of film?
- What are the steps or processes you need to go through to make a film?

One of the first assignments I give a class is to fill out a sheet that answers the following questions:

Name   Age
_____

What do you want to do when you grow up?

_____

If you could do the following activity,
which one would you pick:
  ❑   dance
  ❑   draw
  ❑   write
  ❑   take a picture
  ❑   make music
  ❑   act
_____

What is your favorite movie and why:

_____

If you could work on a film, what would you do?

_____

This seemingly innocent activity lays the groundwork for the roles they'll play for the rest of the workshop. Unbeknownst to them, they've hired themselves as a crew position. By having some basic questions about what they like to do, I can divide them into appropriate roles based on interest.

Begin with an Idea, Concept or Theme

By meeting with the classroom teacher and discussing the curriculum for each week, themes and cross-pollination emerge that combine work from their curriculum with exercises in the film workshop. Reinforce the ideas you present with integrated examples from students' coursework. Try linking the stages of filmmaking with subjects and tasks from their class. Using examples they can relate to from their coursework allows students to integrate advanced film concepts like metaphorical imagery, stories based around social issues, and writing to respond to current events into their videos.

I try to give ten minutes at the beginning and ending of class to reflect on our process and encourage curricular links. By reiterating the expectations for the following week, the students have various ways to absorb the tasks needed to complete the project. As their film teacher, I merely moderate and dig out their knowledge. They are so excited when they discover the ways in which film relates to the bigger picture.

This year, my partnering teacher was interested in social concerns facing fifth-graders. The students were affected by the devastation unfolding around them and on television: the Iraq War, Hurricane Katrina, poverty, homeless animals and gangs—to name a few. They were curious how fifth-graders elsewhere were handling these circumstances. We encouraged each student to write three issues of concern.

Working in groups, they narrowed the concerns down to three, which they presented to the class. In the end, each group pitched their concerns and the class voted on the concepts with these considerations: 1) could we make a film about this subject within the walls of the school? 2) is this a concern we all relate to as fifth-graders? 3) do we like this topic? 4) is it broad enough to support many ideas and people's interests? In the end, the class came up with the following concerns to pursue for their film: no gangs/drugs; no war/peace; and "fifth-grader for president!"

A Good Idea isn't Always a Good Video Topic

How do you judge a film concept? The main component is feasibility and scope of the project. Money, time and labor are some other components to consider. We have representatives from each group "pitch" their concepts to the class and classroom teachers (who act like executive producers). Ultimately we hold the veto power if the idea seems too ambitious or, on the other hand, too limited.

The story for the film "Fifth-Graders for President" was created by class consensus. Once the class decided on their most relevant concerns, groups were created to divide up the many tasks with a focus on each specific idea. Each group had a writer, director, assistant director, art director, and actor. During this developmental phase, the individual groups collaborated to work on the script, completing tasks associated with each department. In the end, the groups met to coordinate and synthesize their ideas into one film. Amazingly, the script pieced together easily.

Organization is Key

Managing the film is an aspect that could easily become a major stress nightmare (especially when you only meet once a week and there are 28 kids who have band practice, ESL, field trips, sick days, etc). It's essential to create an initial syllabus or guide that can ground your thoughts and activities to ensure that the film gets finished. Staying on task is the job not only of the visiting artist and classroom teacher, but also of the students. I am unable to do my work unless everyone contributes and makes sure that we get things done. The role of the filmmaking facilitator is to look into the future and make sure that the activities of the current week are leading to the demands of what needs to be accomplished later on.

A suggestion would be to work with the classroom teacher during the initial planning meeting to gauge their level of commitment and dedication to the film. Allowing some breathing room in the schedule (weeks off from the film workshop) can give teachers a chance to implement some of the film requirements (script writing, actors rehearsal, set designs) into the teaching they do when the artist is absent. Creating a space for them in your lessons to incorporate into their planning ensures that the class will be ready to participate when the artist arrives.

Film is a linear activity and although things don't always go according to plan, the steps to complete a film usually remain the same. Oversee the project as a whole, but don't think you have to do it alone.

Give the Students the Opportunity to Lead

In our film workshop we had three groups working on three different concepts. Everyone in the group was essentially a leader in some capacity (head of writers, actors, directors, art department). This allowed the children to really feel like they were a part of the whole film. Within these groups one dedicated student worked as the assistant director (the person who keeps track of time, deadlines and makes sure everyone in their group stays on task). This position has to have an understanding and respect for the group and is key to keeping things focused and productive.

When you give kids the opportunity to lead, they will take it. They will show up with costumes they drew at home, props their parents gave them and scenes they wrote over the weekend. It's a challenge to find ways to incorporate their hard work into the agenda of the day, but it's also important. One way is to address it in the first ten minutes of class: "Does anyone have anything they'd like to share before we begin the film workshop?" Stay on topic but leave room for surprises.

One day we arrived for the hectic casting day and a student shared that she had invited a police officer to come to class to talk to us about gangs and drugs in their neighborhood. She had attended a Community Policing meeting with her mom, had gone up to the officer, explained the project and invited him. As she finished her enthusiastic story, the officer arrived, ready to be interviewed. Although we weren't expecting him, or ready to begin filming him, we were amazed at the student's ability to coordinate this interview and sent the documentary crew out to film the officer. My assistant and I felt nothing but pride in stepping out in the hall and checking in on them as they asked their pre-prepared questions to the officer. The students had gone from fear of writing and public speaking to setting up an interview on their own with a police officer.

Realistic Equipment and Strategies for Finishing the Film

Fight to get the equipment you need prior to beginning the workshop. You can only stall students so long before they need to start shooting. Make sure that you (or someone familiar with specific video needs) pick out the necessary equipment. Do not overlook certain important things like headphones, cables, extra batteries, tapes, microphone inputs and power sources. It saves money in the long run to acquire the exact equipment needed for the project.

Another suggestion is to pre-label your tapes and pre-stripe them with time code to eliminate time code breaks, which are editing nightmares. I recommend you get a small tape box and keep it in the classroom, locked up, so the tapes are there when you need them and no one has to rely on the film facilitator or assistant.

As filmmakers know all too well, finishing the film is a whole other challenge. Ideally, each classroom would have a computer, editing software and adequate hard drive space to edit in the class. But budget, time and labor does not always allow this. Working in elementary schools, my partner and I struggle to figure out how to finish the films and get them to the students before summer break begins.

What I would suggest is to dedicate a student to post-production and have them log the rushes (raw footage) and keep track of the best takes. This position could begin as soon as shooting starts and requires the dedication and commitment of an individual or two who work well independently. This year we had to hire a college student to help us capture the footage so we could do the finishing work and the editing. It's important to schedule time, money and resources to editing or you could end up with amazing footage for a film that never gets put together. Don't underestimate the time it takes: plan for it.

Positivity, Patience, Clear Goals and a Simple Concept

It is stressful enough to make a film, so eagerness and a positive attitude are essential. Of course, there are days when students don't feel like doing their work, but handling one individual who is off track is easier when we all know our expectations.

Set reasonable goals and manageable expectations. The more you feed a film, the more it grows. It's incredibly easy to create a film monster that you are unable to manage. However, by placing the accountability for the work on the students, they are ultimately responsible for each other and themselves, and enjoy working together with the ultimate goal to get their vision realized.

This year we introduced a field trip to Columbia College Chicago to tour the film facilities and project their finished films in a screening room. After fifteen weeks of hard work, patience, dedication and collaboration, the smiles on their faces as their movie projected were pleasant reminders of the value of all the hard work. Watching the films in a darkened room and giving the students the opportunity to present their work as filmmakers was an excellent culmination to the process. In the end, we pulled the film together, people laughed at the right times, and now everybody has a DVD that they can watch with their friends and family. And it gets easier the second time, right?

TEACHING ARTIST, SUREE TOWFIGHNIA DIRECTS A FILM
SHOOT IN A FIFTH-GRADE CLASSROOM AT CASIMIR
PULASKI FINE ARTS ACADEMY. PHOTO BY JOHN LYONS

FIFTH-GRADE STUDENTS TAKE ON THE ROLES OF
PROFESSIONAL FILMMAKERS AT CASIMIR PULASKI
FINE ARTS ACADEMY. PHOTO BY JOHN LYONS.

The Bridge Project

ACADEMY OF COMMUNICATIONS AND TECHNOLOGY (A.C.T.) CHARTER SCHOOL

Dan Godston
WRITER, TEACHING ARTIST

Theresa Kern teaches science and math to sixth-graders at the Academy of Communications and Technology (A.C.T.) Charter School. Cynthia Weiss asked me if I would be interested in teaching poetry to Theresa's students in conjunction with integrating poetry into the math and science curricula. Theresa was using *Schoolyards to Skylines: Teaching with Chicago's Amazing Architecture,* which is an amazing educational resource created by Jean Linsner and Jennifer Masengarb at The Chicago Architecture Foundation. She and I met to discuss how the Project AIM residency should be structured, and Cynthia Weiss suggested the idea of using "bridges" as a unifying theme for the residency.

Theresa and I developed the Project AIM curriculum together, and we decided that the title of our program should be, "Bridges: Foundations & Expansions." We wanted to create a curriculum wherein the theme of "bridges" could be reflected through the subjects of character development, science, math and poetry. I found some bridge-themed poems that would be good for the program. Those poems included Carl Sandburg's "Clark Street Bridge," Shi Zhecun's "The Arched Bridge," and others. Jean Linsner visited A.C.T. Charter School to help the students learn more about Chicago's movable bridges. Students read and discussed bridge-themed poems, and then they wrote poems inspired by the models we studied.

The theme of bridges was used to approach math (angles, division, subtraction, multiplication, and other concepts) and science (balance, counterbalance, gravity, and other concepts). The students positively responded to poetry as a medium through which those concepts could be creatively addressed and expressed. The students also explored ways by which the theme of "bridges" could be used to think about how human perception relates to artistic expression, (as we read and discussed Lisel Mueller's poem entitled "Monet Refuses the Operation"), "How can we become bridges between cultures?" (as we read and discussed Anna Lazarus' "The New Colossus") and so on. We were discovering how versatile "bridges" could be as a metaphor, and, by doing so, we were learning more about how a good metaphor could be explored in different ways.

After each student had written a body of poems centered around the theme of bridges, we thought about how we could create a project that would provide an opportunity for students to showcase their poems in an interesting and engaging way. A number of murals that contain text adorn the walls in A.C.T. Charter School, and Theresa and I started brainstorming ways the students' poems could be permanently installed at the school.

What about installing an actual bridge at the school? That seemed like an intriguing idea. After getting permission from Executive Director and Founder, Ms. Sarah Howard, and Director of School Operations, Thomas Ivcy, for the bridge project, we bought a 10-foot-long garden bridge from a nearby high school, and the students started painting it. Then the students painted colorful representations of Chicago's movable bridges onto the bridge. Finally, a number of students copied their bridge-themed poems onto the bridge.

After all of our hard work, we had a ribbon-cutting ceremony, and the students performed the poems that were written onto the bridge. Currently, the "Bridges: Foundations & Expansions" bridge can be viewed in A.C.T. Charter School's courtyard.

Keepin' It Real

Cynthium Johnson-Woodfolk
WRITER, TEACHING ARTIST

There is a language that comes from the earliest part of a child that makes it easy for him to write, a language that is as effortless and comfortable as breathing, and it comes from his ethnic background. It is a language that—whenever he hears it—he is whisked away, kidnapped so rapidly by the power of voice, that his pen soars across the page. This is what happened at Crown Community Academy when the children were instructed to examine their communities.

With a milk crate of disposable cameras in hand, we went outside, and there the children began to create, looking for images that, in some way, reflected their lives. They took pictures of many things, but among them the most memorable were close-ups of body parts, (ears, eyes, nose, fists, mouths, etc.) an abandoned garage, two gentlemen walking a Rottweiler, a broken bottle, and a dandelion growing out of a crack in the ground.

"Your stories," I coached, "like these pictures, if you could see them frame-by-frame in your mind, what would they tell?"

For a moment there was silence, then a hand punctuated the air.

"Stuff that bothers me!"

It was Delvin, and he was the perfect picture of innocence, almost ghostlike the way he slid between the crowd, becoming the spokesperson for the class.

"Things that get to me all the time, like that Rottweiler." He motioned toward the two men walking down the alley, and when I turned I could see the black beast's muscles bouncing under its fur. "You know how many of those I have to pass everyday from the four-legged ones to the two?"

Everyone nodded, and in a unified gesture they all folded their hands across their chests.

"He ain't lying!" Porsche confirmed, "'cause sometimes I can be one, too!" She rolled her neck as if it was void of bones, and while the boys nodded the girls did too.

"We get trampled all the time, just like that dandelion do." She pointed to the ground and from every mouth came a unified tune.

"Ummm hmmmmm!"

"What about you, Ms. Cynthium?" Shantiera asked, "Which one of these things identify with you?" And instead of answering I flipped the milk crate over and jumped on top.

"Soapbox," I began, looking each child in the face. "From here your stories begin. What bothers you? What infuriates you? What urges you on? It is your chance to speak, your chance to tell your stories and let the world know who you are, how you feel. This soapbox is your stage and all the world your audience."

They nodded and I could tell by the frantic way they pulled out their notebooks and pens that the story-telling had already begun. I only had to wait for it to hit the page.

Reflections on Housing our Personal Stories

Jamie Lou Thome, BOOK AND PAPER ARTIST
AND Cynthia Weiss

Talk about your process with your students, about the way you move back and forth between narratives and new forms:

When I went to the first planning meeting at Robert Healy Elementary School, the teachers talked about doing a language arts project. We started talking about personal stories because a lot of the students were very smart but didn't necessarily connect writing with personal stories. They were focused on Academic writing and math but didn't consider their family histories or anything related to being first-generation Chinese-Americans.

So how did you decide on the essay form as a starting point?

The teachers and I decided that the students would write an essay and then develop a visual arts project around it. I'd been teaching a class called "Story and Image" at Columbia College Chicago where students were asked to write "passion" papers. Part of writing this paper is exploring specific questions about yourself. I ask all my students to start with their personal stories, belief systems, values and thoughts. I tell them their visual arts projects will be stronger if they write as a way to understand their lives. Our metaphors emerge from the language itself, from thinking and writing our thoughts on paper.

At Robert Healy Elementary School I brought in some pillow cases I created in response to writing I did about grief and loss related to my grandmother. On the first day, I showed them my artists' books and asked, "Is this a book? What makes it a book?" At first they said it has to have pages and a body in some way. It has to have an author, a title, chapters, pages of words. I asked, "What about those books

without words when you were little?" Then I pulled out an Altoids box with visual images inside. We finally concluded that a book has to have a story, be bound in some way, and move in some way (as a narrative sequence). Now they began to see that there were different kinds of structures for books.

How did you shift from essay writing to actually creating new book structures?

I wanted to push the students to the next level of book making—to move away from traditional book forms and focus on how the structure and form of the book pushes the story forward. A book is a container for our stories, but there can be different containers and still be considered books. As they made their books, they were also working on their personal essays and most chose to respond to two themes: 1) family history 2) a moment of personal change. By the fourth week they began thinking more metaphorically about their stories.

Can you talk about your transition exercise? It's really important to think about the strategies we use to help students move across mediums of expression. It's great that you structured a day specifically about that bridge from writing to planning for the book.

We took their essays and started talking about visual images that emerged in their writing. We went through a series of rough drafts, peer editing, final essays, and then read their essays out loud. They broke into peer groups to talk about the "essence" of their essays. I asked them to underline the sentences and words that were most significant or potent. They only had five minutes to do this. They had to then write these words and phrases on a separate sheet of paper. The only criteria were that they be essential and strong. Students then gave each other feedback on their word choices. It was easy to make the leap. Their essays were narrowed down to a poem that was put into the books or influenced them in some way. It helped to move from the essay to the poem to the book. I think that when you take one form of art and learn to transform it into another, it provides evidence of understanding.

It really sounds like you pay close attention to the "materiality of the ideas."

Yes, the whole notion that ideas are embedded in the materials you use. Whether you start with canvas, paper, fabric, paper, everything goes into it. If I'm typing a poem on hand-made paper, you're going to respond differently than if it is written on notebook paper.

What did the students learn? What surprised or excited you?

They went beyond the traditional book form. The majority made boxes with pull-out text and image. They were able to think conceptually and abstractly.

Why do you think stories need a house?

I think of a house as a container. All of our lives—our stuff—are in containers. There are certain places where we hold things, in our bodies, in our minds. Storing memory lets us see which memories are vivid and jewel-like and which are rusted. Memories come out of their houses at weird times in life. I think of the container as a house—a structure—a place to hold our lives. Creating these structures allows students to shape their story literally and metaphorically. It helps us to understand our stories from different perspectives. Working in both the literary and visual arts helps us discover the essence of story.

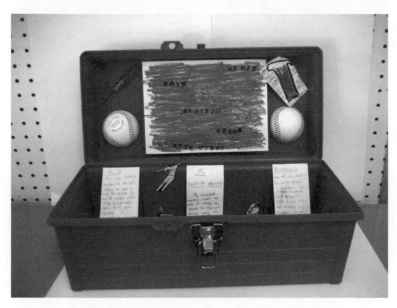

STUDENTS USE TOOLBOXES AND WATER
BOTTLES AS BOOK STRUCTURES DURING
JAMIE LOU THOME'S BOOKMAKING
RESIDENCY AT ROBERT HEALY
ELEMENTARY SCHOOL.

Arts Integration Unit Plans

TITLE OF STRATEGY	AUTHOR(S)	SCHOOL	GRADE	ARTFORM(S)	PAGE
Innter Truth: Mixed Media Self Portraits	Meg Arbeiter, Guillermo Delgado	A.C.T Charter School	12		186
Bridges – Foundations – Expansions: Poetry, Math and Science	Dan Godston	A.C.T Charter School	6		192
Housing Our Personal Stories: Bookmaking and Writing	Jamie Lou Thome	Robert Healy Elementary School	6		198
Choosing Your Own Adventure: Video and Creative Writing	Ai Lene Chor, Julie Buzza	Robert Healy Elementary School	7		204
What's Your Story? Children's Stories by Young Authors	Leah Mayers, Luis Crespo	Thurgood Marshall Middle School	8		210
Poetic Relationships	Jenn Morea	Casimir Pulaski Fine Arts Academy	5–6		216
Bringing Text and History to Life Through Theater	Khanisha Foster	Casimir Pulaski Fine Arts Academy	5–7		222
So Real Video	Suree Towfingha	Casimir Pulaski Fine Arts Academy	5		228
From Scenes to Sprites: Shakespeare with 6th Graders	Tony Sancho	Casimir Pulaski Fine Arts Academy	6		234
What Happens When We Look More Closely: Photography, Poetry and Botany	Deborah Guzmán-Meyer, Julie A. Downey	Albert R. Sabin Magnet School	5		240

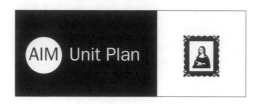

AIM Unit Plan

PROJECT TITLE	# Inner Truth: Mixed-Media Self-Portraits
TEACHER	Meg Arbeiter
ARTIST	Guillermo Delgado
SCHOOL	Academy of Communications and Technology (A.C.T.) Charter School
GRADE	12
ART FORMS(S)	Visual Art
LENGTH OF PROJECT	14 weeks

THE FOCUS OF THE PROJECT

- This project focuses on mixed media self-portraits based on Inner Truth. The work is centered around the question, "How can I express my Inner Truth through visual art and writing?"
- This project focuses on an advanced exploration of abstraction, symbolism and metaphor; as well as inference and interpretation to see, understand, express and support multiple perspectives.

INQUIRY QUESTIONS FOR TEACHERS AND ARTISTS

- How can we get students to express their Inner Truth?
- How can we get students to critically examine the assumptions and conditions of being historically under-served?
- How can we encourage students to expand their Universe of Obligation (the circle of individuals for whom they feel responsible) while honoring their perspectives and experiences?

PRE/POST ASSESSMENT ACTIVITY FOR STUDENTS

- **PRE:** Students reflect and write about the purpose of art and what an artist is. Pre-assessment activities also include "The Seven-Minute Shoe Drawing" (which can be found in the Arts Strategies section of this publication) as well as a "Continuous Line Self-Portrait."
- **POST:** Students revisit "The Seven-Minute Shoe Drawing" to evaluate their growth as artists. Students also create artist statements.

TEXT AND IMAGE SOURCES OF INSPIRATION

- Digital slide show of artists' work dealing with identity and human rights, including: Keith Haring, Goya, Picasso's "Guernica" Mural, Romare Bearden, and photos of past student work dealing with "identity."
- Field trip to see murals by Hector Duarte and Jeff Zimmerman in the Pilsen neighborhood and near west side in Chicago. Studio visit to Guillermo Delgado and Susan Clinard's art studio in Pilsen.
- www.facinghistory.org
- "My Forbidden Face"
- "The Dutchman" by Amiri Baraka
- "The Mask" by Paul Laurence Dunbar
- "The Mask" by The Fugees

TEN KEY VOCABULARY WORDS

1. Perspective
2. Gradients
3. Inference
4. Symbolism
5. Abstraction
6. Monochromatic
7. Human Rights
8. Alienation
9. Composition
10. Juxtaposition

EQUIPMENT AND MATERIALS

"Buffet" of art materials including:
- White glue
- Colored tissue paper
- Assorted brushes
- Watercolor paper
- Mirrors
- Oil pastels
- Watercolor paints
- Pencils
- Markers

WEEK	PRE-ASSESSMENT ACTIVITY
1–4	**LEARNING IN THE LANGUAGE OF THE ARTS	BUILDING A SAFE, CREATIVE SPACE**
1	Introduction to Drawing: Students are immediately immersed in art-making immediately for purposes of assessment and engagement. They learn different drawing techniques that give them more confidence during the brainstorming session; these techniques include contour drawing, continuous line contour drawing, and blind contour drawing.
2	Introduction to Color Theory and working with pastels: Students practice creating custom and basic colors with pastels. Custom colors are created by experimenting and exploring the color wheel. Students assign creative names to the colors they create.
3	Introduction to Composition, Collage and Mixed Media: Students learn about background, middle ground, and foreground. Students learn about, then incorporate the concept of negative and positive space in their artwork.
4	Introduction to Artists (Bearden, Picasso, Goya, Haring) and thematic concepts: Students learn how artists express their ideas as well as the social issues they are passionate about. (We strategically chose to wait until after engaging the students in art-making before presenting this Power Point slide-show examining key artists and pieces exploring human rights).
5–9	**IMMERSION IN A CONCEPTUAL QUESTION OR THEME THROUGH ART-MAKING**
5	Discussion: How can I express my inner truth through visual art and writing (from the individual to the global)? Teacher and teaching artist facilitate a continued study of identity and human rights, plus an introduction to the Universe of Obligation concept as defined by Helen Fein (the circle of individuals for whom you feel responsible).
6	Discussion: Does wearing a mask make you more powerful, less powerful, or both? Why? The teacher leads activities based on "The Mask" by Dunbar a) class "read-aloud" b) small group "think-aloud" of interpretation c) teacher-led discussion examining art.
7	Discussion: What is the purpose of art? What if my truth makes others uncomfortable? Through a slideshow and discussion, the teaching artist introduces the possibility that "Art doesn't have to match the sofa." The class reads aloud "Chicago Picasso" by Gwendolyn Brooks. Students then choose a work of art and begin a deeper examination. How does looking at art make you squirm? Why?
8	Field trip: Artists' studios and public murals in Pilsen as expressions of truth and human rights, exploring issues of immigration, identity, and assimilation.
9	Developing the culminating projects: Self-portraits (using abstraction, symbolism, and a 'buffet' of art materials). Each student begins working on the composition and background for his/her piece, utilizing silhouette techniques.

Column label (vertical, left): ENGAGE (weeks 1–4), IMMERSE (weeks 5–9)

10–14	REVISE, SHARE, AND REFLECT ON ART-MAKING

REFINE

10	Developing the culminating projects (continued). Students re-read journals and underline statements that express Inner Truth and consider how to represent those ideas visually. Guest teaching artist models his own process for mixed media self portraits.
11	Developing the culminating projects (continued) as well as Choices & Critique: Why did I choose this symbol, this color, this arrangement, etc.? Pre-writing artist statements examining his/her process and progress with creating a self-portrait. Should I make changes? What am I trying to say?
12	Students finish projects.
13	Digital audio recording of students' oral reflection: All students sit in a circle and actively listen to one another.
14	Written self-evaluation of self-portrait and arts integration process using art inquiry questions and rubric. (This is the same self-evaluation as used earlier in year, prior to the start of this residency). Artist statements and self-critique.

CULMINATING EVENTS

POST-ASSESSMENT ACTIVITY	PLANS FOR FINAL SHOWING
Classroom exhibits curated by students.	

TEACHER'S REFLECTIONS

"As a humanities teacher, I used to be afraid of engaging students in creating works of visual art. Not all students see themselves as artists, and I have never seen myself as an artist, either. If I feel insecure about my own artistic talents, how could I expect my students to be confident and willing to create visual art? But I learned and created alongside my students. Students commented that they saw me as open to new things and that encouraged them to have an open mind. Watching skeptical students pay close attention to detail and declare, "This is really cool," was worth every bit of anxiety I felt as well as the extra time I spent planning. Now I enjoy creating art with my students."

ARTIST'S REFLECTIONS

"This project has really inspired me to read and write more. I enjoyed the discussions/writing about art in class. It made me miss the frequent dialogue I used to have with my artist community before I got really busy. It's important to talk about art and why/how we make it. The students and Meg were wonderful to work with. I feel lucky to have gotten the chance to participate in their passion for learning."

STUDENTS' REFLECTIONS

"I really got a chance to express how I felt. I learned how to be more open minded about my work and creativity."
"By using objects and pictures, I was able to express myself in a way that I wouldn't normally. It helped me find new and better ways to look at things that are interesting to me." "I learned that you can create art in different ways. Like reading between the lines, you're reading the art. Like when Guillermo showed his paintings and asked us what we saw, I gave my opinion on what I thought the story was behind the painting, and he listened. Everyone has their own story, and no one knows the real truth except the artist." "I won't be buying Jordans anymore."

ILLINOIS STATE FINE ARTS STANDARDS

GOAL #	STATE STANDARD
25.A.5	Analyze and evaluate student and professional works for how aesthetic qualities are used to convey intent, expressive ideas and/or meaning.
26.A.5	Analyze and evaluate how the choice of media, tools, technologies, and processes support and influence the communication of ideas.
26.B.5	Create and perform a complex work of art using a variety of techniques, technologies and resources and independent decision making.
27.B.5	Analyze how the arts shape and reflect ideas, issues or themes in a particular culture or historical period.

ILLINOIS STATE CORE CURRICULUM STANDARDS

GOAL #	STATE STANDARD
4.A.4a	Apply listening skills as individuals and members of a group in a variety of settings.
4.B.5a	Deliver planned and impromptu oral presentations.
16.B.5a	Describe how modern political positions are affected by different ideologies and viewpoints that have developed over time.
2.A.5d	Evaluate the influence of historical context on form, style and point-of-view.

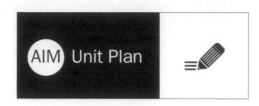

AIM Unit Plan

PROJECT TITLE	Bridges–Foundations & Expansions: Poetry, Math and Science
TEACHER	Theresa Kern
ARTIST	Daniel Godston, Jean Linsner (visiting educator)
SCHOOL	Academy of Communications and Technology (A.C.T.) Charter School
GRADE	6
ART FORMS(S)	Poetry
LENGTH OF PROJECT	6 weeks (12 sessions)

THE FOCUS OF THE PROJECT

This project focuses on students learning about bridges (as physical objects and metaphors), exploring the relationship between poetry and image, and producing short stories or poems about fantastical lands based on math concepts. Each of the following bridge-related themes are focused on throughout the duration of this program: We are building bridges between generations; We are building bridges between disciplines; We are building bridges between art forms; We are building bridges between left- and right-brain ways of thinking; We are building bridges to the past; We are building bridges to the future; and, We are building bridges between dreams and reality.

INQUIRY QUESTIONS FOR TEACHERS AND ARTISTS

How should inquiry questions be used in the context of what else has to be covered in a lesson plan? How can more poetry, math, and science concepts and elements be woven deeply into lesson plans so that students' educational experiences are more meaningful and engaging? How can I, as a poetry instructor, encourage students to combine rigorous research with freeflowing creative expression?

PRE/POST ASSESSMENT ACTIVITY FOR STUDENTS

At the end of each period, students write feedback on what they have learned. Here are some questions for feedback, "What is one thing you remember learning in class today?" "How can we be creative while thinking about bridges?" "What is one thing you have learned about poetry so far this week?" "What is one connection that we can make between math and poetry?" and "Is there anything so far that you find confusing?"

TEXT AND IMAGE SOURCES OF INSPIRATION

- "Clark Street Bridge" by Carl Sandburg
- "Picnic Boat" by Carl Sandburg
- "The New Colossus" by Emma Lazarus
- "The Arched Bridge" by Shi Zhecun
- "A Treasure's Trove" by Michael Stadther
- "Masquerade" by Kit Williams
- "Monet Refuses the Operation" by Lisel Mueller
- A digital slideshow for each poem to be projected.

TEN KEY VOCABULARY WORDS

1. Symmetry
2. Counterweight
3. Impressionism
4. Metaphor
5. Stanza
6. Epiphany
7. Segment
8. Anaphora
9. Blueprints
10. Xieh xieh" ("thank you") and "Ni hao" ("hello")

EQUIPMENT AND MATERIALS

- LCD projector
- Laptop with Powerpoint software
- Student Journals

WEEK	PRE-ASSESSMENT ACTIVITY
1–4	**LEARNING IN THE LANGUAGE OF THE ARTS I BUILDING A SAFE, CREATIVE SPACE**
1	I present a digital slideshow of images of Chicago bridges along with Carl Sandburg's poem "Clark Street Bridge." We talk about connections between a bridge and how a bridge is represented in a poem. I introduce the idea of math poems and write examples on the board. Students write their own math poems using bridge vocabulary. We discuss five styles of bridges and describe how they work.
2	Students compose poems that contain metaphor, an aphora, interesting use of stanzas and line breaks, bridge language, math concepts, and imagery. Students take turns standing in front of the projections of Chicago bridges, and then try to "push them up" or "pull them down." We revisit Sandburg's "Clark Street Bridge" and "Picnic Boat."
3	We read Emma Lazarus' "The New Colossus" and I share a digital presentation based on the poem. We also discuss Shi Zhecun's "The Arched Bridge" and talk about ways that traditional Chinese bridges are different from those found in Chicago. We brainstorm arches that can be found in the world: arches in advertising, nature, architecture. Students are to bring in 3-5 photos from home.
4	We talk about how Ellis Island could be seen as a bridge between America and immigrants' homelands. We discuss the immigrant rallies happening in Chicago and their relationship to physical and metaphoric bridges. Student take out their pictures and sketch the contour of the pictures. Each student puts a piece of paper over his/her contour drawing and writes words about the drawing along the contours. Students also write a poem based on one of the ideas we have discussed this session.
5–9	**IMMERSION IN A CONCEPTUAL QUESTION OR THEME THROUGH ART-MAKING**
5	Students select one "mathland" from these possibilities: Fractionland, Geometryland, Timeland, Multiplicationland, Subtractionlan, or Additionland. Each student writes a short story or poem about an experience in that mathland, adressing the question, "How can your characters use mathematical problems (or magic recipe) to travel, overcome obstacles, capture the treasure, and return home?"
6	Students construct "Fantasy Sandwich" outlines for their stories. The "Top Bun" is the exposition of reality. The "Bottom Bun" is the denouement of reality. The "stuff in the middle" is the fantasy part of a sandwich. Students start writing their poems or stories, making sure that their "Fantasy Sandwiches" are delicious by creating engaging settings, excellent dialogue, and interesting character development.
7	Students are asked to continue working on their story by describing his/her mathland: What does it look like? How big is it? How big are you in this world? What obstacles and creatures do they encounter? Draw pictures of two different kinds of creatures that can be found in your math land. Are they big or small? What do they eat (numbers, fractions, etc.)? Who did they befriend there?

The left margin labels: **ENGAGE** (weeks 1–4), **IMMERSE** (weeks 5–9).

	8	Students focus on revising their stories and poems, making sure they have included math and bridge elements, details that make the writing engaging and exciting, and places where the writing is edited down to make it stronger. Students are asked, "Have you done everything you can to make your writing as original as possible?"
IMMERSE	9	We discuss Impressionism, how painters see bridges, art and disability, and epiphany bridges. Then we talk about the relationship between perception and creation. How would a painter filter what she sees through different painterly styles? We also talk about some artists who have focused on bridges at some point in their careers: Picasso, Da Vinci, Van Gogh, Rembrandt and Claude Monet.
	10–14	**REVISE, SHARE, AND REFLECT ON ART-MAKING**
REFINE	10	We talk about artists who have worked in a number of art forms who have suffered from ailments that have affected their visions and craft, including Beethoven, Van Gogh and others. We read and discuss Lisel Mueller's "Monet Refuses the Operation." I ask students questions after they read it aloud two lines per student.
	11	Students work on computers. I work with students one-on-one to encourage them to include more details to make their poems and stories more vivid and engaging, explore voice more deeply and clear up any grammatical or punctuation issues. We record some students reading their poetry, with musical accompaniment (shakers, kalimba, wooden containers, and so on) by their classmates.
	12	A number of students come out into the courtyard with me. Students draw Chicago's movable bridges which Jean Linsner told them about: single- and double-leaf trunnion bascule bridges, a vertical lift bridge and a few others. Then students start painting the bridges. We write themes around the border of the large painted bridge.

CULMINATING EVENTS	**POST-ASSESSMENT ACTIVITY**	PLANS FOR FINAL SHOWING

There were a number of poetry projects that were part of original plans for this program. They include a project where students were going to interview family members and write poems from others' perspectives (to explore the theme "bridging generations"). There was an idea for a project where students were going to connect with students at another school and create poetry pen pal exchanges (to explore the theme "bridging the classroom with the world"). It's fascinating how this program has developed.

ARTIST'S REFLECTIONS

"It is nice to be able to come in twice, and sometimes three times a week, to accelerate and condense the residency. I was amazed at the poems that the students had written. It hadn't occurred to me to even include this type of lesson plan (session 4) in the curriculum, but I was moved to hear about what had happened at the rallies here in Chicago and elsewhere nationwide. Thematically, what happened, and the issues that people raised during the rallies, relates directly with Emma Lazarus' poem, which we covered the previous week."

STUDENTS' REFLECTIONS

"I learned that we have lots of bridges in Chicago and that there are many different bridges made by different people and I learned that we can make up poems with math.

"[This project] helped me in humanities because we are writing poems in there too."

"I learned that there are bridges that swing and move like see saws. I thought there was only one kind of bridge."

"I learned that bridges are not just things you walk or drive on, they can be your relationships."

"I saw an artistic side to Ms. Kern."

ILLINOIS STATE FINE ARTS STANDARDS

GOAL #	STATE STANDARD
25.B.3	Compare and contrast the elements and principles in two or more art works that share similar themes.
25.B.4	Analyze and evaluate similar and distinctive characteristics of works in two or more of the arts that share the same historical period or societal context.
27.B.3	Know and describe how artists and their works shape culture and increase understanding of societies, past and present.
26.A.3e	Describe how the choices of tools/technologies and processes are used to create specific effects in the arts.

ILLINOIS STATE CORE CURRICULUM STANDARDS

GOAL #	STATE STANDARD
1.A.3b	Analyze the meaning of words and phrases in their context.
3.B.3b	Edit and revise for word choice, organization, consistent point-of-view and transitions among paragraphs using contemporary technology and formats suitable for submission and/or publication.
2.A.3a	Identify and analyze a variety of literary techniques within classical and contemporary works representing a variety of genres.
6.A.3 - B.3	Demonstrate and apply a knowledge and sense of numbers, including numeration and operations, patterns, ratios and proportions.

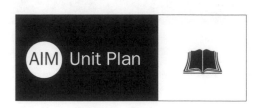

AIM Unit Plan

PROJECT TITLE	# Housing our Personal Stories: Bookmaking and Writing
TEACHERS	Somya Bergman, Michelle Cericola, Rebecca Katsulis
ARTIST	Jamie Lou Thome
SCHOOL	Robert Healy Elementary School
GRADE	6
ART FORMS(S)	Bookmaking and Writing
LENGTH OF PROJECT	14 weeks

THE FOCUS OF THE PROJECT

Students create "artist's books" and compose text for them. Students are allowed to be creative with their housing structures; they can be bottles, CD cases, suitcases, boxes, dioramas, puzzles, etc. Whatever each student needs his or her piece to be, it becomes.

INQUIRY QUESTIONS FOR TEACHERS AND ARTISTS

How can students use art to tell their personal stories?

PRE/POST ASSESSMENT ACTIVITY FOR STUDENTS

During the first and last sessions, students are asked the main inquiry question, "How can I use art to tell my personal stories?" Note how the students' responses have changed.

TEXT AND IMAGE SOURCES OF INSPIRATION

The class looks at artist's books made by the visiting artist, as well as websites of various book artists. During the residency, students read books which deal with various cultural and racial perspectives.

TEN KEY VOCABULARY WORDS

1. Conceptual
2. Artist's book
3. Pamphlet
4. Accordion
5. Structure
6. Housing
7. Theme
8. Signature
9. Awl
10. Folio

EQUIPMENT AND MATERIALS

- paper
- watercolor palettes
- thread, needles
- bone folders (can use popsicle sticks)
- oil pastel sets
- stamping materials for text placement
- imaginations

Students are also asked to bring in personal materials which relate to their stories.

	WEEK	PRE-ASSESSMENT ACTIVITY
	1–4	**LEARNING IN THE LANGUAGE OF THE ARTS	BUILDING A SAFE, CREATIVE SPACE**
ENGAGE	1	The guest artist presents personal artist's books and leads a discussion about the conceptual ideas behind different books.
	2	Students sew a sample structure of a pamphlet book, which they can utilize later.
	3	Students create "accordion" and "shaped" books, and create pop-ups in these structures.
	4	Students begin writing traditional narrative essays related to these four prompts: 1. Tell the story of your family history (maybe even just one family member's story). 2. Tell the story of your life. 3. Tell the story of one important event that impacted your life. 4. Tell the story of your culture or one aspect of your culture.
	5–9	**IMMERSION IN A CONCEPTUAL QUESTION OR THEME THROUGH ART-MAKING**
IMMERSE	5	Students continue to work on narrative essays. With the experience from the previous week in mind, students create 'webs' to assist in organizing their essays. Over the course of the week, students will continue to work on their webs and essays in class.
	6	Students continue to work on narrative essays. Artist and teachers meet to discuss the direction of the artwork and essays. Students are reminded that because the stories are personal, their artist's books will all be unique, and that the choices they make in text and imagery are important.
	7	Students begin to create poems from their texts. They choose the most powerful words and phrases from their text to work with.
	8	Students begin to create housing for their stories. They bring in items that are meaningful to their essays, and start to conceptualize how the stories will be told via the structures.
	9	Students continue to work on their housing structures. Watercolor and oil pastels are utilized to create decorative paper pages that the students can use in their final project.

10–14	REVISE, SHARE, AND REFLECT ON ART-MAKING

<table>
<tr><td rowspan="5">REFINE</td><td>10</td><td>Students continue to work on their book structures. Artist and teachers meet to discuss the direction of the artwork. More watercolor and oil pastel techniques are used.</td></tr>
<tr><td>11</td><td>Students continue to work on their book structures. Students evaluate their choices: Does my housing reflect the story itself or is it something I've chosen simply for ease? Is the housing meaningful to me or to the person the story is about?</td></tr>
<tr><td>12</td><td>Studio day: Students begin to place text on their pieces.</td></tr>
<tr><td>13</td><td>Studio day: Students continue to place text on their pieces.</td></tr>
<tr><td>14</td><td>After a brief work session to make final touches, students present their completed projects during several classroom culminating events.</td></tr>
</table>

	POST-ASSESSMENT ACTIVITY	PLANS FOR FINAL SHOWING
CULMINATING EVENTS	Students present their projects to their peers from other classrooms. The teachers and artists plan on working together to create a space for display and discussion.	

TEACHER'S REFLECTIONS

"Students were always excited when the artist arrived. She began each session by having each student read his/her poem aloud. Students gave each other ideas of how they could make their poems better. I was there during the sessions to participate in the activities and to help guide the students' writing. I also made sure the students had their poems completed each week by the time the artists came. I helped edit the poems that the students chose to type up for the book the artist is making. The project was basically writing different types of poems using different techniques. The artist, herself, did an excellent job of preparing and teaching each lesson."

ARTIST'S REFLECTIONS

"I wanted to push the students to the next level of book making–to move away from traditional book forms and focus on how the structure and form of the book push a story forward. I really believe that thinking abstractly across disciplines will help [the students] later on in their education. At first, I asked them, "How can we use art to tell my personal story?" I got pat answers. By the end, they offered more poignant, metaphorical answers. I think of a house as a container. Creating these structures allows students to shape their story literally and metaphorically. Working in both the literary and visual arts helps us discover the essence of story."

STUDENTS' REFLECTIONS

"I can use art as a way to express my own feelings. I could draw out, make my own, or even use objects that exist in my real life. I can use different colors to show my feelings toward different situations. I can give my story a more colorful outlook by using art. I personally think that art can represent many different things. I chose a water bottle to act as a container of my story." "I can use art to express my thoughts and feelings. Like when I was in a bad mood, I would scribble on my paper really hard. That shows that I'm very mad and angry. When I was in a good mood, I might be very gentle while I drew. Everybody can use art to express their stories, just think."

ILLINOIS STATE FINE ARTS STANDARDS

GOAL #	STATE STANDARD
25.A.3d	Identify and describe the elements of value, perspective and color schemes; the principles of contrast, emphasis and unity; and the expressive qualities of thematic development and sequence.
25.A.3e	Analyze how the elements and principles can be organized to convey meaning through a variety of media and technology.
26.A.3e	Describe how the choices of tools/technologies and processes are used to create specific effects in the arts.
26.B.2d	Demonstrate knowledge and skills to create works of visual art using problem-solving, observing, designing, sketching and constructing.

ILLINOIS STATE CORE CURRICULUM STANDARDS

GOAL #	STATE STANDARD
3.A.2b	Establish central idea, organization, elaboration and unity in relation to purpose and audience.
3.C.3a	Compose narrative, informative, and persuasive writings for a specified audience.
4.A.3c	Restate and carry out multistep oral instructions.
4.B.2b	Use speaking skills and procedures to participate in group discussions.

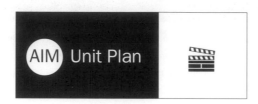

AIM Unit Plan

PROJECT TITLE
Choose Your Own Adventure: Video and Creative Writing

TEACHER Julie Buzza

ARTIST Ai Lene Chor

SCHOOL Robert Healy Elementary School

GRADE 7

ART FORMS(S) Video and Creative Writing

LENGTH OF PROJECT 16 weeks

THE FOCUS OF THE PROJECT

Students will explore the film-making process and create short animated narrative films. They will write their own dialogue and screenplays/scripts using the structure of a short story. Students will work in teams in order to develop protagonists who must deal with a major conflict dealing with survival. Each team will develop their protagonist's looks, personality, fears, ambitions, background, etc. After completing the art-making process, students will be able to define a film and explain its purpose.

INQUIRY QUESTIONS FOR TEACHERS AND ARTISTS

How do students weave their way through the creative process? How do students visualize each shot in their films? How can you construct each scene and character to maximize its effect on camera?

PRE/POST ASSESSMENT ACTIVITY FOR STUDENTS

During week one as well as week sixteen, students respond in their journals to the question, "What is a film?" These responses are compared. Students are encouraged to write original responses.

TEXT AND IMAGE SOURCES OF INSPIRATION

Websites, books, films, exhibitions, openings, news clippings, etc.; Examples of the four genres of film (animated, narrative, documentary and experimental); Young adult survival novels (*Breadwinner, Island of the Blue Dolphins, Hatchet, My Side of the Mountain, Julie of the Wolves*).

TEN KEY VOCABULARY WORDS

1. Narrative
2. Documentary
3. Composition
4. Dialogue
5. Exposition
6. Screenplay
7. Experimental
8. Protagonist
9. Conflict
10. Resolution

EQUIPMENT AND MATERIALS

- cameras & video cassettes
- journals
- materials to construct the characters and the scenes (i.e. construction paper and googly eyes)
- scissors
- small bags to store any little pieces
- tacky goo to temporarily affix the characters and scenes together

	WEEK	PRE-ASSESSMENT ACTIVITY
	1–4	LEARNING IN THE LANGUAGE OF THE ARTS I BUILDING A SAFE, CREATIVE SPACE
ENGAGE	1	Introduction: Students respond to the pre-sampling question, "What is a film?" Students also view last year's documentaries. Throughout the residency, journals will be used not only for recording notes and terms, but also for reflection on questions such as, "What type of film do I like the most (and least) and why?" or "What questions do I have for our video artist?" or "Are there any revisions I would make?"
	2	Film genres: Students view an example of each genre of film (animated, narrative, documentary and experimental). As a class, students create a list of traits for each genre and record these in their journals. Students learn how films are made and are assigned to make a flipbook on the edge of their journals for homework.
	3	Brainstorming survival story ideas: In two small groups, students make a list of possible story lines. The organizer for this exercise contains three columns (character, setting, conflict). These will all be survival stories and need to end positively. The artist and teacher select ten story lines from which students pick one. Students write persuasive arguments to the teacher explaining their picks.
	4	Composition/framing exercise: The video artist (using construction paper frames) discusses composition and framing. Then students use the framing device and their new knowledge of composition to select a frame from a large photo. Students cut out the part of the photo inside the frame and write a creative story about that scene.
	5–9	IMMERSION IN A CONCEPTUAL QUESTION OR THEME THROUGH ART-MAKING
IMMERSE	5	Two-minute films: Students work in teams and select 3-5 images from which they compose a line or two connecting it to a theme. The video artist instructs on the safe and proper way to use the camera. Students work together to record their images and record their voices on tape as well. The homework assignment is to "eavesdrop" on conversations outside of the school and note what they hear.
	6	Two-minute films (continued). The class explores the conversations gathered through the homework assignment and incorporates those into their scripts. Before writing the dialogue of the films, students work in teams to develop their plot lines using the structure of exposition, introduction of initial conflict, rising action, climax, falling action and resolution.
	7	Script writing: Together, the class spends the day reviewing their scripts and looking at them with a "film-maker's eye." They try to visualize the story and the movements. We spend time looking at "Monster" by Walter Dean Myers, which is a young adult novel written as a screenplay.

IMMERSE	8	Storyboard assignment: Each group storyboards their film. Each shot is outlined and labeled with its shot scale. The students color-code the characters in each scene, as well as the sound effects, etc. This is time-consuming, but essential. It helps some groups realize how in-depth their story is. I found it to be a crucial tool during production and post-production.
	9	Construction/Pre-production: The video artist shows the class a model of character made out of construction paper. The class learns how each body part is separate so it can move, walk, jump, etc. Facial parts are also movable in order to show emotion. Several characters might need to be made identical, but in two different sizes for scale. Finally, students begin to construct their characters.
	10–14	**REVISE, SHARE, AND REFLECT ON ART-MAKING**
REFINE	10	Construction/Pre-production: Students draw, cut, create and label individual bags of character parts. Meanwhile, the video artist and teacher roam the space, helping with size, perception and shot scales. Many of the groups progress to background scenes, especially if they only had a few characters.
	11	Shoot/Construction: A few groups start filming. The instruction is limited, like the two-minute videos from earlier in the unit. Staff set up an audio camera in a small room nearby where groups can record their dialogue and sound effects.
	12	Shoot/Construction continued: We want everyone's voice to be heard in the group, so at each stage the students write their own version of the dialogue and then share that with the group. After a group of students has reached a consensus, that group then moves on to the next stage in the writing process.
	13	Shoot/Construction continued: Students compile a list of possible topics to reflect on in their journals. Here is a partial list of our students' ideas: favorite part, least favorite, easiest part, hardest, How did our group cooperate? What terms did I learn? What changes did we make? Did it match my expectations?
	14	Shoot/Reflection: Students respond to the post-sampling question, "What is a film?"

CULMINATING EVENTS	**POST-ASSESSMENT ACTIVITY** PLANS FOR FINAL SHOWING
	We are working with our Fine Arts Coordinator to have a screening of our five films at the Apple store. We are also going to show the films to as many other classrooms as possible.

STUDENTS' REFLECTIONS

"My teacher has a fun side. She is working like an artist."

"Practicing the dialogue helped me in reading."

"It helped me most in language arts with visualizing my poetry and story writing and the dialogue."

"It helped me with teamwork in other classes."

"I learned it's not easy to make a movie, new terms, how to make a movie, writing the dialogues, different scales, different types of movies."

ILLINOIS STATE FINE ARTS STANDARDS

GOAL #	STATE STANDARD
25.A.3e	Analyze how the elements and principles can be organized to convey meaning through a variety of media and technology.
26.A.3e	Describe how the choices of tools/technologies and processes are used to create special effects in the arts.
26.B.3d	Demonstrate knowledge and skills to create 2- and 3-dimensional works and time arts (e.g., film, animation, video) that are realistic, abstract, functional and decorative.
27.A.3b	Compare and contrast how the arts function in ceremony, technology, politics, communication and entertainment.

ILLINOIS STATE CORE CURRICULUM STANDARDS

GOAL #	STATE STANDARD
2.A.3b	Describe how the development of theme, character, plot and setting contribute to the overall impact of a piece of literature.
2.B.3c	Analyze how characters in literature deal with conflict, solve problems and relate to real-life situations.
3.C.3a	Compose narrative, informative, and persuasive writings for a specified audience.
5.C.3a	Plan, compose, edit and revise documents that synthesize new meaning gleaned from multiple sources.

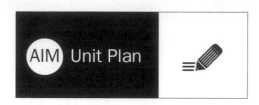

AIM Unit Plan

PROJECT TITLE	## What's Your Story? Children's Stories by Young Authors
TEACHERS	Mary Clare McCarthy, Julienne Backstrom, Diane Simpson, and Carlos Mendez
ARTISTS	Leah Mayers (Book Artist); Luis Crespo (Theater Artist)
SCHOOL	Thurgood Marshall Middle School
GRADE	8
ART FORMS(S)	Drama, Creative Writing, and Book Making
LENGTH OF PROJECT	8 Sessions (4 weeks)

THE FOCUS OF THE PROJECT

8th grade students write children's stories for submission into the city wide Young Authors Program. During each session, the Book Artist reviews, along with the class, parts of the book, book structure and vocabulary. Each week, the Theater Artist leads drama games that explore elements of story and scene. Students come to the front of the class weekly and share their books in progress with their peers for feedback in a modified Critical Response process.

INQUIRY QUESTIONS FOR TEACHERS AND ARTISTS

- Can the experience of writing stories be enhanced by drama and book making?
- Does playing drama games, using the Drawing Response Journals, learning the language of book making, and implementing Critical Response, make the story writing process more fun? Are the stories themselves richer?
- Have these exercises changed the way the students feel about making art, engaging in drama, reading and writing?

PRE/POST ASSESSMENT ACTIVITY FOR STUDENTS

PRE: Write a letter to a trusted friend telling him/her/your story.
POST: Evidence can be found within the finished stories. Students are also given exit slips on which to write their experience using drama and book making to write and present their stories.

TEXT AND IMAGE SOURCES OF INSPIRATION

Liz Lerman's "Critical Response."

TEN KEY VOCABULARY WORDS

1. Folio
2. Codex
3. Drawing Response Journals
4. Colophon
5. Narrative
6. Spine
7. Fore Edge
8. Bone Folder
9. Critical Response
10. Japanese Side Stitch

EQUIPMENT AND MATERIALS

- Hand made book models
- "Japanese Bookbinding" by Kojiro Ikegami
- Drawing Response Journals: 8½" x 14" paper folded & bound with clips

Books
- cover weight colored paper for covers
- 8 ½" x 14" paper
- linen thread
- bee's wax
- scissors
- glue
- bone folder
- markers
- hole punches

AIM Learning Cycle Unit Plan At A Glance

What's Your Story?
Children's Stories by Young Authors

	WEEK	PRE-ASSESSMENT ACTIVITY
	1–4	LEARNING IN THE LANGUAGE OF THE ARTS I BUILDING A SAFE, CREATIVE SPACE
ENGAGE	1	Book Artist (BA) and Theater Artist (TA) introduce project to students. TA engages students in theater warm-up games and exercises. BA assigns homework (pre-writing assignment): consider a story topic that would appeal to a younger child or a social issue important to teenagers and write a letter to a trusted friend telling him/her your story.
	2	TA leads students in theater exercises learned from the previous week. Collect pre-writing assignment. Demonstrate the Critical Response Process with several students' letters. BA leads students in construction of a Drawing Response Journal to be used every class session, as well as during the week, to illustrate their stories.
	3	First drafts of stories due. Class breaks into small groups for Critical Response. One adult in each group facilitates students reading stories aloud, engaging the group in constructive feedback, and makes plans for rewrite. BA leads lesson on illustration using salient details from stories (comic book style). BA hands out Colophon directions, book making checklist, and Critical Response process.
	4	TA selects students to read aloud three scenes from their stories. Led by the TA, each student author directs his/her classmates into tableau of their scenes. The author's peers make observations and ask her/him questions on their work. The author returns to her/his story with the comments of the group. Students exchange stories with partners and read each other's work to make sure the stories are clear, cogent, and entertaining. BA takes first drafts home to read and pose questions for students to answer.
	5–8	IMMERSION IN A CONCEPTUAL QUESTION OR THEME THROUGH ART-MAKING
IMMERSE	5	BA discusses with class the elements of story: audience, relevant details, tense, characters, conflict, etc., in addition to common punctuation, grammar and spelling errors. Starts discussion of book layout: page sequence, book design and binding styles. BA leads group in folding paper for final books and distributing covers.
	6	All stories and drawings due. BA demonstrates binding final books and stitching variations. Students consult Book Making Checklist. Students must bring 3 typed copies of final stories next week.
	7	Assemble final books: paginate, choose illustrations from DRJ for inclusion, punch holes for sewing, hand write Colophon. Class ends with theater games.
	8	Complete all finishing touches on books. Students come to head of class and read their books aloud. Students spend last session exchanging and sharing books. Collect post-writing sample and complete Exit Slips.

POST-ASSESSMENT ACTIVITY   PLANS FOR FINAL SHOWING

We discussed with the students, on the first day of the residency, that their books would be submitted to the city wide Young Authors contest. We also presented the idea of having a school wide Culminating Event where all the books from the four 8th grade classes would be displayed along with the totem poles and masks they made in 7th grade.

The Culminating Event: the four classes of students, teachers, Teaching Artists, AIM staff, members of school community gathered in the theater. Students were selected from each class to come to the podium and share their story. Some of the classes wrote a vignette acting out one story. The totem poles with masks and the books were displayed in the middle of the stage.

ARTIST'S REFLECTIONS

"As teaching artists, we often have dual goals: one is to integrate our art form into our students' literacy learning, and the second is to help our students make aesthetically captivating art work. I don't want kids to make books only to house their poems or make them more apt to seek out new novels, though I do want both of those things to occur. I also want my students to learn the vocabulary of book making, to learn complicated stitches and structures, formal and creative book layout and beautiful, professional looking art objects."

STUDENTS' REFLECTIONS

"I didn't think I could write a book but now I can see that I can write a book."

"I learned that I actually enjoyed writing a story."

"I liked my friend's story because she brought out a problem that many girls face—the pressure to be skinny."

"I liked Jairo's story because when I and other people acted it out we saw that it was interesting."

"It really helped me to decide I want to write books because I really wasn't sure if I liked writing."

"I read more interesting books and write a lot more. I want to do more work and listen."

ILLINOIS STATE FINE ARTS STANDARDS

GOAL #	STATE STANDARD
25.A.3e	Analyze how the elements and principles can be organized to convey meaning through a variety of media and technology.
26.B.3d	Demonstrate knowledge and skills to create 2- and 3-dimensional works and time arts that are realistic, abstract, functional and decorative.
25.A.4	Analyze and evaluate the effective use of elements, principles and expressive qualities in a composition/performance in dance, drama, music and the visual arts.
25.A.2b	Understand the elements of acting, scripting, speaking, improvising, physical movement, gesture and picturization; the principles of conflict/resolution and theme; and the expressive characteristics of mood and dynamics.

ILLINOIS STATE CORE CURRICULUM STANDARDS

GOAL #	STATE STANDARD
3.C.3a	Compose narrative, informative and persuasive writings for a specified audience.
2.A.3d	Identify ways that an author uses language structure, word choice and style to convey the author's viewpoint.
3.B.4b	Produce, edit, revise and format work for submission and/or publication using contemporary technology.
4.A.4c	Follow complex oral instructions.

AIM Unit Plan

PROJECT TITLE	Poetic Relationships
TEACHER	Melissa Padilla, Margarita Garcia
ARTIST	Jenn Morea
SCHOOL	Casimir Pulaski Fine Arts Academy
GRADE	5th/6th
ART FORMS(S)	Poetry
LENGTH OF PROJECT	14 weeks

THE FOCUS OF THE PROJECT

The focus of this project is to create a book of poetry centered around the question, "Where are relationships found?" Students will examine relationships in language, as well as the relationships between language and mathematics, music, and visual arts.

INQUIRY QUESTIONS FOR TEACHERS AND ARTISTS

- How can we deepen our students' understanding of relationships found in language?
- How can we expand our students' definition of "relationship" through an exploration of poetry, music, and visual arts?

PRE/POST ASSESSMENT ACTIVITY FOR STUDENTS

PRE/POST: Students write responses to the question, "Where are relationships found?"

TEXT AND IMAGE SOURCES OF INSPIRATION

- InSite 2000 installation by Valeska Soares
- "Identity is a relational concept...in relation to whom or what do you define yourself, and to which locations?" Kenia Halleck interviewing Gioconda Belli in BOMB Magazine (Winter 2001 No. 74)
- *Boundaries* by Maya Lin
- *Architecture and Geometry in the Age of the Baroque,* by George L. Hersey
- Tesselation patterns on display in Ms. Garcia's classroom made by students

TEN KEY VOCABULARY WORDS

1. Installation
2. Pattern
3. Relationship
4. Symmetry
5. Mathematics
6. Alliteration
7. Onomatopoeia
8. Consonance
9. Assonance
10. Percussion

EQUIPMENT AND MATERIALS

- Journals
- Pens
- Folders
- Copies of model poems
- Supplies for visual arts/music

WEEK	PRE-ASSESSMENT ACTIVITY
1–4	LEARNING IN THE LANGUAGE OF THE ARTS I BUILDING A SAFE, CREATIVE SPACE
1	Introduction: Students write one question that they have about poetry and respond to the question, "What is poetry?" Students then compose Essential Autobiographies (for example: Tell your story in 24 words, 12 words, 6 words, 3 words, and eventually, 1 word).
2	Pre-write: Students write their own definitions of the word "relationship" and respond to the question, "Where are relationships found?"
3	Exploring Poetic Elements: Metaphor and simile.
4	Exploring Poetic Elements: Syntax. Students take a line from poet Sappho and rewrite it 5 different ways, rearranging the words and including every word. Students play with different arrangements by writing the words on index cards and physically moving them to create new arrangements in front of the class. Students also read a poem by Roberto Juarroz (which only uses five words in the whole poem). Students then choose five words and write a poem by arranging it in different ways.
5–9	IMMERSION IN A CONCEPTUAL QUESTION OR THEME THROUGH ART-MAKING
5	Exploring Poetic Elements: Pantoum (Mathematics & Visual Arts tie-in).
6	Exploring Poetic Elements & Form: Line and stanza & calligram. Students read William Carlos Williams' poem "The Red Wheelbarrow." They make a list of objects and images from their country of origin. They choose an object from that list and write a poem about their country in the shape of that object. This prepares them for the calligram work in week 11.
7	Exploring Poetic Elements: Sound (alliteration, onomatopoeia, consonance, and assonance). Students read model poems and identify the poetic elements found within them. Students then write poems employing these elements.
8	Guest Musician (Charles Barbera): Poetry & Percussion. Charles Barbera introduces students to various instruments and musical concepts. Students set their poems to music and perform their pieces for each other.
9	Students write reflections on what they noticed about the relationship between poetry and music.

ENGAGE (weeks 1–4)

IMMERSE (weeks 5–9)

10–14	REVISE, SHARE, AND REFLECT ON ART-MAKING

REFINE	10	Poems of identity and place: Students listen to a lecture on Valeska Soares' *InSite* 2000 installation and engage in a discussion on "borders." Students create poems that explore borders and opposites in both form and content.
	11	Guest visual artist Cynthia Weiss shares models of calligrams and guides students as they make their own calligrams.
	12	Revisions.
	13	Post-write: Students write their own definitions of the word "relationship" and respond to the questions, "Where are relationships found?" and "What differences do you notice between when you first wrote your poem and when you turned it into a calligram?"
	14	Book Release & Reading.

CULMINATING EVENTS	**POST-ASSESSMENT ACTIVITY** PLANS FOR FINAL SHOWING
	We produced a book of student poems titled Poetic Relationships, which students read from at a book release party. Some students also gave performances of their poems at a school assembly in which they combined their talents as poets, actors, and musicians.

TEACHER'S REFLECTIONS

"Students were involved in authentic creation of individual poetry writing. Students were tapping into areas that dealt with very personal topics. Students continue to use the various styles of poetry writing in various subjects. For example, in science and language arts integration, students created a poem using Limerick."

ARTIST'S REFLECTIONS

"I designed the residency around this central question for a number of reasons. I liked the idea of thinking with my students about where relationships are found because relationships signify connections. The more connections that can be found between things, then the more things have a belonging."

For more from the artist, please see "Surprising Relationships: The Oooh's and Ahhh's Between Poetry, Music, Art & Mathematics," an essay by Jenn Morea on page 34.

"My teacher was like a student trying to learn new things and I like that."

"Reading poems helped me to read more fluently and fast."

"It's nice to write what you feel and express it on paper in the form of a poem."

"It helped me in Language Arts to be more descriptive in my language, having a purpose to my piece of writing."

"The activity I most remember is when two people picked out nouns and made similes with the words."

"Like in math, when we were doing symmetry it fit with what we were doing. For example, they both have symmetry."

ILLINOIS STATE FINE ARTS STANDARDS

GOAL #	STATE STANDARD
25.B.3	Compare and contrast the elements and principles in two or more art works that share a similar theme.
25.A.2c	Identify elements and expressive qualities such as tone color, harmony, melody, form, rhythm/meter and dynamics in a variety of styles.
27.A.2a	Identify and describe the relationship between the arts and various environments.
25.B.2	Understand how elements and principles combine within an art form to express ideas.

ILLINOIS STATE CORE CURRICULUM STANDARDS

GOAL #	STATE STANDARD
2.A.3d	Identify ways that an author uses language structure, word choice and style to convey the author's viewpoint.
3.B.3a	Produce documents that convey a clear understanding and interpretation of ideas and information and display focus, organization, elaboration and coherence.
3.B.3b	Edit and revise for word choice, organization, consistent point of view and transitions among paragraphs using contemporary technology and formats suitable for submission and/or publication.
2.A.4b	Explain relationships between and among literary elements and the effectiveness of the literary piece.

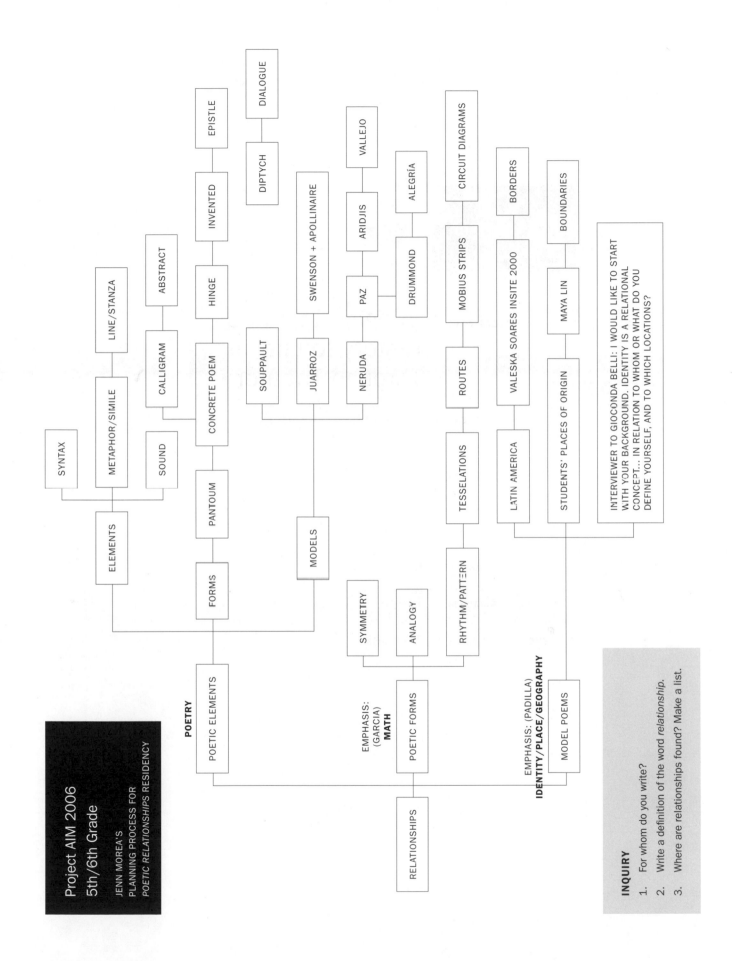

**Project AIM 2006
5th/6th Grade**

JENN MOREA'S
PLANNING PROCESS FOR
POETIC RELATIONSHIPS RESIDENCY

POETRY

- POETIC ELEMENTS
  - ELEMENTS
    - SYNTAX
    - METAPHOR/SIMILE
      - LINE/STANZA
    - SOUND
  - FORMS
    - PANTOUM
    - CONCRETE POEM
      - CALLIGRAM
        - ABSTRACT
      - HINGE
        - INVENTED
          - EPISTLE
          - DIPTYCH
            - DIALOGUE
  - MODELS
    - SOUPPAULT
    - JUARROZ
      - SWENSON + APOLLINAIRE
    - NERUDA
      - PAZ
        - ARIDJIS
          - VALLEJO
        - DRUMMOND
          - ALEGRÍA

MATH

EMPHASIS: (GARCIA)

- POETIC FORMS
  - SYMMETRY
  - ANALOGY
  - RHYTHM/PATTERN
    - TESSELATIONS
      - ROUTES
        - MOBIUS STRIPS
          - CIRCUIT DIAGRAMS

IDENTITY/PLACE/GEOGRAPHY

EMPHASIS: (PADILLA)

- MODEL POEMS
  - RELATIONSHIPS
  - LATIN AMERICA
    - VALESKA SOARES INSITE 2000
      - BORDERS
  - STUDENTS' PLACES OF ORIGIN
    - MAYA LIN
      - BOUNDARIES

INTERVIEWER TO GIOCONDA BELLI: I WOULD LIKE TO START WITH YOUR BACKGROUND. IDENTITY IS A RELATIONAL CONCEPT... IN RELATION TO WHOM OR WHAT DO YOU DEFINE YOURSELF, AND TO WHICH LOCATIONS?

INQUIRY

1. For whom do you write?
2. Write a definition of the word *relationship*.
3. Where are relationships found? Make a list.

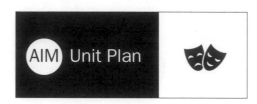

AIM Unit Plan

PROJECT TITLE	Bringing Text and History to Life Through Theater
TEACHERS	Michelle Lugo, Judith Diaz, Candace Guevara, and Valerie King
ARTIST	Khanisha Foster
SCHOOL	Casimir Pulaski Fine Arts Academy, Robert Healy Elementary School
GRADE	5th–7th
ART FORMS(S)	Theater
LENGTH OF PROJECT	14 weeks

THE FOCUS OF THE PROJECT

We will use theater to explore the text(s) each class has been working with in their classrooms. Together, students and teachers will be making text 3-dimensional.

Through the theater-making process, students will gain a greater idea of inference and how theater can be used to fully explore text. By learning the art of theater, students will experience the ins and outs of running a business and how to work in collaboration with their peers.

INQUIRY QUESTIONS FOR TEACHERS AND ARTISTS

- How do you now know the difference between reading a piece of text and performing it?
- How can students use all of the information available to them in the text to develop characters?
- How do we modernize dry history text and make it more accessible and relevant?

PRE/POST ASSESSMENT ACTIVITY FOR STUDENTS

Student reflection questions include: "How do we use character to understand text?" and "How can physical choices highlight text?" In addition, much of the student progress can be observed during performances. Teachers can measure any decline in the amount of judgment students put on themselves and others, learning objectives met, and examples of ensemble work and confident choices.

TEXT AND IMAGE SOURCES OF INSPIRATION

Text used for performances:
- *School House Rock: History*
- *The Witch of Blackbird Pond,* by Elizabeth G Speare
- *Waiting for Anya,* by Michael Morpurgo
- *In the Year of the Boar,* by Bette Bao Lord
- *Jackie Robinson,* by Bette Bao Lord
- *Loser,* by Jerry Spinelli
- *Maniac Magee,* by Jerry Spinelli
- *Esperanza Rising,* by Pam Munoz Ryan
- *The Melancholy Death of Oyster Boy,* by Tim Burton

Films:
- *Nightmare Before Christmas*

Websites:
- Virtual Lighting Lab
- Haunted Mansion
- School House Rock
- Tim Burton
- Creative Drama

TEN KEY VOCABULARY WORDS

1. Ensemble
2. Script
3. Blocking
4. Character
5. Intention
6. Theater
7. Action
8. Status
9. Constitution
10. Narrative

EQUIPMENT AND MATERIALS

- Lights (floor lights, over head stage lights, and spot lights)
- Make-up
- Props
- Set
- Projector
- Laptop computer

	WEEK	PRE-ASSESSMENT ACTIVITY
ENGAGE	1–4	LEARNING IN THE LANGUAGE OF THE ARTS I BUILDING A SAFE, CREATIVE SPACE
	1	This project begins with ensemble-building games that expand theater vocabulary and allow students to create an environment of trust and respect. Some of the games include Filling the Space, Alphabet Aerobics, Partners, Mirror Activities and Steal the Focus. Such games can be found in books by Viola Spolin, Augusto Boal and Keith Johnstone, and can be tailored to fit the classroom.
	2	After using these games to cultivate the only real rule (Respect) students begin to incorporate the texts they've been working on in class. They first work from a midpoint in a text and create tableaus, or frozen moments from the stories. At this point it is important to encourage the students to clear their minds and not plan their actions. They should try to simply react.
	3	From this tableau, students move in silence (in beats of five counts) into a tableau from a previous moment in the story, then return to the midpoint tableau and eventually to a moment in the future. Students are encouraged to use details from the text to create physical characteristics. It is alright if characters are repeated, as each child will bring a different perspective.
	4	As we continue with these activities, we input dialogue by having the students speak their characters' thoughts during each tableau; they speak only when a teacher taps them on the shoulder. Then as the dialogue develops, students return to writing the actual script. Ideally the teacher helps the students create drafts of the script each week while the artist is not in the classroom.
IMMERSE	5–9	IMMERSION IN A CONCEPTUAL QUESTION OR THEME THROUGH ART-MAKING
	5	Students attend a live theater performance, such as School House Rock Live, to transition into the fifth week. This helps the classes understand how the concepts they are learning in the classroom can be transformed into a performance.
	6	During the following few weeks, the class studies theatrical design elements. Students reflect on visual settings and respond to these various surroundings. As we look at different pictures, students discuss what is needed to make the settings more reflective of the text and more interesting to the audience.
	7	Guest Speaker: Jesse Klug, Chicago lighting designer.
	8	Rehearsal.
	9	After each rehearsal of the play, performance notes are given to the students by the teaching artist/director. These scenes are improved upon during the next rehearsal. Students are also asked to reflect on what they have seen and experienced. It is important that the students develop their own opinions about the work, while actively supporting each other.

10–14	REVISE, SHARE, AND REFLECT ON ART-MAKING

REFINE

10–14	In this portion of the unit, we conducted dress rehearsals, performances and class reflections.

CULMINATING EVENTS

POST-ASSESSMENT ACTIVITY	PLANS FOR FINAL SHOWING

We conducted dress rehearsals which ran as full performances. In the future, I would recommend giving the students at least two performances. Students learn so much from their first performance in front of an audience and it is important for them to have the opportunity to apply what they have learned. In addition, teachers facilitated final wrap up sessions in order to collect active feedback about the students' experiences.

TEACHER'S REFLECTIONS

"I feel that Project AIM showed my students that although they have their differences they can come together, use those differences, build on them and create a wonderful piece."

ARTIST'S REFLECTIONS

"This work allows each student to discover their individual voice and figure out how it fits into the whole. It is a key to their intelligence and their future. I am very proud of every student's work."

STUDENTS' REFLECTIONS

"It helped me not to give up on the subjects that I never do well on." "I learned more about the book that we were reading in class. I had a better understanding of the novel that I read." "It help me to be more brave and answer questions in other classrooms." "She taught me not to talk when other people are talking."

"[My teacher] had fun and participated in a lot of games. She is funnier than I thought."

"I learned to work in team and that practice makes it better. I learned you don't have to be afraid of the stage."

"I learned how to use energy. I really like this program. I learned to calm down."

"It got me more active in Kung-Fu."

ILLINOIS STATE FINE ARTS STANDARDS

GOAL #	STATE STANDARD
26.A.3b	Describe the use of the primary tools (body, mind and voice) and the support tools (costumes, scenery, props, lights, make-up, sound) to convey an idea through acting, play-writing and designing a drama or theater activity.
26.B.4b	Create and perform an ensemble drama or theater scene using research, collaboration, characterization and staging in combination with aural and visual technologies (e.g., video, lights, sets, costumes, make-up, sound, props).
27.A3a	Identify and describe careers and jobs in and among the arts and how they contribute to the world of work.
25.A.3b	Understand how the elements of acting, directing, playwriting and designing combine with the principles of tension, rhythm, pattern, unity, balance, repetition and idea to communicate.

ILLINOIS STATE CORE CURRICULUM STANDARDS

GOAL #	STATE STANDARD
1.B.3d	Read age-appropriate material with fluency and accuracy.
1.C.3b	Interpret and analyze entire narrative text using story elements, point-of-view and theme.
2.A.3b	Describe how the development of theme, character, plot and setting contribute to the overall impact of a piece of literature.
5.C.3a	Plan, compose, edit and revise documents that synthesize new meaning gleaned from multiple sources.

AIM Unit Plan

PROJECT TITLE	So Real Video
TEACHERS	Maria Mertz and Sophia Rempas
ARTISTS	Suree Towfighnia and John Lyons
SCHOOL	Casimir Pulaski Fine Arts Academy
GRADE	5th
ART FORMS(S)	Video
LENGTH OF PROJECT	14 weeks

THE FOCUS OF THE PROJECT

For this video-based curriculum, the class works together to create a singular short film collaboration, 10-14 minutes in length. Much of the work focuses on film vocabulary and story development/script-writing.

INQUIRY QUESTIONS FOR TEACHERS AND ARTISTS

What are the social concerns that 5th-graders face?

PRE/POST ASSESSMENT ACTIVITY FOR STUDENTS

PRE: Vocabulary Questions Related to Film
POST: Final Film Production Vocabulary Questions

TEXT AND IMAGE SOURCES OF INSPIRATION

Students are inspired by "Mad Hot Ballroom." They use their interests in current events (immigration issues, Hurricane Katrina, the War in Iraq, etc.) to inform their writings.

TEN KEY VOCABULARY WORDS

1. Composition
2. Art direction
3. Immigration
4. Inquiry
5. Aspect
6. Collaboration
7. Shot stills
8. Design
9. Script
10. Scene

EQUIPMENT AND MATERIALS

- Journals
- Still cameras
- Video cameras
- Microphones
- Tripods
- Computers
- Pens
- Lights

WEEK	PRE-ASSESSMENT ACTIVITY
1–4	**LEARNING IN THE LANGUAGE OF THE ARTS I BUILDING A SAFE, CREATIVE SPACE**
1	Students fill out a survey on their interests as a way to introduce themselves to the teaching artists.
2	Students think about the following question: "To make a successful film, we need… what?" Students collaborate to brainstorm these ideas. The results of this brainstorming become the class "contract" that the students can refer to when they need to refocus their energies (you can also refer to it in order to make sure that everything is on track.)
3	Teaching artists define essential film vocabulary to the class. Students play "Film Jeopardy" to reinforce their learning.
4	Students watch a movie they are familiar with and then incorporate the terms they've learned in their critiques. Students learn to incorporate new vocabulary terms as they analyze the film.
5–9	**IMMERSION IN A CONCEPTUAL QUESTION OR THEME THROUGH ART-MAKING**
5	How do you fill a frame? We introduce concepts of starting with an empty frame and then placing objects in the frame to reveal themes and ideas that the students want to convey.
6	Students begin writing intensively, pulling from their own experiences. They develop their writing into group scripts. Students also take 24 pictures and choose 5-10 of them to incorporate into their films. Students map their scenes in an activity called "story maps."
7	Students head departments and are responsible for each department's activities.
8	Students pitch their scripts/scenes to the class, who then vote on their inclusion into the final script. All individual scripts are combined to make one master script.
9	Crew positions and actors are cast, and they begin shooting the film.

Left vertical labels: ENGAGE (weeks 1–4), °IMMERSE (weeks 5–9)

10–14	REVISE, SHARE, AND REFLECT ON ART-MAKING

	10	Actors rehearse and memorize lines. Directors block the actors. Props are obtained and sets are dressed. All positions are rehearsed. Scenes are timed. Schedule is made for production.
REFINE	11	A script supervisor keeps a master script and checks off completed scenes. Students keep rigorous notes in their journals to assess their process. At each major turning point, students write about the process as a way to learn, touch base, and calm down.
	12	Shooting and Editing (continued).
	13	Teaching Artists review students' journals and assess the process as teachers.
	14	Final "Wrap Party."

CULMINATING EVENTS

POST-ASSESSMENT ACTIVITY PLANS FOR FINAL SHOWING

The final "Wrap Party" took place in a screening room with the students' films projected onto a large screen. Students presented their work to each other and invited family and friends to celebrate. A field trip was also planned to tour Columbia College, introducing them to the film department in an academic setting.

TEACHER'S REFLECTIONS

"At the beginning of the school year, the children were afraid to get up and speak publicly. By the end, because of the film workshop, we couldn't keep them in their seats. They all had the self confidence they needed to speak. They were not only able to find their voice; they were able to project it in public."

ARTIST'S REFLECTIONS

"Working with the students inspired me to remember the enthusiasm we have as children to learn and encouraged me to rekindle that and apply it to the world around me. It reminds me that we need to let go of a fear of trying."

STUDENTS' REFLECTIONS

"During this experience, I learned a lot about the technology, crew, and documentary. It helped me get along with more people and it taught me how to direct and listen. I also started to actually worry about our nation and social issues. I remember before filmmaking I didn't really care about the U.S.A. I decided that I cared for peace, no wars the most because I thought that it would trigger no more gangs, drugs, or war." "This was a good and fun class to take...It involves a lot of hard work and collaboration because you have to work with others. The process isn't really easy as 1, 2, 3...it takes some time just to make a scene, imagine 12...We are having a great experience..."

ILLINOIS STATE FINE ARTS STANDARDS

GOAL #	STATE STANDARD
25.A.3e	Analyze how the elements and principles can be organized to convey meaning through a variety of media and technology.
26.A.3e	Describe how the choices of tools/technologies and processes are used to create specific effects in the arts.
26.B.3d	Demonstrate knowledge and skills to create 2- and 3-dimensional works and time-arts (e.g., film, animation, video) that are realistic, abstract, functional and decorative.
27.A.3a	Identify and describe careers and jobs among the arts and how they contribute to the world of work.

ILLINOIS STATE CORE CURRICULUM STANDARDS

GOAL #	STATE STANDARD
3.C.3a	Compose narrative, informative and persuasive writings for a specified audience.
4.A.3a	Demonstrate ways that listening attentively can improve comprehension.
4.B.4b	Use group discussion skills to assume leadership and participant roles within an assigned project or to reach a group goal.
5.A.3b	Design a project related to contemporary issues using multiple sources.

AIM Unit Plan

PROJECT TITLE	# From Scenes to Sprites: Shakespeare with 6th Graders
TEACHERS	Neeta Agrawal, Eileen Kahana
ARTIST	Tony Sancho
SCHOOL	Casimir Pulaski Fine Arts Academy
GRADE	6th
ART FORMS(S)	Theater
LENGTH OF PROJECT	14 weeks

THE FOCUS OF THE PROJECT

In this project, students will gain the skills and confidence necessary in order to work together as an ensemble and produce a stage performance of a work by Shakespeare. Our goal is to encourage deeper student engagement and interest in reading through the theater process. Students will be taught criteria needed to assess strong personal work. They will also be able to assess their growth by comparing rehearsals to actual performances.

INQUIRY QUESTIONS FOR TEACHERS AND ARTISTS

How can theater improve students' reading, inference and overall student life? How can we implement Shakespeare into a 6th grade classroom with excitement and enthusiasm? How can we teach students to have ownership of this project? Can this process teach students to creatively collaborate and give constructive criticism, despite any differences they may have in the classroom? Will these lessons spill out into the other areas of their education? What will students learn about theater through the production process itself?

PRE/POST ASSESSMENT ACTIVITY FOR STUDENTS

Both before and after the project, students are asked questions about their knowledge of theater, acting and ensemble. Reflection and critique happen on a daily basis. Students reflect on two inquiry questions at the beginning and end of the project: "How do you feel about performing in front of others?" and "What do ensemble members need from each other in order to perform?"

TEXT AND IMAGE SOURCES OF INSPIRATION

A Narrative, Film and Script of "A Midsummer Night's Dream."

TEN KEY VOCABULARY WORDS

1. Diction, Articulation
2. Projection
3. Monotone
4. Designer
5. Ensemble
6. Tactics
7. Obstacle
8. Conflict
9. Objective
10. Technical

EQUIPMENT AND MATERIALS

- journals
- copies of text and monologues
- fabrics
- prints
- paints
- foam board
- tape

WEEK	PRE-ASSESSMENT ACTIVITY
1–4	LEARNING IN THE LANGUAGE OF THE ARTS	BUILDING A SAFE, CREATIVE SPACE

	WEEK	PRE-ASSESSMENT ACTIVITY
ENGAGE	1	In order to break the ice and separate the residency sessions from the regular school day, students learn theater games such as Zip Zap Zop, Imagining a Ball, Color Command, What Are You Doing and Telling a Lie. Students also learn tongue twisters and voice exercises that encourage them to enunciate words clearly, develop memory skills and speak effectively with timing, rhythm and fluency.
	2	Using a narrative of Shakespeare's "A Midsummer Night's Dream," we introduce the story. We focus on the personal perspectives of the characters in order to keep the text relevant. Two inquiry questions are posed: "How do you feel about performing in front of others?" and "What do ensemble members need from each other in order to perform?" Students discuss and write responses in their journals.
	3	We conduct exercises with the text memorized; encouraging ensemble, body and voice concentration, listening/direction and partnering.
	4	Students re-read for comprehension and self-selection of characters. Students are focused because they know that everyone will have a part and participate in the end product. Many of the scenes are duplicated by other classes, providing a healthy, competitive spirit between the different classrooms.
	5–9	IMMERSION IN A CONCEPTUAL QUESTION OR THEME THROUGH ART-MAKING
IMMERSE	5	We hold a mini-culminating event where the students warm-up together and then perform their pieces for the whole class, utilizing everything they have grasped from the first week to the fifth week. These performances are recorded so that the tape can be played back for the students. They will be able to hear the improvements in their voices during performance.
	6	Each class is set up as an actual theater company, with the teachers and guest artist as the directors. Staff assign both a stage manager and technical director for each class. The stage manager (SM) acts as the go-between among the actors and the directors. The technical director (TD) is the go-between among the designers and directors.
	7	After the characters are assigned, teachers create other non-performing tasks for the rest of the class. Under the supervision of the TD, any students who are not performing are split into two groups: the costume designers and the set designers. Each of these smaller groups is assigned a supervisor.

IMMERSE	8	With this structure in place, everyone in the class is responsible for a specific element of the production, as well as for the entire group as a whole. Students work in self-selected groups of actors, assistant directors, set and costume designers. They rehearse and refine scenes for the final production.
	9	The actors are guided by the SM and the teaching artist, while the designers are guided mostly by the classroom teacher and the TD. Both the SM and the TD help to keep their groups running and organized.
	10–14	REVISE, SHARE, AND REFLECT ON ART-MAKING
REFINE	10	Rehearsal: Theater, being the collaborative form that it is, forces students to challenge each other and to resolve any issues they have with one another.
	11	Rehearsal: The natural pressures of wanting to produce a quality production keeps the student on track.
	12	Final Dress Rehearsal for an audience of 2nd and 3rd-graders.
	13	Performance.
	14	Reflection: Students watch a videotape of their performance. We hold a positive critical feedback session focusing on the things the students have done well and discuss what they would do differently after this experience. They discuss and then write in their journals the answers to the two inquiry questions, as well as reflect on how drama has helped them with reading.

CULMINATING EVENTS

POST-ASSESSMENT ACTIVITY   PLANS FOR FINAL SHOWING

From the moment we decided to go with a Shakespearean text, our journey has been geared toward the culminating event. In preparation for the final performance, we invited 2nd and 3rd-graders to our dress rehearsal. Doing this gave our students a chance to feel the reactions of a live audience.

TEACHER'S REFLECTIONS

"The kids were constantly helping each other with memorizing lines, etc. I witnessed their sense of pride and positive attitude to work together. My students walked away from this project with new self-esteem as a result of performing and seeing the culminating activity. Their feelings of success came from weeks of group work, cooperation, trust and a genuine caring environment. This project was an effective method to motivate students, encourage active learning and develop critical thinking, communication and decision-making skills."

ARTIST'S REFLECTIONS

"As a product of Chicago Public Schools I have a direct connection with the culture many of my students live in. I have found, in my theatrical training, that many alternative avenues can help a student to find new ways of learning. While growing up I had difficulties with reading, and discovered in college that I have a reading disability. My interest and love for performance pushed me to improve. However, it was my Shakespeare class that taught me a new way to teach myself to read. This, in combination with my voice training for the stage, gave me new insight into grammar, punctuation, phonics and breath. It helped me to break text down to its very basic components."

STUDENTS' REFLECTIONS

"I learned from Mr. Sancho to express how you feel, and when you're acting to also express how the character feels."

"I learned how to do Shakespeare's work and understand it." "I can read louder and know more words because the script was hard. " "I see a few words that I have heard on stage and I think it's nice to tell people about them." "I learned from the artist that you need to speak clearly so the audience could hear you talk." "When I have to give oral presentations for science or social studies, I'm not as scared talking in front of the class as I used to be." "I learned how to be more responsible." "[Our teacher] is funnier. She does more things with the arts now."

ILLINOIS STATE FINE ARTS STANDARDS

GOAL #	STATE STANDARD
25.A.2b	Describe various ways the body, mind and voice are used with acting, scripting and staging processes to create or perform drama/theatre.
25.B.2	Understand how elements and principles combine within an art form to express ideas.
26.B.2b	Demonstrate actions, characters, narrative skills, collaboration, environments, simple staging and sequence of events and situations in solo and ensemble dramas.
27.B.2	Identify and describe how the arts communicate the similarities and differences among various people, places and times.

ILLINOIS STATE CORE CURRICULUM STANDARDS

GOAL #	STATE STANDARD
1.A.3b	Analyze the meaning of words and phrases in their context.
2.A.3a	Identify and analyze a variety of literary techniques within classical and contemporary works representing a variety of genres.
4.A.3b	Compare a speaker's verbal and nonverbal messages.
4.A.3d	Demonstrate the ability to identify and manage barriers to listening.

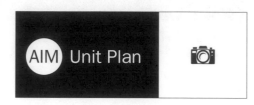

AIM Unit Plan

PROJECT TITLE	# What happens when we look more closely?: Photography, Poetry, and Botany
TEACHERS	Ms. Alcala, Ms. Escobar, Ms. Torres
ARTIST	Deborah Guzmán-Meyer, Julie A. Downey
SCHOOL	Albert R. Sabin Magnet School
GRADE	5th
ART FORMS(S)	Photography and Poetry
LENGTH OF PROJECT	14 weeks

THE FOCUS OF THE PROJECT

Students become explorers of botany, using photography and writing skills to document primary research of an individual plant and its environment. Arts lessons in preparation for field study at the Garfield Park Conservatory reinforce fifth grade science units such as "Comparing Living Things," inherited traits and adaptation, and photosynthesis. Students write about how it feels to be photographed, and sensory observations of botanical subjects. They also interview families about their relationship to plants and place, food and memory.

INQUIRY QUESTIONS FOR TEACHERS AND ARTISTS

What do we learn from looking closely at the world around us? What is the difference between writing from something that is right in front of you, to writing from a photograph or a memory?

> "...There is work to do. There is light to make... Be aware. Be awake. Be resistant. Be your ancestors. Be your future. Be alive. Be alive."
>
> – Suheir Hammad

PRE/POST ASSESSMENT ACTIVITY FOR STUDENTS

PRE: Students respond to the following questions in their journals, "What is the difference between writing about something that is in front of you or that is in a book?" and "What do you know about where your parents grew up?" POST: Students respond to the questions, "How did photography and creative writing help you learn about your plant?" and "What do you now know about photography and/or writing that you didn't know before?"

PRE/POST ASSESSMENT ACTIVITY FOR STUDENTS

- **PHOTOGRAPHY:** Terry Evans, Museum of Contemporary Photography. Adobe Digital Kids Clubs
- **SCIENCE:** Brooklyn Botanic Garden. Garfield Park Conservatory. RD Home Handbooks, House Plants, Ed Brookes. Ciencias, Science, 5th grade science book in English and Spanish, by Foresman
- **PROSE:** La Familia by Garcia, "For Dinner/Para la cena." by Ligon: "Runaways." Lithographs, 1993
- **POETRY:** "La luna, un platano" Morfín; "The Moon, a Banana" Islante. "Lifting Lava" Downey. "Adaptación" and "Adaptation" Guzmán Meyer. "Street Poems" Froman. "Poetry at Play" Burg. "Seeing Things" Froman. "Flicker Flash" Graham. "Snake Date" Balderston, "A Weak Poem" McGough

TEN KEY VOCABULARY WORDS

1. Inherited
2. Conservatory
3. Photosynthesis
4. Composition
5. Botany
6. Climate
7. Simile
8. Bellows
9. Environment
10. Species, Genus, Family

EQUIPMENT AND MATERIALS

- digital cameras, batteries, memory sticks
- firewire cords
- computer with photo editing and layout software, firewire port
- photo quality printer, ink, and paper
- construction paper
- hole punch
- 12" x 12" cardstock
- string or yarn
- clothesline
- wooden clothespins
- live flowering plants (Gardenia).

	WEEK	PRE-ASSESSMENT ACTIVITY
	1–4	LEARNING IN THE LANGUAGE OF THE ARTS I BUILDING A SAFE, CREATIVE SPACE
ENGAGE	1	Family, Language, Food, and Culture: Students write a memory related to gardening, cooking, eating, or a plant. Students read their work and discuss language of family. Read "Picking Cactus" by Carmen Garcia. Students are also photographed in a chair with a white background.
	2	Near and Far/Before and After: Students write how it feels to be photographed. Students view a plant and use frames to observe close up and far away views.
	3	Parts and Whole: Students learn about cause/effect and parts/process. Discuss the origins of names and link to science discussion of genus/species/plant names. Plan for interviews with parents and their connection to a plant from country of origin.
	4	Time and Place: Students view Terry Evans' aerial photographs of Chicago taken from a hot air balloon. Students write about the familiar and unfamiliar, experimenting with similes and metaphor in writing. The focus is on perspective-taking in writing and photography. Students read Martin Espada's poems and write poetry in response to questions of time and place.
	5–9	IMMERSION IN A CONCEPTUAL QUESTION OR THEME THROUGH ART-MAKING
IMMERSE	5	Location: Students take a walk around the neighborhood and get acquainted with foliage. Students take photographs of their surroundings. Students write a postcard to someone not yet born describing their present locations. Students discuss their parents' countries of origin.
	6	Preparation and Process, Making Choices and Editing: Prepare for trip to Garfield Park Conservatory. Students view their photographs of the area and make selections for their postcards.
	7	Garfield Park Conservatory Field Trip: Students take photographs of plants found in parents' country of origin. Students write about their plants and their experience at the conservatory.
	8	Making Choices/Editing: Students view contact sheets of images from field trip. Students select three photographs and write about why they like them. Introduce students to Liz Lerman Critical Response by selecting 5 photographs for review.
	8	Metaphor: Students paste three photographs on white board and view botanical samples. Students write about their photographs and explain the parts using metaphor as a main poetic element.

10–14	REVISE, SHARE, AND REFLECT ON ART-MAKING

<table>
<tr><td rowspan="5">REFINE</td><td>10</td><td>Art Promotion: What is an Art Show? Students create ideas for a public program and decide on whom to invite to the show. Students plan snacks and venue.</td></tr>
<tr><td>11</td><td>Principles of Design and Layout: Teaching artists give several sizes of the same image and students cut and paste their botanical samples. Students create a program for the Sabin Art Show. Create Invitations.</td></tr>
<tr><td>12</td><td>Design Trends/Time and Place: Students view designs from various decades in the United States and in other countries. They finalize layouts and send invitations to their guests (or hand deliver) for the upcoming gallery opening event.</td></tr>
<tr><td>13</td><td>Why are Art Shows Important? Students prepare for the Text and Image show called "Talkin' Back." They view images from other students' in previous years and troubleshoot the final work. The class discusses the process of creating a show and hanging work; they decide what should go where and select final pieces.</td></tr>
<tr><td>14</td><td>Show and Tell: Gallery opening event at the school, during which they promote the Talkin' Back show at the Museum of Contemporary Photography. Students greet guests and serve snacks. They explain the project to attendees and document the event. Each student has a job for this event.</td></tr>
</table>

CULMINATING EVENTS	POST-ASSESSMENT ACTIVITY	PLANS FOR FINAL SHOWING
	We created a gallery exhibit and hosted a gallery opening event at the school for peers, family, and friends.	

TEACHER'S REFLECTIONS

"I believe students in room 301 had a wonderful experience. They enjoyed learning how to use the camera. They had a lot of fun. In writing, they were able to understand how to get details to help them to describe in their writing."

"Throughout the entire process, the students were engaged and worked cooperatively with the camera equipment, and their peers. The final product displays their excellent artistic work and will be an unforgettable experience."

"The whole experience was amazing because we were able to connect photography with science, as well as being able to research the plant to get information on the genus, species, family, etc."

ARTIST'S REFLECTIONS

"This project inserts photography and creative writing into a science learning experience and it transforms it by giving each individual child different tools for learning, and making them the authors of their own learning materials. We are creating a more layered way of learning, placing the child in the center of their own learning experience through, researching, photographing and investigating."

STUDENTS' REFLECTIONS

"Photography and writing helped me learn more about my plant by showing me the texture, and showing me more info about my plant."

"I like the toolbox we did. I really had some fun with it. I like the comparing part. I really liked it, especially when we had to draw our plant in words."

"I did not know how to focus on things. When I took a picture I did not care about the background. Now I do care."

"I liked that we got to do something very creative and fun. Something that we can keep for always."

"You were able to actually go on a fieldtrip and go to the conservatory, and write, and take pictures of different plants."

ILLINOIS STATE FINE ARTS STANDARDS

GOAL #	STATE STANDARD
25.A.3d	Identify and describe the elements of value, perspectve and color schemes; the principles of contrast, emphasis and unity; and the expressive qualities of thematic development and sequence.
26.A.2e	Describe the relationships among media, tools/technology and processes.
26.A.2f	Understand the artistic processes of printmaking, weaving, photography and sculpture.

ILLINOIS STATE CORE CURRICULUM STANDARDS

GOAL #	STATE STANDARD
12.A.2a	Describe simple life cycles of plants and animals and the similarities and differences in their offspring.
11.A.3c	Collect and record data accurately using consistent measuring and recording techniques and media.
12.B.2b	Identify physical features of plants and animals that help them live in different environments.
13.A.3c	Explain what is similar and different about observational and experimental investigations.

Epilogue
DIALOGUES AND DEBATES

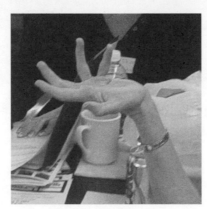
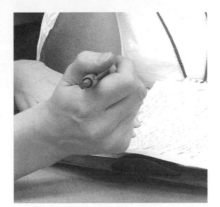

Epilogue

DIALOGUES AND DEBATES

Cynthia Weiss and
Amanda Leigh Lichtenstein

We've come to the end of our book, and in a way, the end of our spiral, where we are discovering new intentions for this work. Ending this book is also a beginning, a chance to renew and ignite conversations that will inform our practice and bring us closer to one another in a collective mission to awaken future generations. Even as we write and edit this collection of essays and artifacts, the landscape of arts integration changes and shifts to raise new questions and issues. If we know anything at all, it's that this work is complex and layered, political and spiritual, pedagogically significant and in many ways an ethical obligation to young people. At the close of this book, we are left with as many questions as answers:

- What happens when teachers and artists look at their work from a researcher's lens?
- How does learning in specific art forms impact literacy?
- How do we continue to engage reluctant learners through the arts?
- What are we learning about the use of documentation as assessment?
- How can we improve our understanding of assessment and evaluation in the arts by sharing tools, instruments and ideas across programs?
- How does looking closely at student work affect our pedagogy and our art-making?
- What is the kind of training and institutional support needed to provide teaching artists with a respectable living wage?
- Are we creating a new genre of art-making with students?
- In what ways do teaching artists influence the aesthetics of their students' final products?
- In what ways do students affect the studio aesthetics of teaching artists?
- What are the specific benefits and challenges of the arts at each developmental stage?
- How do arts partnerships contribute to whole school change?
- What are sustainable infrastructures to insure that the work continues when the artists and/or funding leaves?

- How do we demonstrate the power of arts integration to parents?
- What role does the imagination play in affecting social change?
- How can we continue to use the arts to promote understanding and empathy across race, religion, class, gender and culture?
- How do the arts democratize schools and communities?
- In what ways is a teaching artist an agent of change?
- How do the arts invite students to discover their own agency in the world?
- How do arts organizations, school systems and funders work together to ensure the continuity of funding for arts integration?

As we end our book, one particular student comes to mind: Porsha, the student mentioned in Tricia Hersey's essay, "The Connection." Porsha, now an eighth-grader, is about to graduate from Crown Community Academy. Porsha has had the opportunity to work with Project AIM writers Tricia Hersey, avery r. young, Cynthium Johnson-Woodfolk, and Amanda Leigh Lichtenstein.

Recently, Porsha was one of the stars in a Project AIM multimedia installation/spoken word performance called "The Algebra of Awareness: Coming of Age in the Age of AIDS." Porsha clearly stole the show with her fierce writing and her equally fierce performance when she personified "AIDS" in a raging piece called "Dear Body." Her forceful presentation style took our breath away.

When asked about her experience with Project AIM, she explained, "I've worked for four years [with different writers]. I've always liked writing…but it's only now that I'm ready to speak my truth."

At the close of this book, we ask ourselves and you, our readers: How do we continue to inspire our students and ourselves to speak our truths?

Appendix

Building An Assessment Matrix

AS A BLUEPRINT FOR PROGRAM IMPLEMENTATION AND EVALUATION

Dr. Barbara A. Holland

U.S. DEPARTMENT OF EDUCATION'S
FUND FOR THE IMPROVEMENT OF POSTSECONDARY EDUCATION (FIPSE)
PROJECT AIM EVALUATOR

(Excerpt from Barbara Holland's 2006 FIPSE/Project AIM Final Evaluation Report)

The Project AIM evaluation process was guided by a planning matrix created by the project team during the first year of the grant. The collaborative process of building the matrix also served in an unexpected way to help focus and organize implementation of the core components of the overall program. In the matrix, the team identified major evaluation goals and then developed core concepts and measurable or observable indicators for each concept. These matrices guided the design and selection of evaluation instruments as well as the analysis and presentation of findings.

This carefully designed process for organizing and implementing evaluation activities ensured a complete examination of all dimensions of the program's objectives. Our attention to the collection of impact data was comprehensive and inclusive. Teachers completed evaluative exit slips at every professional development event, Teacher Artists (TAs) provided samples of their teaching journals and lesson plans, and participated in an annual focus group with the external evaluator. Principals participated in either focus groups or interviews. School students were asked to complete a brief survey at the end of the TA's project unit. Most valuable of all, perhaps, has been the investment in systematic and direct observation of TAs, teachers and school students working together in classrooms. Unlike other program evaluation models that rely largely on self-reported data from each of these participant groups, observational data provided direct evidence of the actual interactions, experiences and impacts of project activities on participants. Therefore, each year's evaluation report became a valuable guide for program improvement and helped to shape the next year's program strategies.

In this final year of the FIPSE grant, we found that this careful approach to linking evaluation to program improvement provided a rich and deep understanding of the key ingredients essential to a quality arts integration partnership between Columbia College Chicago and the partner schools. Though some challenges remain (learning never ends!), the thorough attention to evaluation continues to indicate areas for improvement and enrichment of program strategies and outcomes, especially and ultimately for student learning improvement.

Editor's Note Cynthia Weiss

The Project AIM assessment matrix was an invaluable tool that served as a blueprint to create, refine and evaluate our program. Barbara Holland gracefully guided the Project AIM team to create the matrix through days of careful consensus building and discussion in the fall of 2003. That participating team included; Julie Simpson, Joanne Vena, April Langworthy, Sadira Muhammad, Lisa Hutler and Cynthia Weiss.

The clear objectives described in the following were a touchstone that helped us keep our vision consistent and coherent. This assessment matrix in turn informed the creation of our program's current Logic Model and has insured a meaningful continuity of Project AIM beyond the FIPSE grant. We highly recommend that new projects adapt a similar planning process where program staff, stakeholders and evaluators come together to define priorities and name the hopes and dreams of an emerging program.

Project AIM/FIPSE Assessment Matrix

1 | Assessment Matrix

Goal: to establish sustainable partnership infrastructures at targeted Chicago Public Schools, guided by a Steering Committee at each school

CONCEPTS *What do we want to know?*	INDICATORS *How will we know it?*	METHOD	SOURCE	TIMING
Relationships between College and School	college faculty/reps meet regularly with school team and individuals	Artifacts, Meetings, Calendars	CCAP	Ongoing
	school staff is aware of college resources and opportunities	Focus Group & Interviews	School Teachers & Principals	End of Year
Systems and Plans for AIM Applications/ Growth	classroom schedules accommodate arts integration strategies	Artifacts	School	End of Year
	teachers use planning time to develop AIM curriculum	Reflections	Teachers	End of Year
	administrators incorporate the use of AIM model in overarching school plans	Artifacts & Interviews	Principals	End of Year
	principals articulate expectations for teachers to integrate the AIM model	Interviews, Focus Groups & Artifacts	Principals	End of Year
	AIM artists/staff facilitate teacher's capacity to plan and implement arts integrated curriculum	Journals, Reflections & Focus Groups	Artists	End of Year
Leadership Density	teachers model strategy and process of AIM for other teachers	Exit Slips, Curriculum Fair	Teachers	Year Two
	teacher/leaders acting as leaders of steering committee and/or grade /content area meetings projects	Meetings & Observation	Teachers	Ongoing
	principals articulate value and importance of AIM programming	Interviews	Principals	End of year
Resource Development	school plans include continued support for artists in the classroom	Artifacts	Schools SIPAAA	Annually
	teachers/arts specialists partner to develop arts-integrated curriculum	Focus Groups, Artifacts, Notes, Agendas	Teacher	Ongoing
	CCC departments engage in planning for cultural school partnerships	Notes, Photos, Agendas, Observation	Departmental Staff	Ongoing

2 | Assessment Matrix

Goal: to train Columbia College Chicago (CCC) faculty and teaching artists to deliver arts-integrated programming to elementary students

CONCEPTS *What do we want to know?*	INDICATORS *How will we know it?*	METHOD	SOURCE	TIMING
CCC Teaching Practice	Faculty/AIM teaching artists use AIM strategies in CCC courses	Focus Groups & Artifacts	Faculty & Artists	Annual
	AIM faculty collaborates across departments and disciplines	Meetings & Focus Groups	Faculty & Artists	Annual
	AIM faculty integrate student learning outcomes to include community-based learning in planning, delivery & assessment	Meetings & Focus Groups	Faculty & Artists	Annual
CCC Artists teaching to CPS students	teaching artists adapt their specific art form to meet the needs of CPS students & teachers	Journals, Focus Groups & Reflections	Artists & Teachers	Annual
	teaching artists extend the delivery of their art form to promote student literacy	Journals, End Of Year Reflections, Lesson Plans, Vocabulary	Artists & Teachers	Annual
	teaching artists use their art forms to promote engaged learning	Journals, Observations & Reflections	Artists & Teachers	Annual
CCC Faculty Professional Responsibility	AIM artists and departmental representatives plan, lead & initiate project @ CPS & CCC sites which partner with CCAP resources	Journals, Focus Groups & Reflections	Artists, Teachers, Departments, Interviews	Annual
	Departmental representative participate in CCAP sponsored workshops	Artifacts & Meetings	CCAP	Ongoing
Teaching Artist Attitudes	respect for public education and challenges school teachers face	Journals, Focus Groups & Reflections	Artists & Teachers	Annual
	artists believe they function as change agents for classroom teaching	Journals, Focus Groups & Reflections	Artists & Teachers	Annual
Curriculum	teaching artists create curriculum that utilizes arts process to engagement in the reading/writing process (parallel processes)	Artifacts & Observation	Schools & Teachers	Annual
	teaching artists incorporate key concepts in art making with key concepts in CPS core curriculum	Journals, Focus Groups & Reflections	Artists & Teachers	Annual
	teachers and artist collaborate to create arts and teach integrated curriculum	Journals, Focus Groups & Reflections	Artists & Teachers	Annual

3 | Assessment Matrix

Goal: to enhance student engagement and achievement in learning

CONCEPTS *What do we want to know?*	INDICATORS *How will we know it?*	METHOD	SOURCE	TIMING
Student Engagement	students participate in class discussions	Observation, Journals, Focus Groups & Reflections	Teachers & Artists	Ongoing
	students are physically engaged in the lesson and their own learning process (ref. TAJ)	Observation, Journals, Focus Groups & Reflections	Teachers & Artists	Ongoing
	students are actively involved in their own learning by engaging in decision-making processes (ref. TAJ)	Observation, Journals, Focus Groups & Reflections	Teachers & Artists	Ongoing
	students interact in ways that promote peer learning	Observation, Journals, Focus Groups & Reflections	Teachers & Artists	Ongoing
Student Achievement	students articulate new understanding of arts concepts	Artifacts & Observation	Students	Ongoing
	students demonstrate reading comprehension	Artifacts & Observation	Students	Ongoing
	students are fluent readers/writers	Artifacts & Observation	Students	Ongoing
	students have command of arts and subject area vocabulary	Artifacts & Observation	Students	Ongoing

4 | Assessment Matrix

Goal: for professional development in arts education
for CPS teachers and administrators

CONCEPTS *What do we want to know?*	INDICATORS *How will we know it?*	METHOD	SOURCE	TIMING
Curriculum Development	teachers/school arts specialists partner to develop arts-integrated curriculum	Focus Groups & Artifacts	School	Annually
	lessons incorporate arts-integrated engagement strategies	Artifacts	School	Annually
(IMPACT ON) Teachers & Attitudes	teachers advocate for arts in the classroom	Focus Groups, Reflections & Interviews	Teachers, Principals	Annually
	teachers view their role in the classroom in a different way	Reflections & Focus Groups	Teachers	Ongoing
	teachers/specialists view each other as partners	Reflections & Focus Groups	Teachers	Ongoing
	teachers view students active engagement as a essential part of the teaching/learning process	Observation, Reflections & Focus Groups	Teachers, Artists	Annually

5 | Assessment Matrix

Goal: to involve national and local responders as an advisory committee to aid with both
local implementation and national dissemination of the training model

CONCEPTS *What do we want to know?*	INDICATORS *How will we know it?*	METHOD	SOURCE	TIMING
Inform the Field	internal (CCC), local and national organization and individuals will be aware of the AIM model	Artifacts & Observation	Logs, Inquiry, Meetings, Websites, Publications, Curriculum Fair And Exhibit	Year Two
	best practices for AIM will be presented and discussed at AEP, NAE, FIPSE, ASCD			
Planning for Year III	created curriculum materials, website, video, power point presentations	Artifacts & Observation	Logs, Inquiry, Meetings, Websites & Publications	Year Three
	articles will be written for publication in education journals			

UNIT PLAN TITLE

TEACHER(S)

ARTIST(S)

SCHOOL

GRADE

ART FORM(S)

OVERVIEW & BIG IDEAS FOR UNIT

GUIDING QUESTIONS FOR UNIT

INTENTIONS FOR TEACHING & LEARNING As a result of this unit, what do you want your students to know and be able to do in the following areas?

ART FORM(S) AND PROCESS:

ACADEMIC CONTENT AREA(S):

SOCIAL/EMOTIONAL DEVELOPMENT:

TEXT & IMAGE SOURCES OF INSPIRATION

TEN KEY VOCABULARY WORDS

1)
2)
3)
4)
5)
6)
7)
8)
9)
10)

EQUIPMENT & MATERIALS

unit plan **AIM**

PRE-ASSESSMENT ACTIVITIES FOR STUDENTS

PLANS FOR DOCUMENTATION

☐ journals ☐ photos ☐ audio ☐ video ☐ exit slips ☐ _____
other

WEEK	CREATE A SAFE COMMUNITY OF LEARNERS	LEARNING IN THE LANGUAGE OF THE ARTS

ENGAGE

1

2

3

4

WEEK	IMMERSION IN THE BIG IDEAS

IMMERSE

5

6

7

8

WEEK	REVISE & SHARE	PERFORM & EXHIBIT	REFLECT & ASSESS
9			
10			
11			
12			
13			

REFINE

DESCRIPTION OF CULMINATING EVENT(S)

POST–ASSESSMENT ACTIVITIES FOR STUDENTS

TEACHER'S REFLECTIONS

ARTIST'S REFLECTIONS

STUDENTS' REFLECTIONS

ILLINOIS STATE FINE ARTS STANDARDS

state standard/goal #	state standard/goal #	state standard/goal #	state standard/goal #

ILLINOIS STATE CORE CURRICULUM STANDARDS

state standard/goal #	state standard/goal #	state standard/goal #	state standard/goal #

PROJECT TITLE

ARTIST

ART FORM

CONTEXT

DESCRIPTION

CHALLENGES

VARIATIONS

DESIGNING CURRICULUM THROUGH

Big
Ideas

1. What is the Big Idea you would like to use to organize your teaching?

2. Why is this idea important?

3. How can this Big Idea help your students make personal connections and to connect concepts across subject areas?

4. What are the essential questons you have about this Big Idea?

Big Idea Concept Web

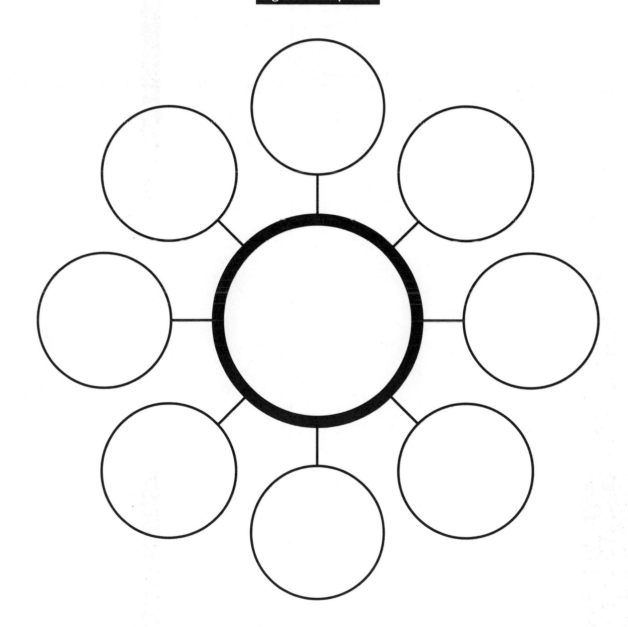

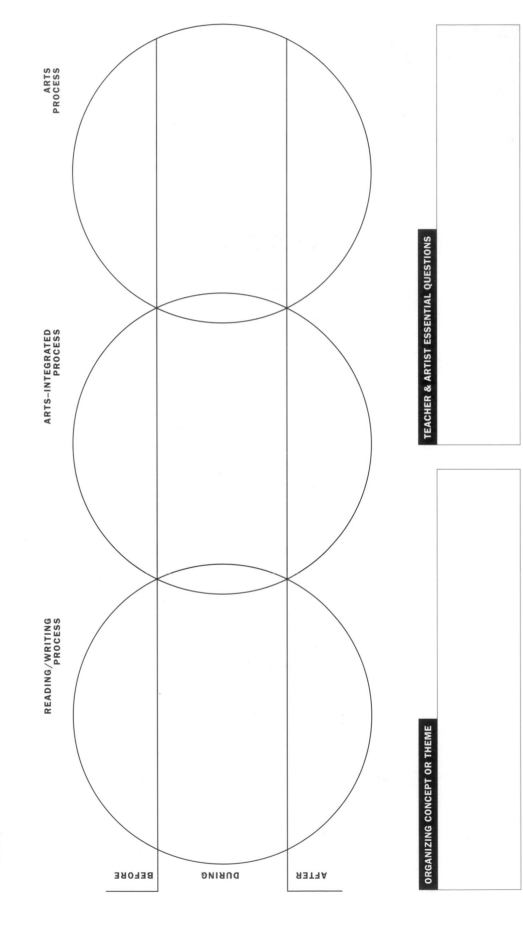

AIM ARTS INTEGRATION MENTORSHIP

parallel processes

READING/WRITING PROCESS

ARTS–INTEGRATED PROCESS

ARTS PROCESS

BEFORE

DURING

AFTER

TEACHER & ARTIST ESSENTIAL QUESTIONS

ORGANIZING CONCEPT OR THEME

ADAPTED BY CYNTHIA WEISS, LYNETTE EMMONS, AMANDA LICHTENSTEIN, AND DR. DR. GAIL BURNAFORD, FROM RENAISSANCE IN THE CLASSROOM: ARTS INTEGRATION AND MEANINGFUL LEARNING. EDITED BY GAIL BURNAFORD, ARNOLD APRILL, AND CYNTHIA WEISS. NEW YORK, NY: TAYLOR & FRANCIS GROUP, LLC (FORMERLY LAWRENCE ERLBAUM), 2001.

Parallel Processes across Reading, Writing, and the Arts

WRITING PROCESS	VISUAL ART MAKING PROCESS	READING PROCESS
Before Writing • Reading high-quality writing • Making personal connections • Finding Voice • Oral Storytelling	**Before Art-Making** • Reading high-quality artwork • Making personal connections • Finding Voice & perspective • Observation	**Before Reading** • Reading high-quality writing • Making personal connections • Finding Author's Voice & perspective • Activating Prior Knowledge
During Writing • Visualization–Seeing in the minds' eye • Brainstorming ideas • Recording in journals • Writing first drafts • Researching information • Sharing writing with peers • Comparing drafts with Intentions • Revising & refining • Improvisation • Writing second drafts • Complete writing	**During Art-Making** • Visualization–Seeing in the minds' eye • Gathering images • Recording in sketchbooks • Making rough sketches, create storyboards • Researching visual information • Sharing sketches with peers • Comparing rough sketches with Intentions • Revising & refining • Improvisation • Adding details, color, background, etc. • Complete art work	**During Reading** • Visualization–Seeing in the mind's eye • Entering Text as active Reader • Recording in journal/literature log • Making connections, asking questions, altering predictions • Researching information-Add known to the unknown • Sharing reading/Partner reading • Responding to questions/ predictions/connections • Re-reading for clarity & purpose • Entering the story world, imagining • Making inferences • Complete text or book
After Writing • Publishing • Sharing work with an audience • Reflecting and Assessing work • Deepening personal connections	**After Art-Making** • Exhibiting • Sharing work with an audience • Reflecting and Assessing work • Deepening personal connections	**After Reading** • Discussing book with others (Literature Circles, Book Talk) • Retelling story • Reflecting and Assessing work • Deepening personal connections

Bibliography, Resources, Links

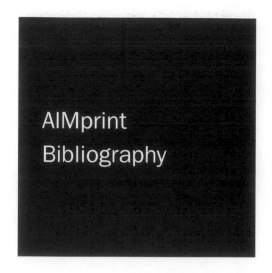

AIMprint
Bibliography

Albers, Randall K. *"No More Lip Service: Voice as Empowerment in a Story Workshop Composition Class."* Charleston, SC: NCTE Presentation, 1989.

Atwell, Nancy. *In the Middle: Writing, Reading, and Learning with Adolescents.* Portsmouth: Boynton/Cook, 1998.

Ayers, W., Klonsky, M.m & Lyon G. (Eds.). *A Simple Justice: The Challenge of Small Schools.* New York: Teachers College Press, 2000.

Baraka, Amiri. *"Dutchman."* Cherry Lane Theatre, New York. 1964. William Morrow & Company, 1976.

Booth, Eric. *"Expanding the Range of Essential Skills of 21st Century Artists."* The Creative Campus: The Training, Sustaining, and Preserving of the Performing Arts in American Higher Education. New York, NY: American Assembly, 2004.

Burnaford, Gail, Arnold Aprill, and Cynthia Weiss. Eds. *Renaissance in the Classroom: Arts Integration and Meaningful Learning.* New York, NY: Taylor & Francis Group, LLC (formerly Lawrence Erlbaum), 2001.

Brzoska, Deborah. *"Designing Arts-Centered Interdisciplinary Curriculum."* Professional Development Opportunities for Teachers. Washington, DC: The Kennedy Center, 2000.

Catterall, James S. *"The Arts and the Transfer of Learning."* Critical Links: Learning in the Arts and Student Academic and Social Development. Ed. Richard J. Deasy. Washington, DC: Arts Education Partnership, 2002.

Clyde, Jean Anne. *"Stepping Inside the Story World: The Subtext Strategy—A tool for connecting and comprehending International Reading Association"* (2003). *Beyond Reading and Writing: Inquiry, Curriculum, and Multiple Ways of Knowing,* 2000.

Deasy, Richard J., and Lauren Stevenson. *Third Space: When Learning Matters.* Washington, DC: Arts Education Partnership, 2005.

Delillo, Don. *The Body Artist.* New York: Scribner, 2001.

Dunbar, Paul Laurence. *"We Wear The Mask." Lyrics of Lowly Life.* New York, NY: Dodd, Mead, and Company, 1896.

Eisner, Elliot. *The Arts and the Creation of Mind.* New Haven, CT: Yale University Press, 2002.

Eisner, Elliot. *The Kind of Schools We Need: Personal Essays.* Portsmouth, NH: Heinemann, 1998.

Erickson, H. Lynn. *Concept-Based Curriculum and Instruction: Teaching Beyond the Facts.* Thousands Oaks, CA: Corwin Press, 2002.

Erickson, H. Lynn. *Stirring the Head, Heart, and Soul: Redefining Curriculum and Instruction.* Thousands Oaks, CA: Corwin Press, 2000.

Freire, Paulo. *Pedagogy of the Oppressed.* New York, NY: Continuum Books, 1993.

Greene, Maxine. *Releasing the Imagination: Essays on Education, the Arts, and Social Change.* San Francisco, CA: Jossey-Bass, 1995.

Hindley, Joanne. *In the Company of Children.* Stenhouse Publishers: York, Maine, 1996.

Hughes, Langston. *"Theme from English B."* 1949.

Jensen, Eric. *Arts with the Brain in Mind.* Alexandria, VA: ASCD, 2000.

Kozol, Jonathan. *The Shame of the Nation: The Restoration of Apartheid Schooling in America.* New York, NY: Crown, 2005.

Labov, William. *Language in the Inner City: Studies in the Black English Vernacular.* Philadelphia, PA: University of Pennsylvania Press, 1972.

Lee, Harper. *To Kill a Mockingbird* (reissue edition). Lebanon, IN: Warner Books, 1988.

Lerman, Liz, and John Borstel. *Critical Response Process: A Method for Getting Useful Feedback On Anything You Make, from Dance to Dessert.* Takoma Park, MD: Liz Lerman Dance Exchange, 2003.

Livingston, Jane. *The Art of Richard Diebenkorn,* Whitney Museum of Art in association with University of California Press: Berkeley, 1997.

Perry, Theresa, and Delpit, Lisa D. *The Real Ebonics Debate: Power, Language, and the Education of African American Children.* Boston, MA: Beacon Press, 1998.

Pinar, William F. *What is Curriculum Theory?* Lawrence Erlbaum Publishers, Mahwah, NJ, 2004.

Putnam, Robert. *Bowling Alone: The Collapse and Revival of American Community.* New York, NY: Simon & Schuster, 2000.

Rabkin, Nick, and Robin Redmond. Eds. *Putting Arts in the Picture: Reframing Education in the 21st Century.* Chicago, IL: Columbia College Chicago, 2004.

Seuss, Dr. *Green Eggs and Ham.* New York, NY: Random House, 1960.

Smith, Ralph. *"Aesthetic Education: Questions and Issues."* Arts Education Policy Review, vol. 106, no. 3 (Jan/Feb 2005): 19-34.

Solnit, Rebecca. *Wanderlust: A History of Walking.* New York, NY: Viking Penguin, 2001.

Wilheim, Jeffrey D. *You Gotta Be the Book: Teaching Engaged and Reflective Reading With Adolescents.* New York, NY: Teachers College Press, 1997.

Zemelman, Daniels, and Hyde. *Best Practice Today's Standards for Teaching and Learning in America's Schools-Heinemann Portsmouth,* New Hampshire 2005 (p. 283).

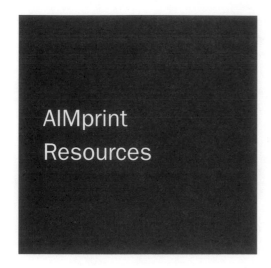

AIMprint
Resources

Ayers, William. *To Teach.* New York: Teachers College Press, 2001.

Bizar, Marilyn, and Harvey Daniels. *Methods That Matter: Six Structures for Best Practice Classrooms.* York, ME: Stenhouse Publishers, 1998.

Blecher, Sharon, and Kathy Jaffee. *Weaving in the Arts: Widening the Learning Circle.* Portsmouth, NH: Heinemann, 1998.

Booth, Eric. *"Expanding the Range of Essential Skills of 21st Century Artists." The Creative Campus: The Training, Sustaining, and Preserving of the Performing Arts in American Higher Education.* New York, NY: American Assembly, 2004.

Campbell, Dorothy, and Linda Harris. *Collaborative Theme Building: How Teachers Write Integrated Curriculum.* Upper Saddle River, NJ: Pearson Allyn & Bacon, 2000.

Catterall, James S. *"The Arts and the Transfer of Learning."* Critical Links: Learning in the Arts and Student Academic and Social Development. Ed. Richard J. Deasy. Washington, DC: Arts Education Partnership, 2002.

Clark, Edward. *Designing & Implementing an Integrated Curriculum: A Student-Centered Approach.* Brandon, VT: Holistic Education Press, 1996.

Cleveland, William. *Art in Other Places: Artists at Work in America's Community and Social Institutions.* Amherst, MA: Arts Extension Service Press, 2000.

Community Arts Partnership Consortium. *Art/Vision/Voice.* Columbia College Chicago and Maryland Institute College of Art, 2006.

Cooper, Mark. M*aking Art Together: How Collaborative Art-Making Can Transform Kids, Classrooms, and Communities.* Boston, MA: Beacon Press, 2006.

Corbett, H. Dickson, Belinda Williams, and Bruce L. Wilson. *Effort and Excellence in Urban Classrooms: Expecting, and Getting, Success With All Students.* New York, NY: Teachers College Press, 2002.

Cornett, Claudia. *Creating Meaning Through Literature and the Arts: An Integration Resource for Classroom Teachers (3rd ed.).* Upper Saddle River, NJ: Pearson Education, 2007.

Csikszentmihalyi, Mihaly. *Flow: The Psychology of Optimal Experience.* New York, NY: Harper, 1990.

Drake, Susan. *Creating Integrated Curriculum: Proven Ways to Increase Student Learning.* Thousand Oaks, CA: Corwin Press, 1998.

Edwards, Carolyn, Lella Gandini, and George Forman, eds. *The Hundred Languages of Children: The Reggio Emilia Approach—Advanced Reflections.* Westport, CT: Ablex Publishing, 1998.

Finberg, Carol. *Creating Islands of Excellence: Arts Education as a Partner in School Reform.* Portsmouth, NH: Heinemann, 2004.

Flynn, Robert, and Eugene McKinney. *Paul Baker and the Integration of Abilities.* Fort Worth, TX: Texas Christian University Press, 2003.

Freeman, Carol, Karen R. Seashore, and Linnette Werner. *"Models of Implementing Arts for Academic Achievement: Challenging Contemporary Classroom Practice."* Center for Applied Research and Educational Improvement: University of Minnesota, 2003.

Freire, Paulo. *Teachers as Cultural Workers: Letters to Those Who Dare Teach (Expanded edition).* Boulder, CO: Westview Press, 2006.

Gablik, Suzi. *The Reenchantment of Art.* London: Thames & Hudson, 1992.

Gardner, Howard. *Frames of Mind: The Theory of Multiple Intelligences.* New York, NY: Basic Books, 1985.

Gardner, Howard. *The Unschooled Mind: How Children Think and How Schools Should Teach.* New York, NY: Basic Books, 1993.

Gelmon, Sherril, Barbara Holland, Amy Driscoll, Amy Spring, and Seanna Kerrigan. *Assessing Service-Learning and Civic Engagement: Principles and Techniques.* Providence, RI: Campus Compact, Brown University, 2001.

Goudvis, Anne, and Stephanie Harvey. *Strategies That Work: Teaching Comprehension to Enhance Understanding.* York, ME: Stenhouse Publishers, 2000.

Henna, Judith Lynne. *"In My Opinion: The Teaching Artist's Armament."* Teaching Artist Journal, vol. 2, no. 2 (2004): 104-106.

Heath, Shirley Brice, and Adelma Roach. *"Imaginative Actuality: Learning in the Arts During the Non-School Hours."* Champions of Change. Carnegie Foundation for the Advancement of Teaching, 1996.

Hetland, Lois, Ellen Winner, Shirley Veenema, and Kimberly M. Sheridan. *Studio Thinking: The Real Benefits of Visual Arts Education.* Teachers College Press: New York, NY, 2007.

Hooks, Bell. *Teaching to Transgress.* New York, NY: Routledge, 1994.

Jacobs, Heidi Hayes. *Mapping the Big Picture: Integrating Curriculum & Assessment.* Association for Supervision and Curriculum Development, 1997.

Kaprow, Allan. *The Blurring of Art and Life.* Berkeley, CA: University of California Press, 1992.

Labov, William. *Language in the Inner City: Studies in the Black English Vernacular.* Philadelphia, PA: University of Pennsylvania Press, 1972.

Larson, Renya. *"Training in the Teaching Arts: A Study from the Paul A. Kaplan Center for Educational Drama."* Teaching Artist Journal, vol. 1 (2004): 12-19.

Lauritzen, Phyllis, and Nancy Lee Cecil. *Literacy and the Arts for the Integrated Classroom: Alternative Ways of Knowing.* White Plains, NY: Logman, 1994.

Lerman, Liz. *"Art and Community: Feeding the Artist, Feeding the Art."* Community, Culture and Globalization, ed. Don Adams and Arlene Goldbard. New York, NY: Rockefeller Foundation, 2002.

Lindsley, Elizabeth. *"Teaching Artist as Teacher Trainer."* Teaching Artist Journal, vol. 4, no. 1 (2006).

Lippard, Lucy. *Public Art: Old and New Clothes.* New York, NY: The New Press, 1997.

McClaren, Peter. *"Critical Pedagogy: A Look at the Major Concepts." Critical Multiculturalism: Uncommon Voices in a Common Struggle.* Westport, CT: Greenwood Publishing, 1995.

Nachmanovitch, Stephen. *Free Play: Improvisation in Life and Art.* New York, NY: Putnam, 1990.

Oreck, Barry, Susan Baum, and Heather McCartney. *"Artistic Talent Development for Urban Youth: The Promise and the Challenge." Champions of Change.* National Research Center on the Gifted and Talented: University of Connecticut, 2005.

Schwarzman, Mat. *Beginner's Guide to Community-Based Arts.* Oakland, CA: New Village, 2005.

Smith, Ralph. *"Aesthetic Education: Questions and Issues." Arts Education Policy Review,* vol. 106, no. 3 (Jan/Feb 2005): 19-34.

Tharp, Twyla. *The Creative Habit: Learn It and Use It for Life.* New York, NY: Simon & Schuster, 2003.

Torp, Linda, and Sara Sage. *Problems as Possibilities: Problem-Based Learning for K-16 Education.* Alexandria, VA: ASCD, 2002.

Tudge, Jonathan, and Barbara Rogoff. *Peer Influences on Cognitive Development: Piegetian and Vygotskian Perspectives.* London: Routledge, 1999.

Wah, Lee Mun. *The Art of Mindful Facilitation.* Berkeley, CA: StirFry Seminars & Consulting, 2004.

Wilheim, Jeffrey D. *Action Strategies for Deepening Comprehension.* Jefferson City, MO: Scholastic Professional Books, 2002.

Wilheim, Jeffrey D. *Improving Comprehension with Think-Aloud Strategies: Modeling What Good Readers Do.* Jefferson City, MO: Scholastic Professional Books, 2001.

Wolf, Dennie Palmer, and Dana Balick, eds. *Art Works! Interdisciplinary Learning Powered by the Arts.* Portsmouth, NH: Heinemann, 1999.

Publications
Available Online

Afterschool Training Toolkit: Promising Practices in the Arts. Austin: Southwest Educational Development Laboratory (SEDL) (2006), http://www.sedl.org/afterschool/toolkit/art/index.html

Authentic Connections: Interdisciplinary Work in the Arts. The Consortium of National Arts Education Associations, http://www.mpsaz.org/arts/integration/pdf_files/interart.pdf

Burnaford, Gail, Sally Brown, James Doherty, and H. James McLaughlin. *Arts Integration Frameworks, Research, and Practice: A Literature Review*. Arts Education Partnership (AEP), 2007. http://aep-arts.org/publications/index.htm

Champions of Change: The Impact of Arts on Learning. Arts Education Partnership and The President's Committee on the Arts (1999), http://www.aep-arts.org/publications.htm#ChampChange

Creating Quality Integrated and Interdisciplinary Arts Programs. Arts Education Partnership (2003), http://www.aep-arts.org/publications.htm#CreatingQuality

Goldbard, Arlene. New Creative Community: The Art of Cultural Development, http://newvillagepress.net/publications.html

Learning through the Arts: A Research Journal on Arts Integration in Schools and Communities. Irvine: Center for Learning through the Arts, http://repositories.edlib.org/clta.lta

Learning through the Arts. National Endowment for the Arts, http://www.arts.gov/pub/ArtsLearning.pdf

Living with and Teaching Young Adolescents: A Teacher's Perspective, http://www.nmsa.org/moya/new2002/pk_related_teaching.html

National Standards for Arts Education. The Kennedy Center Arts Edge, http://artsedge.kennedy-center.org/teach/standards.cfm

Art and Education Websites

A+ Schools Network, http://aplus-schoolsuncg.edu.edu

Americans for the Arts, http://www.artsusa.org

Art Resources in Teaching (ART), http://www.artresourcesinteaching.org

Arts Education Partnership (AEP), http://www.aep-arts.org

Arts for Learning, http://www.artsforlearning.org

The Arts in Every Classroom, http://www.learner.org/channel/workshops/artsineveryclassroom/index.html

ArtsEdNet, http://www.getty.edu/artsednet

ArtsLit: The ArtsLiteracy Project at Brown University, http://www.artslit.org/home.html

Break Arts: International Arts Education Collaborative, http://www.breakarts.org.

Center for Applied Research and Educational Improvement (CAREI), http://education.unm.edu/CAREI

Chicago Arts Partnerships in Education (CAPE), http://www.capeweb.org

Columbia College Chicago, http://www.colum.edu.

Columbia College Chicago Center for Community Arts Partnership, http://www.colum.edu/ccap/about.

Columbia College Chicago Center for Arts Policy, http://www.colum.edu/cap.

Community Arts Network (CAN), http://www.communityarts.net

Curriculum Integration: Middle School Educators Meeting the Needs of Young Adolescents, http://www.nscu.edu/chass/extension/ci/index.html

Facing History and Ourselves, http://www.facinghistory.org

Integrative Curriculum in a Standards-Based World, http://www.nmsa.org/research/res_articles_integrated.htm

Lincoln Center Institute for the Arts in Education, http://www.lcinstitute.org

UIC Spiral Art Education, University of Illinois Chicago, http://www.uic.edu/classes/ad/ad382/index.html

Walloon Institute, http://www.wallon.org

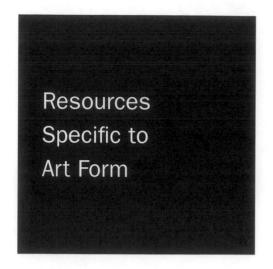

Resources Specific to Art Form

Book and Paper Arts

Columbia College Chicago, Center for Book and Paper Arts, http://www.bookandpaper.org

The Book Arts Web, http://www.philobiblon.com

Dog Eared Magazine, http://www.dogearedmagazine.com

Dance

Clark, Veve, and Sarah Johnson, eds. *Kaiso! Writings by and About Katherine Dunham (Studies in Dance History).* University of Wisconsin Press, 2006.

Foundation for Community Dance, http://www.communitydance.org.uk

Liz Lerman Dance Exchange Toolbox, http://www.danceexchange.org

McGreevy-Nichols, Susan, Helene Scheff, and Marty Sprague. *Dance About Anything. Human Kinetics:* Champaign, IL 2006.

Reedy, Patricia. *Body, Mind, and Spirit in Action : A Teacher's Guide to Creative Dance* Luna Kids Dance: Berkeley, California, 2003. http://www.lunakidsdance. com/LunaBook.html

Weikart, Phyllis. *Teaching Movement & Dance: A Sequential Approach to Rhythmic Movement.* Ann Arbor: High/Scope Press, 2003.

Film/Photography

Student Curriculum in Photography, http://www.scphoto.com

Youth Learn, http://www.youthlearn.org/learning/activities/multimedia

Teaching Photo: A Newsletter for Photography and Imaging Educators, http://www.teachingphoto.com

Music

Barrett, J.R., C.W. McCoy, and K. Veblen. *Sound Ways of Knowing: Music in the Interdisciplinary Curriculum.* New York, NY: Schirmer, 1997.

Garland, Trudi Hammel. *Math and Music: Harmonious Connections.* Lebanon, IN: Dale Seymour, 1995.

Jenson, Eric. *Music with the Brain in Mind.* San Diego, CA: Brain Store Inc., 2000.

Levene, Donna. *Music through Children's Literature: Theme and Variations.* Portsmouth, IN: Teachers Ideas Press, 1993.

Theatre

Boal, Augusto. *Theatre of the Oppressed.* New York: Theatre Communications Group, 1979.

Greer, Richard Owen. *"Out of Control in Colquitt: Swamp Gravy Makes Stone Soup." The Drama Review,* vol. 40, no. 2 (1996): 103-130.

Literacy Connections: Reader's Theater, http://www.literacyconnections.com/readerstheater.php

McKean, Barbara. *A Teaching Artist at Work: Theatre with Young People in Educational Settings.* Portsmouth, NH: Heinemann, 2006.

Schechner, Richard. *Believed-In Theatre.* New York, NY: Routledge, 1997.

Swados, Elizabeth. *Teaching Teenagers Theater.* London: Faber & Faber, 2006.

Writing/Poetry

Academy of American Poets, http://www.poets.org.

Collom, Jack and Sheryl Noethe, eds. *Poetry Everywhere: Teaching Poetry Writing in School and in the Community.* New York, NY: Teachers and Writers Collaborative, 1994.

Eleveld, Mark, ed. *The Spoken Word Revolution: Slam, Hip-Hop & The Poetry of a New Generation.* New York, NY: Sourcebooks MediaFusion, 2003.

Lamott, Anne. *Bird by Bird: Some Instructions on Writing and Life.* New York, NY: Anchor, 1994.

Morice, David. *The Adventures of Dr. Alphabet: 104 Ways to Write Poetry in the Classroom and in the Community.* New York, NY: Teachers and Writers Collaborative, 1995.

Marzan, Julio. *Luna, Luna: Creative Writing Ideas from Spanish, Latin American, and Latino Literature.* New York, NY: Teachers and Writers Collaborative, 1996.

National Gallery of the Spoken Word, http://www.ngsw.org.

The Poetry Center of Chicago, http://www.poetrycenter.org.

The Poetry Foundation, http://www.poetryfoundation.org.

Solomon, Dorothy, ed. *Inside Out: Creative Writing in the Classroom.* Salt Lake City: Utah Arts Council, 1989.

Teachers & Writers Collaborative, http://www.twc.org.

Visual Arts

The Art Room, http://www.arts.ufl.edu/art/art_room

Chicago Public Art Group, http://cpag.net/home/

Education at the Getty: Art & Language Arts, http://www.getty.edu/education

Efland, Arthur. *Art and Cognition: Integrating the Visual Arts in the Curriculum.* New York, NY: Teachers College, 2006.

Youth Learn, http://www.youthlearn.org/learning/activities/multimedia

Exquisite Corpse, http://en.wikipedia.org/wiki/exquisite_corpse and http://www.exquisitecorpse.com

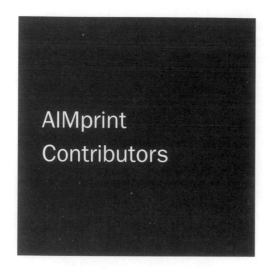

AIMprint Contributors

Meg Arbeiter has been teaching English, history, and humanities in Chicago Public Schools for the past five years, the last three at the Academy of Communications and Technology (A.C.T.) Charter School in West Garfield Park. She currently serves as the humanities department chair at A.C.T., the on-site lead teacher for the A.C.T.– Project AIM partnership, and a member of the Chicago Teacher Leadership Team for *Facing History and Ourselves*. Additionally, she was selected to be a member of the first U.S. delegation for Beyond Borders, a program piloted by Seeds of Peace in 2004-05 that brought educators from the U.S. and the Middle East together. Meg received her National Board Certification in 2007.

Barlow is a practicing professional visual artist, arts advocate and arts educator, who has worked as a teaching artist with Project AIM for the last four years. He is the founding artistic director of the Violent Injury Prevention Center at Children's Memorial Hospital. He holds concurrent teaching positions with Columbia College Chicago, The School of the Art Institute of Chicago, Museum of Contemporary Art Chicago, and Marwen Arts Foundation in Chicago. His studio is in the historic Fine Art Building at 410 South Michigan Avenue, a center for creative expression in the heart of the city. Barlow earned his M.F.A. from the School of the Art Institute of Chicago and his B.F.A. from the Henry Radford Hope School of Fine Arts at Indiana University and has exhibited widely throughout Chicago.

George Bailey is a writer, teacher and musician who lives in Oak Park, IL. He teaches English Composition, Literature and basic public speaking in the English Department of Columbia College Chicago. He believes that "arts saves your life."

Eric Booth As an actor, Eric performed in many plays on Broadway, Off-Broadway and around the country. As a businessman, he started a small company, Alert Publishing, that in seven years became the largest of its kind in the U.S. analyzing research on trends in American lifestyles. As an author, he has had four books published. His most recent, *The Everyday Work of Art,* won three awards and was a Book of the Month Club selection. Eric was the Founding Editor of the new quarterly Teaching Artist Journal, now produced by the Center for Arts Policy at Columbia College Chicago. In arts learning, he is currently on the faculty of Juilliard, and has taught at Stanford University, NYU, Tanglewood and Lincoln Center Institute (for 25 years), and he has given classes for every level from kindergarten through graduate school. He started the Art and Education program at Juilliard, and now leads Juilliard's new Mentor Program. He was the Faculty Chair of the Empire State Partnership program (the largest arts-in-education project in America), and held one of six chairs on The College Board's Arts Advisory Committee for seven years. He serves as a consultant for many organizations, cities and states and businesses around the country and is a frequent keynote speaker on the arts to groups of all kinds.

Emmy Bright is a fiber artist and arts educator who also enjoys writing. She came to Chicago in 1995, attended the University of Chicago, and took a degree in Art History.

Since then, she has worked organizing and directing Arts and College Access programs for organizations in Chicago. She worked with the Center for Community Arts Partnerships and serves on the board of Cooperative Image Group. She received a Master's degree in Arts in Education in 2007 from the Harvard Graduate School of Education.

Deborah Brzoska is a nationally recognized leader in arts education who has worked with teachers, school districts and arts organizations in more than forty states on interdisciplinary learning and arts assessment. A former dancer and choreographer, Deb was the founding principal of an award-winning arts-centered public school and has been a school designer for the Small Schools Project, funded by the Bill and Melinda Gates Foundation. Deb is known for her lively workshops as a national presenter for The Kennedy Center's Partners in Education program and she has written about arts education for the Arts Education Partnership and The College Board.

Luis Crespo is a graduate of the Columbia College Chicago Theatre Department. Luis is an actor and has worked as a teaching artist for Project AIM for five years. He has been an ensemble member of The Artistic Home in Chicago since 2002 and has had the pleasure of training, performing and becoming part of the Artistic Home family. He has directed a one-act and late night production at Home, as well as taught performance to teenagers through the Association House of Chicago. He has worked with Free Street Theatre and Young Chicago Authors.

Julie A. Downey is a writer, activist, and photographer from Chicago, IL. She has worked with Project AIM as a teaching artist for five years. Julie A. Downey (AJ Viola) often combines text and image; she recently began accompanying musicians with photographic projections. "Dying and Decay" is a collaboration with Chicago musician Tristan James and Los Angeles screenwriter Denise Cruz. Julie has taught writing, photography, collage, photojournalism and magazine editing for: Gallery 37, After School Matters, Young Chicago Authors, East Village Youth Program and Evanston Arts Center. She has also been interviewed for her activist work on CAN-TV, Indymedia Video, WZRD, and the United Front podcast.

Dan Godston is a poet, writer, and musician, and has worked as a teaching artist with Project AIM for the last five years. He also teaches for the Poetry Center of Chicago and in the English Department at Columbia College Chicago. In 2006 he was one of few teaching artists world-wide to present at the UNESCO World Conference on Arts Education. His poetry and fiction have appeared in Chase Park, Versal, 580 Split, Kyoto Journal, California Quarterly, after hours, and other magazines, and his nonfiction has appeared in print and websites, such as Teaching Artist Journal, Afropop Worldwide, and The Jazz Institute of Chicago Newsletter. He composes music and plays the trumpet and other instruments. Joel Wanek, Jayve Montgomery, and he perform as The Ways & Means Trio.

David A. Flatley, Executive Director of the Center for Community Arts Partnerships (CCAP) at Columbia College Chicago, has more than a decade of experience in developing and implementing educational and intercultural initiatives designed to improve teacher practice and student achievement, and affect whole-school change. His work supports both national and international groups— most recently the Scottish Arts Council and Scottish Educational Authority as they work to replicate the arts integration model developed by David and his team through the Chicago Teacher's Center. He has an M.A. in Arts Administration from the University of Wisconsin-Madison and a B.S. in Business Administration from the University of Illinois-Champaign. He received his practitioner's certification in intercultural communications through the Intercultural Communications Institute in Portland, Oregon. David currently serves as vice chair of the Americans for the Arts' Arts Education Council.

Khanisha Foster is a Chicago actor who has been teaching with Project AIM since 2005. She also works at Sabin Magnet School and Pulaski Fine Arts Academy with the Center for Community Arts Partnerships Community Schools after-school programs. She has developed arts integrated curriculum that promote literacy through the arts. She graduated from Columbia College Chicago in 2002, and just recently finished her training with Steppenwolf Theatre Company in Chicago. You can see her in the film *Chicago Boricua* and look for her future onstage endeavors.

Amanda Leigh Lichtenstein writes poetry creative nonfiction. Her creative writing appears in *Another Chicago Magazine, Contrary, Painted Bride Quarterly,* and others. Essays on teaching poetry appear in *Teachers & Writers, Teaching Tolerance, Children's Book Council* and *Teaching Artist Journal*. She has worked as a community poet in Chicago for eight years and frequently travels as a writer, consultant and educator. In 2006, she presented at UNESCO's first World Conference on Arts Education as a Teaching Artist. She consults and partners with Urban Gateways: The Center for Arts Education, CAPE, Center for Community Arts Partnerships and Project AIM, Chicago Public Schools, the Museum of Contemporary Photography, Lane Community College in Eugene, OR, and the Chautauqua Arts Council of Jamestown, NY. She earned her Ed.M. in Arts in Education at the Harvard Graduate School of Education and recently co-founded Breakarts, an international arts and education collaborative whose mission is to partner with schools and communities around the world through the arts to encourage young people to narrate the stories of their lives.

Leah Mayers is a book artist and has been a teaching artist for Project AIM since 2002. She also teaches in the Education Department at Columbia College Chicago and is one of four founders of Vespine Gallery and Studios in Chicago.

Deborah Guzmán-Meyer is a native New Yorker who grew up in the Dominican Republic. She is a teaching artist with Project AIM and Gallery 37, and founding member of Standard Usage Project an artist collective. She received an MFA in Photography from Columbia College Chicago and has exhibited throughout the United States.

Barbara A. Holland, Ph.D., is Director of the Learn and Serve America National Service-Learning Clearinghouse, funded by the Corporation for National and Community Service. She is also a Senior Scholar at Indiana University-Purdue University Indianapolis. Her research agenda focuses on organizational change in higher education with an emphasis on the role of community engagement and its impacts on institutions, faculty, students and community partners. She has been an evaluator for Columbia College arts partnership programs since 1997.

Tricia Hersey is a poet who has been teaching youth how to scream and write their truths in Chicago for over seven years. She was a teaching artist for Project AIM for two years and currently coordinates after-school tutoring programs for Chicago Public Schools.

Shawn Renee Lent holds the position of Arts Integration Program Specialist at Columbia College Chicago's Center for Community Arts Partnerships (CCAP), and is a choreographer and teaching artist. Shawn holds a masters degree in Arts in Youth & Community Development from Columbia College, a post-graduate certificate in Youth Arts Development from the University of London, as well as a BFA in theatre/dance from Millikin University. Ms. Lent is a former employee of Jacob's Pillow Dance Festival in Massachusetts and from 2001-2003, Shawn volunteered in London's East End as a youth worker, community development worker, and dance critic.

John Lyons is an Emmy Award winning documentary filmmaker. A graduate of Chicago's Columbia College, he has produced, directed, shot and edited films in various areas of the humanities, often taking him around the country and the world. He co-produced and directed, *Too Flawed to Fix: The Illinois Death Penalty Experience,* and signed on as editor *In a Time of Siege: Voices in the Wilderness Defying War and Sanctions in Iraq*. He co-produced half hour segments of both films for broadcast on ABC-WLS Chicago, the former earning him a Midwest Emmy award, and the latter earning him an Emmy nomination. He has also made films about youth political activism, humanitarian trips to Bolivia and Mexico, and is shooting an ongoing oral history project featuring civil rights veterans of Benton County, Mississippi. He lives in Chicago with his wife Jessica and daughter Catie.

Cecil McDonald Jr. is an award-winning photographer and teaching artist with Project AIM. He received an MFA in Photography from Columbia College Chicago and was a recipient of the Albert P. Weisman Memorial Scholarship. He has taught at Trinity Christian College, and exhibited his work widely in Chicago and across the United States including; the Catherine Edelman Gallery, Beverly Art Center, Schopf Gallery on the Lake, Vespine Studios & Gallery, the Nova Art Fair, Philadelphia African American Art Museum, and Leica Gallery in New York.

Jenn Morea is a poet and teaching artist with Project AIM and Chicago Arts Partnerships in Education (CAPE). She has also taught in the English Department at Columbia College Chicago, at Young Chicago Authors and at Marwen, and has led teacher workshops at Louisiana State University in Baton Rouge.

Sadira Muhammad is the Project AIM Program Coordinator; she provides coordination for the Arts Integration Mentorship (AIM) project including work in event production, professional development, budget management, and vendor relations. Prior to CCAP, she worked for the education foundation arm of Ariel Capital Management in support of one of CPS' smaller schools, Ariel Community Academy. There, she also provided support administration. Sadira comes to the field of arts and education with a wealth of knowledge in public relations (legal field) and performance art administration. Sadira is a performing artist (professional ethnic folkloric dancer) and has worked, and currently works, in her art form as a teaching artist and a professional development specialist as part of her job at CCAP.

Lisa Redmond received her Bachelor of Arts Degree from Roosevelt University. She is currently completing a Master of Fine Arts degree in Creative Writing here at Columbia College. She is a teaching artist within Columbia's Center for Community Arts Partnerships. She has worked with the Arts Integration Mentorship Program (Project AIM) and the Gaining Early Awareness and Readiness for Undergraduate Programs (GEAR-UP) program. She was a student editor for the Fiction Writing Department's anthology, Hair Trigger 25, which won the Columbia (University) Scholastic Press Association's Gold Crown Award. She is a fellow within the Illinois Consortium for Educational Opportunity Program (ICEOP) for the years 2002/2003 and 2003/2004. She has also won the finalist award for the John Schultz and Betty Shiflett Story Workshop Scholarship for the years, 2002, 2003, and 2004.

Tony Sancho is an actor, visual artist, musician, and martial artist. He has been involved in community-based art work for 16 years. He works with students ranging from sixth-grade to adult. Currently, Tony teaches acting and voice training for the stage at Columbia College Chicago, and is a teaching artist with Project AIM. Currently Tony is in training with the Steppenwolf Theatre Company in Chicago. His Chicago-area theater credits include companies such as the Goodman, Victory Gardens, Remi Bumppo, and Teatro Vista. Tony is also an ensemble member of Teatro Vista, the only Equity Latino Theater in the Midwest. His latest film, *On the Downlow,* was released in January, 2007. You can also find him on the Chicago music scene performing with his band, The Luna Blues Machine.

Mathias "Spider" Schergen is an award winning artist and educator at Edward Jenner Academy of the Arts, where he has worked as an Art Specialist for 14 years. He is a lead teacher liaison to Project AIM. Spider was the recipient of the Golden Apple Award for Excellence in Teaching in 2005. He has exhibited his assemblage sculptures in galleries throughout Chicago including the ARC Gallery and Hot House.

Jamie Lou Thome is a teaching artist in Chicago and is one of the four founders of Vespine Gallery and Studios. She received her MFA in Interdisciplinary Book and Paper Arts from Columbia College Chicago in 2000, and is currently enjoying making art, learning Italian, and hanging out with her family.

Suree Towfighnia is an independent filmmaker, director of photography and freelance director/producer from Chicago. Her documentary, *Tampico* (2006), winner of the Studs Terkel Award, chronicles a woman's struggle to survive by performing her family's music in the subways of Chicago. Suree's other recent projects include *Standing Silent Nation* (2006), which follows a Lakota Indian family as they battle to grow industrial hemp on their lands. Suree studied history and Latin American studies at the University of California, Santa Cruz. She earned her MFA in documentary film from Columbia College Chicago, where she co-founded Prairie Dust Films with Courtney Hermann in 2002.

Joanne Vena is currently the Director of School Partnerships at the Center for Community Arts Partnerships at Columbia College Chicago. Prior to her arrival in 2001, she was the Director of Arts Education for the Illinois Arts Council and helped to create several grant programs that linked artists and communities of learners together in conjunction with the State of Illinois and the National Endowment for the Arts. She is an artist with a MFA from the School of the Arts Institute of Chicago.

Joel Wanek is a photographer, educator and musician in Chicago. He teaches photography at many of the city's premier arts organizations including the Museum of Contemporary Photography, Center for Community Arts Partnerships and Marwen Foundation. He received a BA in Photography & Cinematography from Webster University and carried out advanced studies at Columbia College Chicago and the Center for Documentary Studies.

Cynthia Weiss is the Associate Director of School Partnerships/Project AIM at the Center for Community Arts Partnerships at Columbia College Chicago in the Center for Community Arts Partnerships. She directs Project AIM, an Arts & Literacy project that places teaching artists in Chicago Public School classrooms to partner with teachers on arts-integrated curriculum. Cynthia was a founding member of Chicago Arts Partnerships in Education (CAPE). She is co-editor with Gail Burnaford and Arnold Aprill of the book, *Renaissance in the Classroom: Arts Integration and Meaningful Learning.* Cynthia received her MFA in Painting from the University of Illinois at Chicago. She is an award-winning public artist, painter, and educator. As a member of the Chicago Public Art Group, Cynthia directs large-scale public art projects that invite community participation.

Cynthium Johnson-Woodfolk received her BA from Columbia College Chicago and is currently completing both an MA in the Teaching of Writing and an MFA in Creative Writing. She is a teaching artist with Project AIM, and has worked with Columbia's Center for Community Arts Partnerships, as well as Saturday Scholars, Act/Write, and the Story Workshop®Institute (SWI). Cynthium won the Academic Excellence award, Hermann Conaway Leadership award, Dwight Follett Fellowship and was a fellow in the Illinois Consortium for Educational Opportunity Program for 2004/2005. Her work appears in Hair Trigger 9, 10, 25, and 26.

avery r. young has been a staple in the spoken word community since 1996. He teaches spoken word performance and creative writing for Project AIM, Young Chicago Authors, and in the Juvenile Detention Center. He has been performed in the Hip Hop Theatre festival, Lollapolooza, and Steppenwolfe Theatre. A finalist of 2006 Illinois Art Fellowship Grant, he classifies his style of writing and performance as "urban hymns you find at a sunday mornin juke joint." Blending spoken word, jazz and gospel, his work challenges ideals of racism, politics, sexuality and language. His work for schools and community organizations has made him not only an artist but an advocate for social dilemmas such as H.I.V., gender consciousness and cultural competency. He edited 'absractvision' and is an advice columnist fo 'Say What' magazine. His writing has been published in Callaloo, Warpland and *Teaching Artist Journal.* He is currently performing works from his play, "me n'em: cullud boi schitz".

AIMprint
Index

* *n* indicates notation

Index
(by author)